Reconciliation Discourse

# Discourse Approaches to Politics, Society and Culture (DAPSAC)

The editors invite contributions that investigate political, social and cultural processes from a linguistic/discourse-analytic point of view. The aim is to publish monographs and edited volumes which combine language-based approaches with disciplines concerned essentially with human interaction – disciplines such as political science, international relations, social psychology, social anthropology, sociology, economics, and gender studies.

## General Editors

Ruth Wodak and Greg Myers
University of Lancaster

Editorial address: Ruth Wodak, Bowland College, Department of Linguistics and English Language, University of Lancaster University, Lancaster LA1 4YT, UK
r.wodak@lancaster.ac.uk and g.myers@lancaster.ac.uk

## Advisory Board

Volume 27

Reconciliation Discourse. The case of the Truth and Reconciliation Commission
by Annelies Verdoolaege

# Reconciliation Discourse

The case of the Truth
and Reconciliation Commission

Annelies Verdoolaege

Ghent University

John Benjamins Publishing Company

Amsterdam / Philadelphia

The paper used in this publication meets the minimum requirements of American National Standard for Information Sciences – Permanence of Paper for Printed Library Materials, ANSI z39.48-1984.

Library of Congress Cataloging-in-Publication Data

Verdoolaege, Annelies.
   Reconciliation discourse : the case of the Truth and Reconciliation Commission / Annelies Verdoolaege.
      p.   cm. (Discourse Approaches to Politics, Society and Culture, ISSN 1569-9463 ; v. 27)
   Includes bibliographical references and index.
      1. South Africa. Truth and Reconciliation Commission. 2. Reconciliation--Political aspects  South Africa. 3. Reconciliation--Social aspects--South Africa. 4. Discourse analysis--Political aspects--South Africa. I. Title.
   DT1974.2.V47      2008
   968.06--dc22                                                                     2007040633
   ISBN 978 90 272 2718 8 (Hb; alk. paper)

John Benjamins Publishing Co. · P.O. Box 36224 · 1020 ME Amsterdam · The Netherlands
John Benjamins North America · P.O. Box 27519 · Philadelphia PA 19118-0519 · USA

For Zaïna and Kalifa

After the gruelling work of the Commission I came away with a deep sense – indeed an exhilarating realisation – that though there is undoubtedly much evil about, we human beings have a wonderful capacity for good. We can be very good. *That* is what fills me with hope for even the most intractable situations.

Archbishop Desmond Tutu (1999b: 205)

# Table of contents

# Preface

Converting my Ph.D. dissertation into a book has been a great challenge to me. This book can be seen as the culmination of four years of intensive doctoral research, and the means to spread my ideas and findings both within and beyond the academic community. I should first of all express my gratitude towards John Benjamins Publising Company who gave me the opportunity to engage in the process of reworking my doctorate and making it accessible to the larger public. In addition, I should also thank Professor Jan Blommaert, whose academic network brought me into contact with John Benjamins. Throughout my doctoral research Professor Blommaert was a source of inspiration and enlightenment, stimulating my thinking at each stage of the project, but also leaving me a great deal of intellectual freedom. It was he who stirred in me a love for Africa and who ignited my fascination for Critical Discourse Analysis and for questions of power, identity and ideology it embraces. I am grateful to all of my colleagues at the Department of African Languages and Cultures. They were responsible for a peaceful and at the same time very inspiring work atmosphere. I should definitely thank Karel Arnaut, Inge Brinkman, Meryem Kanmaz, Katrijn Maryns, Gilles-Maurice de Schryver, Michael Meeuwis, Ngo Semzara Kabuta, Marga Peters, Marijke Van Petegem and Cécile Vigouroux for their support and friendship – and David Chan from the English Department for checking my English.

This book stands as an expression of my love for South Africa and my admiration for its people. Therefore, I would especially like to emphasise how grateful I am to my South African friends and fellow researchers: Kay McCormick, Mary Bock, Chris and Biebie van der Merwe, Christine Anthonissen, Fiona Ross, Patricia Shariff, Theo du Plessis, Annelie Lotriet, and Antjie Krog. Without their input and guidance I would not have been able to gain the insight into South African society that informs much of this book. Many foreign Africanists, linguists or TRC specialists have given me valuable advice and supported me in my first tentative attempts to discover the international academic scene. They have offered me tremendous opportunities to become familiar with academic competences like chairing, presenting and networking. Let me just thank Chris Youé, Bogumil Jewsiewicki, Lars Buur, Stephen Ellis, Ineke Van Kessel, Jim Collins, John Daniel, Deborah Posel, and Lyn Graybill.

Finally, this book and my life in academia would not have been possible without my family members. I am extremely grateful to my parents, Raymond Verdoolaege and Viviane Plets, for their unconditional love and support in all of my endeavours over the past thirty years. Thanks to them I have always been able to fulfil my dreams. I especially thank them for their open-mindedness and for teaching me some of the most important human values. My brother Geert, even though also finishing his Ph.D., was always prepared to help me out with ICT problems, and he and his girlfriend Lien were often there just to have a chat or to baby-sit. And then there is Kalifa, my husband; he became very familiar with the terms 'reconciliation', 'truth' and 'TRC' and he heard me talking endlessly about Foucault, Bourdieu or Archbishop Tutu. Nevertheless, he always listened to me and he often provided timely help when I encountered problems or did not know how to proceed. Above all, he often had to miss me for many days or weeks, when I attended a conference or went on a research trip to South Africa. He never objected to any of my plans, so it is mainly thanks to his patience and tolerance that my research has come to a successful end. I should of course also mention our little daughter Zaïna, who was born a few months after I defended my Ph.D. and who experienced the writing of this book at first hand. She is now my source of joy, happiness and inspiration and I hope that the conclusion of this project will allow me to spend even more time with her and her daddy.

# Acronyms

| | |
|---|---|
| AC | Amnesty Committee |
| ANC | African National Congress |
| APLA | Azanian People's Liberation Army |
| AWB | Afrikaner Weerstandsbeweging |
| AZAPO | Azanian People's Organisation |
| CDA | Critical Discourse Analysis |
| CSVR | Centre for the Study of Violence and Reconciliation |
| DA | Discourse Analysis |
| GHRV | Gross Human Rights Violations |
| HRV | Human Rights Violations |
| HRVC | Human Rights Violations Committee |
| ICTJ | International Centre for Transitional Justice |
| IDASA | Institute for a Democratic Alternative for South Africa |
| IFP | Inkatha Freedom Party |
| IJR | Institute for Justice and Reconciliation |
| IMN | Ideological Master Narrative |
| ISA | Ideological State Apparatus |
| KSP | Khulumani Support Group |
| LFP | Language Facilitation Programme |
| MK | Umkhonto we Sizwe |
| NEC | National Executive Committee |
| NGO | Non-governmental organisation |
| NP | National Party |
| PAC | Pan-Africanist Congress |
| RRC | Reparation and Rehabilitation Committee |
| SABC | South African Broadcasting Corporation |
| SACP | South African Communist Party |
| SADF | South African Defence Force |
| SAP | South African Police |
| TRC | Truth and Reconciliation Commission |
| UDF | United Democratic Front |
| UN | United Nations |

CHAPTER 1

# Introduction

## 1.1 The TRC and discourse?

South Africa's apartheid regime unofficially came to an end with the release of Nelson Mandela in February 1990. However, it was not until the first democratic elections, on the 27th of April 1994, that democracy was officially introduced in the southern tip of Africa. In the years between these two crucial events there was much speculation with regard to the peaceful coexistence of South African population groups. Apartheid had been so dehumanising to millions of people, so many South Africans had had their lives destroyed as a result of state security violence or because of activities carried out by the liberation forces, that the entire world wondered how the various groups in South Africa could ever be united. It was crystal-clear that the atrocities committed under apartheid had to be addressed, in one way or another. Trying to construct a new society without reflecting on apartheid was not an option. Forgetting the brutality of the past might well lead to massive acts of revenge, or even civil war.

Attempting to unify South Africa – and even starting the process of reconciling South Africans – became a task assigned to the Truth and Reconciliation Commission (TRC). In this way, the TRC became one of the most significant phenomena in South African history. The Truth and Reconciliation Commission can in fact be considered as one of *the* symbols of South Africa's change to liberty. By devoting attention to apartheid victims and perpetrators and by formulating visions for the future, the Commission embodied the entire transitional process. Today, the Commission continues to be analysed and to be reflected upon, with academics and journalists trying to grasp its consequences and its effect on present-day South Africa. Moreover, because of the worldwide media attention it has received, its charismatic chairperson, Archbishop Tutu, and the recognition it gained in South Africa itself, the South African TRC has become widely regarded as a model of how societies can deal with traumatic pasts. In fact, the Commission has been taken as an instructive example in many other post-conflict countries, such as Sierra Leone, Liberia or Indonesia (see http://www.ictj.org/en/index.html).

Through the South African Truth and Reconciliation Commission, perpetrators and victims of apartheid started to listen to each other and, to a certain extent, they also tried to understand each other. Testifying, complaining, apologising, venting one's rage, expressing one's grief, disappointment or despair, all of these discursive practices took a central position in the proceedings of the TRC. They were all used to give form and content to the Commission. It was through these discursive practices that South Africans got to know one another and that they started to rethink the apartheid past. There are many ways in which TRC discourse can be analysed: attention can be paid to the role of the interpreters, the original language of the testifiers can be scrutinised, or one can try to understand the interaction between perpetrators, their lawyers and the commissioners. In this book, I have focussed on the language constructed at the hearings of the Human Rights Violations Committee (HRVC), the sub-committee of the TRC where the apartheid victims could testify about what had happened to them under apartheid.

In contrast with the Amnesty hearings, these victim hearings were aimed much more at national unity and reconciliation. The issues of personal and national reconciliation were raised in these testimonies, along with the question of a peaceful and unified future for South Africa. My idea was to analyse this human rights violations discourse and to find out what the repercussions of this language might be on South African society. Such a linguistic approach is absolutely innovative in the field of TRC studies, even more so because I decided to use Critical Discourse Analysis (CDA) as my theoretical point of reference. The relation between TRC discourse and power in society will therefore take a central position in this work, whereby power will mainly be conceptualised as the power to unify and to reconcile. How was TRC discourse – defined here as 'reconciliation discourse' – created during the hearings of the HRV Committee; how did this discourse impact on South African society; did this discourse help in establishing a unified nation with reconciliation-oriented citizens; and what lessons can be drawn for other countries struggling to deal with a violent past? These are the main questions that will be addressed in this book. While discussing these themes, a lot of contextual information will be provided and theoretical issues will be illustrated by means of quotes taken from the transcribed TRC testimonies. The elaborate bibliography at the end of this book will be an extremely useful tool for anyone interested in present-day South African politics or in conflict resolution by means of truth and reconciliation commissions.

## 1.2    Central proposition of this book

In this work the South African Truth and Reconciliation Commission will be regarded as a mechanism to produce power through discourse. Importantly, as will become clear towards the end of this text, the exertion of power will predominantly be regarded as a positive and highly productive aspect. One of the main findings will be that the term reconciliation was conceptualised in an open-ended manner at the TRC victim hearings. Consequently, this term could also be interpreted in various ways in post-TRC South African society, resulting in the extension of its power to a large number of socio-political and cultural domains. According to my findings, it is possible that the reconciliation-oriented master narrative of the HRV hearings was deliberately constructed in a polysemic and vague manner. As a result, the majority of South Africans could relate to the concept of reconciliation, turning it into a highly inclusive term. Because of this vagueness the debate on reconciliation was sustained and is ongoing today; reconciliation became South Africa's national symbol, meaning that by keeping the debate on reconciliation going, the nation constantly gives meaning to its proper existence. In addition, the TRC consciously addressed all South Africans and tried to involve all of them in its process – this in an attempt to establish an inclusive national unity. This issue was also part of the inclusive superstructure of the Commission. All of these beneficial effects of the TRC proceedings may well signal the Commission as one of the factors leading to peace and stability in the South Africa of the late 1990s and the early 21st century.

It is important to emphasise that this study can be seen as an exploration of the semantic layeredness of the term reconciliation. Throughout this text I will consider reconciliation as a very vague and ambiguous term; as a term most people assume they can define, but which in reality seems to be extremely complex and polysemic. On a purely abstract level, it is a term we could give an ideal-typical interpretation – such an interpretation can be useful for the sake of clarity, also in this research. In the course of this text, though, we will understand that at the TRC the actual – and highly diverse – interpretation of the term was only revealed through discursive practices.

## 1.3    Theoretical framework

Since I looked at a socio-political phenomenon from a discursive perspective, I turned to conceptual frames available in the field of Critical Discourse Analysis. Some of the aims of CDA are to explore power relations among discourse participants and to reveal how – ideologically coloured – power can be expressed through language. By reading through all of the HRV testimonies it became clear that specific discursive patterns could be distinguished – discursive patterns based on external rules, but also patterns that were constructed at the HRV site itself. These patterns emerged significantly through the dynamic of relations, mainly power relations between commissioners and testifying victims, but also between testifiers and the audience or between testifiers and some of the contextual features (media, discursive setting, etc.). As with any institutional situation, power relations took shape through interaction between discourse participants.

To analyse and understand these relations, the insights obtained from CDA were helpful. However, I should stress that the CDA research I consulted solely functioned as background to my theoretical framework. In addition, as claimed by Fowler (1996:8), Van Dijk (2001:98) or Fairclough (2001b:121) CDA does not contain clear-cut methodologies. CDA insights or ideas always have to be applied creatively – they should never be adopted indiscriminately. Much attention should always be paid to contextual features, which means that CDA theories necessarily should be adapted to the historical, geographical, or socio-political context of the discourse under investigation.

So, CDA was regarded mainly as a source of inspiration, rather than a fixed theoretical framework. The framework I then developed consisted of a combination of Blommaert's theory on discursive layering and of the notion of the archive as developed by Foucault. My basic aim became the deconstruction of the HRV archive to reveal the discursive rules of formation that came into existence at the HRV hearings. In order to understand this archive I discussed the ways in which this HRV discourse was layered on ideological, historical and identity levels. The purpose of this theoretical framework was to gain insight into the power relations exercised at the HRV setting. Since the TRC can be seen as a state institution that has had a considerable impact on South African society, I was also interested in the implications of these internal power relations on post-TRC South Africa. For this aspect of my research I mainly appealed to post-structural theories from scholars such as Althusser, Bourdieu, Gramsci and again Foucault. Clearly, my theoretical framework did not consist of ready-made theories copied from other domains of the humanities. Instead, I tried to construct an inventive frame which borrows from a number of other disciplines, but which is adapted to a very specific contextual situation. This frame has been implemented in a particular way, in order to gain insight into a unique phenomenon and – to a lesser extent – into a unique contemporary society.

## 1.4    Some general remarks

As a Belgian researcher, analysing the TRC and its impact on present-day South African society posed a number of problems. To begin with, the main part of the TRC process had been finished about three years earlier; my investigation would thus necessarily be retrospective. In addition, by not living and working in South Africa full-time, I would never come close to gaining insight into this complex society. I therefore explicitly decided to study the TRC from the perspective of an outsider, meaning that I would be an outsider both with respect to history and with respect to geography. TRC discourse would be analysed without being influenced by emotional aspects that were present in South Africa at the time of the TRC process. Also current day sensitivities surrounding the TRC and South Africa's post-apartheid socio-political life would have a minor impact on this re-search project. As a result, my knowledge of the TRC and of South Africa itself was to be based largely on primary and secondary material such as publications and audio-visual data. Bearing the outsider's perspective in mind, the findings made at the end of this monograph will not be called conclusions, but rather sug-gestions. I will try to gain insight into a part of the TRC process and I will propose an impact of the TRC on post-apartheid South Africa – all of these suggestions, though, will be formulated cautiously and provisionally.

Further, my point of departure in this study is the analysis of HRV discourse, on the basis of Critical Discourse Analysis. However, I should stress that the data used are much too inaccurate and incomplete to conduct a detailed discourse analysis or conversation analysis. Moreover, I will be using translated material, which makes it rather impossible to study grammatical constructions or lexical choices. Instead, this work analyses contextualised interaction patterns between groups of individuals, the ways in which this interaction is influenced by the so-cio-political and historical situation and the power these constructed discursive meanings might exert on South African society. Central to this book is the notion of reconciliation: the manner in which this concept was constructed at the HRV hearings; the ways in which it was conceptualised by the testifying victims; and the ways in which it reverberated through South African society at large. There-fore, South Africa's apartheid victims and their visions on the past and the future are the central focus of this work. All this develops in connection with issues such as the media, the power of state institutions and South Africa's attempts at building a reconciled nation. Discourse will be my main tool to deconstruct this intricate network.

To sum up, the aim of this study is to analyse how, through a certain type of *reconciliation discourse* constructed at the HRV hearings, a reconciliation-ori-ented reality took shape in post-TRC South Africa. Basically, it is an investigation of the long-term implications of a truth commission's activities on a traumatised post-conflict society. Conflict resolution and especially conflict resolution by using restorative instead of retributive mechanisms is an internationally relevant research domain. This book hopes to add to this expanding field on truth commissions as a means of peacekeeping. Although the TRC will be approached critically at certain points, the idea is to demonstrate the value of truth commissions and the constructive contribution of the TRC to a relatively stable and tolerant post-apartheid South Africa.

# CHAPTER 2

# The South African Truth and Reconciliation Commission

## 2.1 How it all began

The idea of a truth commission for South Africa first came from the African National Congress (ANC). As soon as the ban on the ANC was lifted, in February 1990, accusations were levelled against the party that it had committed human rights violations in some of its training camps in Tanzania and in other southern African countries. The response of the ANC was to set up its own internal investigation commissions, amongst others the Stuart, the Skweyiya and the Motsuenyane Commissions. These Commissions confirmed that gross human rights violations had taken place in the camps during the time of exile, findings that were accepted by the National Executive Committee (NEC) of the ANC. However, in response to the Motsuenyane Commission's report the NEC did call upon the government to "set up, without delay, a Commission of Inquiry or Truth Commission into all violations of human rights since 1948" (Boraine 2000c: 12).

It was especially professor Kader Asmal who, at his inaugural lecture at the University of the Western Cape on the 25th of May 1992, gave form and content to the ANC's proposal to establish a truth commission once a political settlement had been reached. It was also in 1992 that others started to consider the idea of a truth commission for South Africa, for instance members of the Institute for a Democratic Alternative for South Africa (IDASA) after their visit to Eastern Europe. Upon their return they decided to organise two conferences in order to discuss the possibilities and modalities of a truth commission in South Africa. The first conference would be a preparatory conference, focusing on Eastern European and Latin American countries and their experiences in dealing with a traumatic past. This conference was called 'Dealing with the Past' and it was held in Cape Town in February 1994. It was Dullah Omar, the newly appointed Minister of Justice, who, on the 27th of May 1994, announced to parliament the decision of the government to set up a commission of truth and reconciliation. The second conference in preparation for the Commission was held in Cape Town, in July 1994; this conference was called 'The South African Conference on Truth and Reconciliation' and its focus was more on South African participants – such as representatives from South Africa's human rights organisations and political parties – than on international guests (Boraine 2000c: 43; Boraine & Levy 1995: xxii).

In the summer of 1994 the stage for the truth commission was set and the work of drafting the Bill could begin. It took about four months of consultation, negotiation and legislation before all of the political parties reached an agreement; it was only in November 1994 that the Promotion of National Unity and Reconciliation Bill was published by the newly appointed government. The bill was signed into law in July 1995 and came into effect on the 15th of December 1995 (Boraine 2000c: 71). It was this Promotion of National Unity and Reconciliation Act 34 of 1995 (from now on 'TRC Act') by which the Truth and Reconciliation Commission was established.

Importantly, this Act was prepared in an extremely transparent way: the draft bill was distributed to non-governmental organisations all over South Africa; seminars and workshops were held to help people understand the philosophy behind the Commission; the findings of these workshops and seminars were made available to the people working on the bill; thousands of booklets explaining the main ideas of the Commission were distributed; and also a number of radio programmes on the TRC were broadcast (Boraine 2000c: 50).

All this resulted in the setting up of a very unique institution.


## 2.2    Formal aspects of the Truth and Reconciliation Commission

Hayner (2001: 14) uses the term 'truth commission' to refer to institutions that share the following characteristics: (1) truth commissions focus on the past; (2) they investigate a pattern of abuses over a period of time, rather than a specific event; (3) a truth commission is a temporary body, typically in operation for six months to two years, and completing its work with the submission of a report; and (4) these commissions are officially sanctioned, authorised and empowered by the state.

The South African TRC was called into existence in the Promotion of National Unity and Reconciliation Act No. 34 of 1995. This Act provided the framework within which the establishment of the Commission and its mandate had to be understood. The mandate of the Commission, as set out in the TRC Act, was very ambitious. The Act stated that the TRC was to "promote national unity and reconciliation in a spirit of understanding which transcends the conflicts and divisions of the past by

1. establishing as complete a picture as possible of the causes, nature and extent of the gross violations of human rights which were committed during the period from the 1st of March 1960 to the 5th of December 1993;
2. facilitating the granting of amnesty to persons who make full disclosure of all the relevant facts relating to acts associated with a political objective and comply with the requirements of this Act;
3. establishing and making known the fate or whereabouts of victims and restoring the human and civil dignity of such victims by granting them an opportunity to relate their own accounts of the violations of which they are the victims, and by recommending reparation measures in respect of them;
4. compiling a report providing as comprehensive an account as possible of the activities and findings of the Commission contemplated in paragraphs (1), (2) and (3), and which contains recommendations of measures to prevent the future violations of human rights" (TRC Report 1998, 1/4: 54).

The TRC was seen as a bridge-building process between a past of injustice, discrimination and intolerance and a future founded on the recognition of human rights, democracy and equality. One of the main tasks of the Commission was to uncover as far as was possible the truth about past gross violations of human rights; it was believed that this task would be necessary for the promotion of reconciliation and national unity.

Crucial for the functioning of the TRC and its ultimate success was the selection of commissioners. The appointment of commissioners followed a very democratic and transparent pattern. To begin with, many organisations, political parties, churches, individuals, and so on were invited to nominate people to serve on the Commission. In the end, 299 nominations were received. A committee, specially appointed by President Mandela, then made a first selection, public hearings were held and finally the committee sent twenty-five names to the President. People who were selected had to be capable of passing judgement impartially, they were not allowed to have an explicit political profile and they should not be potential amnesty applicants. In consultation with his Cabinet President Mandela selected fifteen commissioners from this list of twenty-five (Boraine 2000c: 71). He also added two new names in order to increase the representativeness of the Commission (Shea 2000: 25).

The final group was extremely diverse: Black, Brown, White and Indian, old and young, jurists, ministers, writers, academics, doctors and parliamentarians, people who had been on different sides of the struggle, representatives of all main religions in the country (Meiring 1999: 14). According to Krog (1998a: 36) the final list of TRC commissioners was fairly predictable: the Afrikaner members were Wynand Malan and Chris de Jager, the English-speaking members were

Alex Boraine, Mary Burton, Wendy Orr and Richard Lyster, the Indian members were Fazel Randera and Yasmin Sooka, and the Coloured members were Denzil Potgieter and Glenda Wildschut. The selected Black commissioners consisted of Dumisa Ntsebeza, Bongani Finca and Khoza Mgojo on the male side, and of Mapule Ramashala, Hlengiwe Mkhize and Sisi Khampepe on the female side. Archbishop Tutu was appointed as the chairperson of the TRC and the Methodist minister Alex Boraine became the deputy chairperson. Although members of the Commission came from each of South Africa's population group, it is important to note that the South African languages were not as well represented.

In addition to the commissioners, the TRC Act also allowed for the appointment of additional committee members to serve on the Human Rights Violations and Reparation and Rehabilitation Committees. These committee members had to assist the commissioners and they had to ensure that the membership of the Committees was representative in terms of race, gender and geographical origin (TRC Report 1998, 1/6: 137).

Apart from the selection of the commissioners, it was also important for the TRC to be granted sufficient resources in order to be operational. On a financial level the TRC had 196 million Rand at its disposal: 165 million allocated by the South African government and 31 million in foreign donations. In addition, 400 staff members worked for the Commission, either to carry out investigations regarding past human rights abuses, or to deal with the administrative matters of the TRC (Eyskens 2001: 26). At the second meeting of the Commission, in January 1996, it was agreed that the national office would be located at 106 Adderley Street in Cape Town. To structure and coordinate the proceedings of the Commission, four regional centres were established in Cape Town, Durban, East London and Johannesburg. Each of these regional centres was led by a commissioner (TRC Report 1998, 1/3: 45).

## 2.3    The TRC ready for operation

The TRC officially began work in December 1995 and according to the TRC Act it was given eighteen months to finish its work. The Commission consisted of three subcommittees: the Human Rights Violations Committee, the Amnesty Committee and the Committee on Reparation and Rehabilitation. In addition, the Commission retained a permanent Investigation Unit as an integral component. The Investigation Unit consisted of a staff of approximately fifty people and it was led by commissioner Ntsebeza. In a first phase, the Investigation Unit was required to provide an investigative service to the Commission's subcommittees (especially the Human Rights Violations Committee and the Amnesty Committee) and to initiate independent investigations as determined by the Commission. In a second phase, the Investigation Unit had to corroborate claims made by victims or witnesses in their statements or submissions to the other Committees (TRC Report 1998, 1/11:331). Although the Investigation Unit was considered to be one of the four cornerstones of the TRC, it was especially the three Committees that attracted most attention.

### 2.3.1 The Human Rights Violations Committee

The Human Rights Violations Committee (HRVC) was one of the most important components of the TRC. It was especially the media that brought this Committee to the attention of the national and international public; in this way the HRVC became the public face of the TRC.

The duties and functions of the HRVC were clearly stipulated in section 14 of the TRC Act. With reference to gross violations of human rights the Committee was mandated, amongst other things, to enquire into systematic patterns of abuse, to try to identify motives and perspectives, to establish the identity of individual and institutional perpetrators and to designate accountability for gross human rights violations (TRC Report 1998, 1/10:267). According to the TRC Act 'gross violation of human rights' referred to "the violation of human rights through the killing, abduction, torture or severe ill-treatment of any person" (TRC Act, article ix).

The HRVC was made up of ten commissioners and ten committee members. The commissioners were:

> Archbishop Desmond Tutu (Chairperson, Cape Town)[1]
> Ms. Yasmin Sooka (Vice-Chairperson, Johannesburg)
> Mr. Wynand Malan (Vice-Chairperson, Johannesburg)
> Dr. Alex Boraine (Cape Town)
> Ms. Mary Burton (Cape Town)
> The Revd. Bongani Finca (East London)
> Mr. Richard Lyster (Durban)
> Mr. Dumisa Ntsebeza (Cape Town)
> Adv. Denzil Potgieter (Cape Town)
> Dr. Fazel Randera (Johannesburg)

---

1.   The regional offices in which these people were located are indicated between brackets.

The Human Rights Violations Committee members were:[2]

> Dr. Russell Ally (Johannesburg)
> Ms. June Crichton (East London)
> Mr. Mdu Dlamini (Durban)
> Ms. Virginia Gcabashe (Durban)
> Ms. Pumla Gobodo-Madikizela (Cape Town)
> Mr. Ilan Lax (Durban)
> Mr. Hugh Lewin (Johannesburg)
> Ms. Judith 'Tiny' Maya (East London)
> Ms. Motho Mosuhli[3] (East London)
> Adv. Ntsikilelo Sandi (East London)
> Ms. Joyce Seroke (Johannesburg)

The HRVC had a number of duties, among which were the setting up of public awareness initiatives to communicate the mandate of the Commission to the wider population and the contacting of various structures and organisations to encourage individuals to appear before the Commission. Two of their most important tasks were to initiate the statement taking process and to organise public hearings.

The taking of statements developed along a number of phases. Statement takers were recruited, trained and then sent out to record oral testimonies of apartheid victims. This happened in close cooperation with local organisations; especially social and religious institutions helped to inform people about the TRC and they encouraged individuals to give statements to the TRC. These statement takers tried to reach as many people as possible both in the rural and the urban areas. People could also approach the Commission on their own initiative by going to one of the branches of the TRC to submit a statement. In this way, the HRVC gathered close to 22,000 statements, covering 37,000 violations; this is more than any other previous truth commission had achieved (Graybill 2002: 8). The statements were then corroborated, verified and processed by means of an electronic database (TRC Report 1998, 1/10: 282).

The HRVC was also in charge of organising public hearings. In each of the regions the Human Rights Violations Committee selected a number of statements for public hearing. About 10% (1819 more precisely) of the victims who gave

---

2.  In this text, the terms 'commissioner' and 'committee member' will be used interchangeably. Usually, the term 'commissioner' will be used, for the sake of clarity and because also in the HRV transcriptions only this term is used.

3.  Tiny Maya resigned from the Commission at the end of 1997 and she was replaced by Motho Mosuhli.

written statements were selected to appear at the public hearings (Kgalema & van der Merwe 2003: 2). In selecting the testifiers a number of criteria were taken into account: their stories had to be representative for the experiences of many people in the region; they had to be able to resist the pressure and stress such a public hearing would involve; and they had to be able to express their ideas in a straightforward manner (TRC Report 1998, 5/1: 5; Buur 2000a: 159). Unfortunately, because there are no statistics or figures available on public HRV testifiers, we do not have a clear idea as to the break down of the testifiers in terms of gender, age, population group and regional background.

At these victim hearings considerable attention was paid to the individual personae of the victims. Simultaneous interpreting services were set up in order to allow people to testify in the language they preferred and psycho-social support was provided for the testifying victims and their families – for instance, during their testimonies victims were constantly assisted by 'briefers', staff members of the TRC who had been trained in order to psychologically support survivors of human rights violations.

Apart from the public victim hearings, the HRVC also held theme hearings and institutional hearings. Theme hearings were hosted with the aim of understanding patterns of abuse and motives of gross human rights violations. As with the public victim hearings there was a focus on victims, but their testimonies were important on a group level rather than on an individual level. Amongst others, theme hearings were held on the experiences of women, youths and children, on the issue of military service, and on a number of notorious events – such as the Soweto 1976 uprising, the killing of the 'Guguletu Seven', the Bisho massacre or the 'Trojan horse' incident in Cape Town (TRC Report 1998, 1/10: 281).

Institutional hearings focused primarily on organisations as opposed to individuals within those organisations. The idea behind the institutional hearings was to gather information on the role of certain institutions under apartheid. These hearings examined the prison system, the media, the legal system, the role of business during apartheid, the health care sector, the faith communities, the state security system, the role of the armed forces, and the involvement of the former state in chemical and biological warfare. In each of these hearings representatives of the institution in question came forward to talk about the way their institution had functioned during the apartheid era (TRC Report 1998, 1/10: 280). Some of these hearings were quite successful, like the hearings on the health care sector; others were disappointing, like the hearings in which the legal sector was scrutinised (Dyzenhaus 1998).

The first HRV public hearing took place in East London, on the 15th of April 1996. From then onwards, hearings were organised all over the country in locations as diverse as local churches, town halls and schools. All in all, almost 90 hearings took place in over 63 places; the last public victim hearings took place in Cape Town in May 1997, and the last special hearings in June 1998 (Meiring 1999: 380). The national as well as the international media devoted a lot of attention to the hearings of the HRVC. They were covered in newspaper articles daily; over the radio people could listen to live recordings of the hearings; the HRVC was a recurring item on the news, and special television programmes of these victim hearings were broadcast weekly (Wilson 2001a: 21).

The Committee on Human Rights Violations has been one of the most impressive aspects of the TRC. Hundreds of apartheid victims were given a voice and were offered a platform to talk about their experiences in the past. These testimonies revealed the extent to which apartheid has had a pernicious influence on the daily lives of many South Africans. In a later section attention will be paid to some of the positive and negative features of this Committee, features that will be crucial for the overall understanding of the TRC process.

## 2.3.2 The Amnesty Committee

In many other countries where truth commissions have been established, the amnesty procedure was often a separate legal mechanism (see Hayner 2001). In South Africa, however, the Amnesty Committee (AC) was an integral part of the TRC. The Committee was given the power, though, to decide independently who was going to be granted amnesty.

The primary function of the AC was to consider applications for amnesty that were made in accordance with the provisions of the TRC Act. Following the Act, the AC consisted initially of a chairperson, a vice-chairperson and three other members; these members had to be South African citizens, they should be appropriately qualified and they should be representative of the South African community. Because of the heavy workload, the number of members was increased on two occasions in order to complete the process in the shortest possible time. The final Committee included six High Court judges, eight advocates and five attorneys, and its national office was based in Cape Town (TRC Report 1998, 1/10: 266).

The final date for the submission of amnesty applications was midnight on the 30th of September 1997 and the total number of applications received before the deadline was 7127 (TRC Report 1998, 1/10: 266). In the first phase, only a few people applied for amnesty, but as time went on more apartheid perpetrators came forward to ask for pardon from the AC (Boraine 2000c: 122). The number of amnesty applicants dramatically increased after high level members of the security forces and the liberation movements came forward – mostly because people

were implicated in earlier applications and were afraid of prosecution if they did
not appear before the TRC. Few applications came from members of the National
Party, the Inkatha Freedom Party and the former South African Defence Force;
the majority of applicants were members of the liberation movements or of the
former South African Police (Graybill 2002: 67).

There were a number of strict criteria to comply with before amnesty could be
granted and most of the applicants – 5392 – were refused amnesty. Initially, applicants could apply for amnesty with respect to any offence committed between the
1st of March 1960 and the 6th of December 1993. This cut-off date was later extended to the 10th of May 1994. In addition, the criminal act had to be associated
with a political motive. This meant that offences committed for personal gain, or
out of personal malice, ill will or hatred were not eligible for amnesty (Hayner
2001: 43). Most importantly, in order to qualify for amnesty, applicants had to
make a full disclosure of their crimes, including the naming of those who had
ordered the offence. Finally, the AC took into account the proportionality of the
crime as well, by trying to find out whether the crime was proportional to its motives. The amnesty applicants were not required to show remorse when confessing
their human rights violations. When amnesty was granted, applicants were to be
free of all civil and criminal liability. In addition, the facts and revelations made
known at the hearings of the AC could never be used as evidence against the accused in a court of law. If amnesty was refused, the accused ran the risk of being
prosecuted in the future (TRC Report 1998, 1/5: 123).

Not all of the amnesty applications could be dealt with in public hearings;
the AC did not have enough time to do so. Applications were divided into three
groups: 'hearable matters' (those applications involving gross human rights violations and requiring a public hearing), 'chamber matters' (applications involving
violations of human rights which were not 'gross' as defined by the Act and which
did not require a public hearing – they were considered by the AC in chambers),
and 'possible refusals' (applications that, at least superficially, did not qualify for
amnesty in terms of the Act – these applications first had to be corroborated by
the Investigation Unit) (TRC Report 1998, 1/10: 269; Eyskens 2001: 31; Wilson
2001a: 23). The public amnesty hearings lasted from the 20th of May 1996 till the
20th of July 1998. The activities of the TRC were suspended on the 29th of October 1998, but the Amnesty Committee was authorised to continue until it had
completed its work – the President dissolved the Amnesty Committee with effect
from the 31st of May 2001 (TRC Report 2003, 6/1: 18).

### 2.3.3 The Reparation and Rehabilitation Committee

The TRC Act gave a large number of responsibilities to the Committee on Reparation and Rehabilitation (RRC). Amongst others, this Committee had to consider matters referred to it by the Human Rights Violations Committee and the Amnesty Committee; it had to gather evidence relating to the identity, fate and whereabouts of victims, and the nature and extent of the harm suffered by them; and it had to make recommendations to the President on measures for reparation and rehabilitation of victims and on measures to be taken to restore the human and civil dignity of victims (TRC Report 1998, 1/10: 284). The Committee was also involved in planning, preparing and conducting different hearings held throughout the country. Some of the event hearings (for example, the children and youth hearings) were the specific responsibility of the RRC.

The RRC consisted of five commissioners and five committee members and its head offices were located in Johannesburg. The RRC was soon confronted with two difficult issues: it was not at all clear who would qualify for reparations, nor was it clear what these reparations would consist of. In the course of the hearings of the Committee for Human Rights Violations, it became clear that the requests of some victims were quite modest. People sometimes asked for a memorial or a tombstone for their dead family members. Others wanted their deceased loved one to be exonerated, after he or she had been wrongly branded as a collaborator of the apartheid regime. Some victims, however, expected financial compensations and that was quite a problem for the Committee. The TRC did not have enough financial means at its disposal to financially compensate those victims. It could only formulate noncommittal recommendations, but the final decision lay in the hands of the government.

Since individual compensations would be difficult to realise, attention was paid to collective or symbolic reparations. Collective reparations included the improvement of infrastructure, medical care or education facilities in certain local communities, while symbolic reparations included the building of monuments, the issuing of death certificates, the organisation of ceremonial reburials, and the renaming of streets, schools and buildings after fallen heroes (TRC Report 1998, 5/5: 187).

## 2.4    The TRC as a favourable phenomenon

The TRC was clearly unique in a number of respects and many critics are convinced that the Commission has played a crucial role in shaping post-apartheid South Africa. A large number of articles, books and dissertations have tried to explain the favourable characteristics of the TRC in comparison to truth commissions in other countries. Let me highlight some of these positive features.

According to a number of scholars (amongst others Minow 1998:331 and Mooney 1998:215) a first positive achievement of the TRC concerned the airing of victims' personal experiences. For many victims the act of telling about their suffering under apartheid was psychologically very important and a healing experience (Govender 1998; Fourie 1999; Rakate 1999). It was often extremely difficult to relive the past, but most people were very relieved after having opened their hearts to the Commission. By telling their stories, victims realised that their suffering had not been a private matter, but that it had been part of a social experience in which millions of people played a role. In this way it became easier for them to deal with the past trauma and with the powerlessness and humiliations they had been confronted with for so many decades (Minow 1998:67). For many of the victims it was not only important mentally to tell their personal stories, but also to hear the truth from the mouth of the perpetrators. For many years they had been kept in the dark concerning the whereabouts of their loved ones and they were often relieved to finally learn the truth (Goodman 1999:181).

The disclosure of 'the truth' was clearly one of the aspects of the TRC highly valued by many victims (see also the research carried out by the Centre for the Study of Violence and Reconciliation in Johannesburg in 2001 as reported in for example Chapman 2003a, 2003b; Kgalema & van der Merwe 2003; Phakathi & van der Merwe 2003 and Picker 2003). It was especially important that through these testimonies everybody in South Africa had been obliged to confront the terrible past. For many months South African society was flooded with information about the TRC. Every day the written as well as the spoken media devoted attention to the proceedings of the Commission, through special programmes and live broadcasts. Children were given special courses on the TRC at school and many civil society associations or church groups set up information sessions. No one in South Africa – and beyond – could deny the apartheid past anymore, and this was psychologically very significant for many of the victims. For the first time in their lives, their suffering was acknowledged and they felt respected and valued by society. Many of them had wanted the world to know about the past and therefore they greatly appreciated the opportunity given to them to tell their stories in public.

A significant number of scholars are convinced that, in addition to the benefits of 'truth' disclosure, the second component of the TRC – the reconciliation part – has also been a success. Many publications argue that the aim of the TRC was not to achieve reconciliation, but rather to start a process of reconciliation (Godobo-Madikizela 1997; Parlevliet 1998a; Mxolisi 2000; Villa-Vicencio & Verwoerd 2000). A number of critics are convinced that this aim has been achieved

(Meiring 1999; Tutu 1999b; Boraine 2000c; Gibson 2004). According to them, South Africans have started to listen to each other, since the TRC brought about a culture of debate and open discussion. In this way, people have started to get to know each other better and this might be the beginning of a more reconciled society. Some recent surveys from the Institute for Justice and Reconciliation in Cape Town indicate that parts of the South African population seem to have a positive attitude towards reconciliation and forgiveness, indeed (IJR 2004).

At the Human Rights Violations hearings, victims sometimes expressed individual feelings of reconciliation or forgiveness. At the Amnesty hearings, encounters between victims and perpetrators took place and also there the audience could witness some amazing moments of reconciliation (see Tutu 1999b: 120). These individual instances of reconciliation were often the result of the actual encounters between victims and perpetrators. A number of victims stated that the opportunity to meet the person who committed the human rights violation was one of the major benefits of the TRC (Picker 2003: 18).

A number of critics argue that, in addition to facilitating precious moments of individual reconciliation, the TRC also helped to bring about a certain kind of reconciliation on a national level. According to these scholars, this is the case because through the establishment of a collective memory the TRC succeeded in achieving national unity (see Asmal, Asmal & Roberts 1997: 121; Lapsley 1998: 750 and Minow 1998: 345). In earlier times, these authors argue, black and white South Africans regarded each other as two distinct groups who happened to live together in the same country. After the proceedings of the TRC they saw each other as civilians of South Africa who were obliged to work together in order to build a new nation. The revelations of the TRC showed that each and every South African had a history in common, a history that could no longer be neglected and that brought about solidarity and feelings of togetherness.

Finally, the TRC is often considered as a model for so-called 'restorative justice' (Carnegie Council 1999; Llewellyn & Howse 1999; van Zyl 1999; Villa-Vicencio 2000b). The basic idea behind this kind of justice is not to achieve individual satisfaction or compensation, but to establish equality, humanity and respect among members of a society. Restorative justice is about restoring victims, offenders and communities, so according to some critics it is an ideal way to address issues of justice in transitional contexts. Because of the advantages of restorative justice, a number of scholars are convinced that the TRC delivered justice to the victims (Chapman 1999; Ndebele 1999; Rakate 1999). They claim that the TRC tried to pay tribute to the victims and that justice was also achieved through the perpetrator's shame of public exposure and through the reparation policy (McGregor 2001). Therefore, according to Archbishop Tutu (1999b), the chairman of the TRC, the South African model could be adapted and then implemented in conflict situations all over the world, such as Congo, Angola, Sudan or the Middle East (see also Derrida 1999: 129).

## 2.5    Negative critiques on the TRC

Right from the start the TRC was severely criticised by a number of political parties. The National Party and the Inkatha Freedom Party, for instance, were convinced that the TRC was merely an instrument in the hands of the ANC and that its decisions were biased. They claimed that the TRC did not fully investigate the ANC gross human rights violations and that it brought about a view on the past favourable to the ANC. Indeed, according to some critics the TRC was politicised through the selection of commissioners – they said that the majority of the appointed commissioners could be considered as pro-ANC, through the amnesty process and through the controversies on reparations and prosecutions (Robins 1998b: 11; Shea 2000; Cleveland 2002: 14). I will come back to this item in 7.8.

A second major form of critique came from a number of apartheid victims who were convinced that the TRC process was unjust. Perpetrators who appeared before the TRC and who met the criteria in order to be granted amnesty were acquitted from any civil or criminal liability. These individual perpetrators had to confess their crimes in public, which turned out to be a very difficult task on a psychological and a social level. Nor was the granting of amnesty guaranteed and perpetrators who did not come forward could still be prosecuted. Nevertheless, many apartheid victims were convinced that the TRC process was perpetrator-friendly and that real justice solely involved the judicial prosecution and punishment of perpetrators. A number of victims manifestly disagreed with the TRC and some of them – for example the family of Steve Biko – even challenged the amnesty principle of the TRC before court. They claimed that the amnesty procedure was unconstitutional, since the South African Constitution states that every citizen has the right to seek recourse in the court of law when he or she feels wronged (Motala 1995; Manda 1996). Many victims felt that the TRC robbed them of any sense of personal justice since perpetrators went free, without any moral or material compensation for the victims. In addition, due to the inefficiency of the South African legal system and to the lack of evidence implicating perpetrators, there was only a very slight chance that perpetrators who had not come forward or who had been refused amnesty would be prosecuted in the future. Victims were also convinced that many perpetrators had only told their version of a certain human rights violation, while they doubted that this version came anywhere near 'the truth'.

With regard to the truth, a number of commentators wondered about the extent to which the TRC had actually revealed the truth about the apartheid past. An 'objective truth' had definitely not been revealed, since each witness had talked about reality from his or her own personal perspective (Adam 1997; Henderson 2000). In particular because of practical problems it had been difficult for the TRC to reveal the whole apartheid truth – the main problem being that the old government had destroyed a huge amount of incriminating evidence, especially in the period 1990–1994. Another problem was that thousands of victims had indeed told their stories before the TRC, but that the vast majority of South Africans had not come forward. The response of high-ranking officials was especially disappointing, and the testimonies of those who did come forward had often been unbelievable (Dunn 1997: 34; Stanley 2001: 532). There was a general impression that while minor officials did come forward for fear of prosecution, their superiors got away. People like the former Presidents Botha and de Klerk refused to take their responsibilities and this was a huge disappointment to many South Africans (Goodman 1999: 179). Certain political groups, like the Inkatha Freedom Party and the Pan-Africanist Congress also boycotted the Commission.

All of these aspects caused critics to argue that the Commission had only revealed a partial truth and definitely not 'the truth' about the apartheid past (Mamdani 1997; Pigou 2003). In the words of Michael Ignatieff (1997: 8): "All that the truth commission could achieve was to reduce the number of lies that can be circulated unchallenged in public discourse."

With regard to reconciliation, critics admitted that there had been instances of individual reconciliation during the TRC hearings or as a result of the hearings. Nevertheless, certain people argue, reconciliation is such a personal feeling that it cannot be imposed by an official institution like the TRC (Hamber & Wilson 1999; Stanley 2001). It is therefore questionable that individual reconciliation was brought about by the TRC, especially since reconciliation would be enhanced by signals of repentance, by apologies from apartheid leaders, or by white acknowledgement of past wrongdoings – elements that were often lacking during the TRC process (Pauw 1998).

The failure to realise material changes in the lives of apartheid victims is often seen as one of the biggest shortcomings of the TRC, and more specifically of the Reparation and Rehabilitation Committee. In the TRC Act provisions were made to grant material compensation to the victims of apartheid – these reparations were to compensate for the amnesty given to some of the apartheid perpetrators and were seen as crucial for the reconciliation process. The RRC was to make recommendations to the President on appropriate measures for reparation and rehabilitation of victims and on measures to be taken to restore the human and civil dignity of victims (TRC Report 1998, 1/10: 284).

Many victims and survivors of human rights violations expected the TRC to provide monetary reparations for them in exchange for their participation in the hearings. A first problem regarding this idea was that the TRC could only recommend reparations to the government – they were not brought into effect immediately. The second problem was that the government was not keen on establishing an effective reparations policy. It was only in April 2003 that President Mbeki ruled that the government would provide a one-off grant of 30,000 Rand to those individuals designated by the TRC (Stoppard 2003). This offer left many apartheid victims – and also people closely connected to the TRC such as Wendy Orr (2000a) and Zenzile Khoisan (2001) – very disappointed; from the start of the process onwards they had expected a much more substancial amount of money.

I have been quite elaborate in discussing the positive and negative features of the TRC. This discussion will turn out to be indispensable in order to grasp the remainder of this work, especially the analysis of the victim testimonies in later chapters. For now, it is important to realise that it is very difficult to be unambiguously positive or negative about the TRC. We could tentatively argue that it was a praiseworthy undertaking, necessary for the future of South Africa. Many of its features, though, could have been improved and some of its anticipated achievements or results turned out to be failures.

## 2.6    Language at the HRV hearings

Since this research involves a discursive analysis of the language used at the HRV hearings, it is necessary to give some background information on this highly complex HRV discourse. I will first dwell on the concrete use of language at the HRV hearings; in section 2.7. TRC discourse will be approached from a Foucaultian point of view.

The TRC Act (Section 11 (f), Chapter 25) stipulates that "appropriate measures shall be taken to allow victims to communicate in the language of their choice" (http://www.doj.gov.za/trc/trc_frameset.htm), which means that right from the start the TRC was confronted with the complexities of South Africa's multilingualism. The statements of the victims who told their stories to the TRC were taken down in the home language of the victim. These statements were supposed to be translated into English, but according to du Plessis & Wiegand (1997: 15) this was seldom done in practice.

About 10% of the victims who had given statements were then selected to tell their stories in public. Considering the victim-orientedness of the HRV hearings, special attention was paid to ensuring that the victims would feel at ease when testifying. Therefore, the victims were allowed to tell their stories in the languages of their choice, even if these languages fell outside of the eleven official languages of South Africa (TRC Report 1998, 10/1:282). In practice, most of the languages used at the hearings fell within the group of official languages.

This multilingual provision demanded the establishment of an extensive interpreting service. The Language Facilitation Programme (LFP) of the University of the Free State was among the agencies that were approached to render this service. It was the LFP that assisted the TRC in the training of the interpreters and the management of the interpreting service. The LFP's team of interpreters covered practically all possible combinations of the eleven official languages, so each hearing displayed a unique language situation. Never before had such an extensive and continual interpreting service been supplied in South Africa, never before had so many interpreters been trained and employed simultaneously and never before had the different African languages been used so consistently on such a scale in a high status function[4] (du Plessis & Wiegand 1997:13).

The LFP's agreement with the TRC stipulated that no more than four languages would be used per hearing. The channels available to listeners at the hearings were standardised as follows:

- Channel 1: Afrikaans (if requested, otherwise the channel was dead)
- Channel 2: English
- Channel 3: dominant language of the region
- Channel 4: additional language of the region (du Plessis & Wiegand 1997:21).

The fact that English service was provided at every hearing is an indication of the TRC's language policy to use English as the main language of communication. According to a preliminary analysis carried out by du Plessis & Wiegand (1997), an Afrikaans translation service was provided at 64.9% of the hearings. This is a surprisingly high figure, since only a small percentage of the victims spoke Afrikaans. This figure could be attributed to a deliberate symbolic gesture on the part of the Commission: by supplying an Afrikaans interpreting service they tried to get the Afrikaans speakers more involved, which would enhance their favourable feelings towards the TRC. Of the African language services, the Xhosa, Zulu and Sotho services were used most extensively.

A commonplace in the field of translation studies is that interpreting always involves a reconstruction and a re-composition of the original discourse. According to Walter Benjamin (quoted in Asad 1993:189) a translation has to try to "give voice to the *intention* of the original, not as reproduction, but as harmony, as a

---

4. 'African language' is a controversial term in current day South Africa. Although the term LOTAE (Language Other Than Afrikaans and English) is claimed to be a better alternative (see du Plessis & Wiegand 1997), I will use the term 'African language' for practical reasons.

supplement to the language in which it expresses itself, as its own kind of *inten-tion.*" (in Buur 2000a: 213). Although the term 'translating' was given a word-ori-ented reading at the TRC (Blommaert & Slembrouck 2000: 29) – the interpreters were not *supposed* to interpret or evaluate the victims' discourse, it goes without saying that neutrality or objectivity were out of the question. It lies beyond the scope of this work to talk about the difficulties interpreters encounter when try-ing to reformulate the intention of the original. However, since the data used for this analysis consist predominantly of translated material, it is useful to give an idea of the problems the interpreters came across at the Human Rights Violations hearings.

Compared to the Amnesty hearings, language at the HRV hearings was more informal and the vocabulary tended to be of a more general nature. The testimo-nies were often heavily charged with emotion and they usually displayed a strong narrative structure. Importantly, the narrative technique could differ consider-ably from victim to victim: some victims were extremely eloquent and went into great detail when recounting their apartheid experiences; others were hesitant, needed a lot of feedback from the facilitator, or talked very incoherently. The ma-jority of interpreters did not have a lot of experience in simultaneous interpreting and they could be unfamiliar with different language varieties as used during the hearings. Indeed, since the TRC victims came from different regional and social backgrounds and belonged to different age groups, there could be a wide variety of different speech styles. Moreover, the TRC victims were described as 'ordinary people' and most of them did not have any experience in public speaking. They tended not to take into consideration their rate or volume of speech and many times the facilitators had to urge testifiers to speak up or to speak slower, with an eye to the interpreters (du Plessis & Wiegand 1997).

Many HRV interpreters found their work extremely stressful. They had to listen to horrifying stories for many days in a row and especially to identify with the victims was very demanding emotionally. This emotional component made interpreting at the HRV hearings very difficult. Although the debriefing service offered to the commissioners and officials by the TRC was also available to the interpreters, more attention could have been paid to these psychological features in the course of the training period (du Plessis & Wiegand 1997: 18).

In addition, it was often difficult for interpreters to find a balance between, on the one hand adhering to the *ideal* discourse of a positivist translator, and on the other hand the *practice* of interpretation, where the emotional persona could not be dismissed. The interpreters could try to maintain their objective, profes-sional persona, but this desired distance with the victim sometimes collapsed. As Buur (2000a: 231) testifies, interpreters sometimes gave their translated words a particular emotional tone in order to stress a victim's humanity or mental situation. Although this was against the code of professional conduct, it seemed to be an unavoidable aspect of HRV interpreting.

It was a general rule at the TRC that the commissioners tried to communicate in the victims' own languages – this was possible to a certain extent since the HRV Committee consisted of commissioners from different linguistic groups in South Africa. More often, though, the chair of the hearing or the commissioner who acted as facilitator did not speak any of the languages of the testifying victim. Yasmin Sooka and Denzil Potgieter, for instance, knew both English and Afrikaans, but since the testifiers were mainly non-Afrikaans – African – speakers, they mostly used English. Alex Boraine often functioned as the chair of the hearing and he always spoke English. Also Desmond Tutu, although he sometimes used several languages when opening the hearings, usually spoke English when leading a testifier. This means that even when commissioners and testifiers had a common language, English was sometimes preferred as the language of interaction.

Not only commissioners, but also victims themselves sometimes reverted to English, without this being their mother tongue. As mentioned before, it was indeed the language policy of the TRC to use English as a communication language – although clear efforts were made to value each of the languages spoken by the testifiers. This language policy became manifest in several distinct ways, in addition to the concrete language practice at the hearings. The Official TRC Website, for instance, solely exists in English. All of the public testimonies given at the TRC are available on this website, but it is only the English discourse – of the testifier, but more often of the interpreter – that was transcribed. Only very rarely were some words or sentences transcribed in the original language and this mostly happened when the testifiers uttered Afrikaans phrases. As we will see later, this use of Afrikaans often had a pragmatic meaning.

When comparing the transcriptions as available on the website with the language of the interpreters as heard on the video and audio tapes, you notice that they are not always identical. The language of the interpreters formed the basis for the English transcriptions, but at certain points this language was edited before being put on the website (personal conversation with TRC interpreters from the University of the Free State, June and November 2003). It would be interesting to explore when and why there is a difference between the English translations at the actual hearing site and the transcribed English, but at this point I will not go further into this linguistic feature.

Also the TRC Final Report is written entirely in English. It is only the brochure 'Time to Act', which was published by the Institute for Justice and Reconciliation and which contains a summary of the TRC recommendations as found in the Final Report, that was translated in Afrikaans and in Xhosa (http://www.ijr. org.za/broch.html). The fact that the meta-language of the Commission was English, i.e. the language through which the TRC was defined and conceptualised, is another indication of the hegemony of English in the proceedings of the TRC. Key notions like repentance, forgiveness or reconciliation, for example, were English terms, which could not always be easily translated in the other South African languages (Derrida 2002:66).

The media seemed to assist the TRC in realising its English-oriented language policy. The South African Broadcasting Corporation (SABC) recorded each of the testimonies on video and audio tape. Each of these testimonies existed in several different linguistic versions: there was the original language as spoken by the commissioners and testifiers, there was always a version in English, usually also in Afrikaans, and also in the two dominant languages of the region. Apparently, each of these four or five different versions was taped separately by the SABC – so for each of the testimonies four or five video and audio recordings should be available at the SABC archive (personal conversation with TRC interpreters from the University of the Free State, in June and November 2003). However, when fragments of the hearings were shown in the news or in special programmes, it was always the English version that was used. Also when live footage of the hearings was broadcast on national television, only this English version was made available. In this way, both the national and the international audience got to know the TRC through the English language-medium.

This language policy of the TRC is understandable considering the international appearance of the Commission. The TRC wanted to stand as an example of restorative justice, not only in South Africa, but in the entire world. In particular the Final Report and the TRC website aimed at an international audience, so the choice of English was self-evident. However, the fact that basically everything was translated into English tells us that we should be cautious when interpreting the testimonies that were originally made in a different language (Derrida 2002:64). Within the circles of discourse analysis (see Hymes 1981:38; Duranti 1997:137; Hutchby & Wooffitt 1998:92; Cameron 2001:43) it is a commonly held principle that researchers should work with original data; secondary material and translations are to be avoided. Since the data for this research predominantly consist of English translations, it is important to stress that I am well aware of this interpretation issue. When discussing my data in a later chapter I will come back to the reasons for using the translated material after all.

## 2.7   Discourse at the HRV hearings

At different stages of the TRC process different types of discourse seemed to be constructed. There is a long tradition of treating discourse in linguistic terms, either as a complex of linguistic forms larger than the single sentence or as 'language-in-use', so linguistic structures actually used by people (Blommaert 2005: 2). In this book the term *discourse* is understood in a Foucaultian sense, for instance as explained in his 'L'Archéologie du Savoir' from 1969. The most general and the vaguest way in which Foucault has used *discourse*, as he explains in this work, is by referring to "a group of verbal performances", so "that which was produced by the groups of signs" (Foucault 2002: 107). More specifically, though, Foucault sees *discourse* as denoting a "group of statements that belong to a single system of formation", such as "clinical discourse, economic discourse, the discourse of natural history, psychiatric discourse" (Foucault 2002: 107–108). In this definition, a 'discursive formation' is the "principle of dispersion and redistribution of statements". Importantly, this system of formation goes beyond the idea of discourses as particular linguistic systems and encompasses, amongst others, the material settings of discourses, their institutional sites, etc. (Pentzold & Seidenglanz 2006: 63). It is this more specific definition of discourse that I will use in this work.

In its day-to-day running, the most common discourse used at the TRC was that of *legal discourse*: the setting at the hearings resembled a courtroom setting and terminology used included *cases, witnesses, findings, testimonies, evidence, subpoenas*, etc. (Stibbe & Ross 1997: 20). It was especially at the hearings of the Amnesty Committee, where apartheid perpetrators came forward to apply for amnesty, that the dominant discourse was legal. Truth finding was the main concern at these hearings and the participants included lawyers, solicitors and judges, all of whom were familiar with the adversarial kind of legal discourse. The hearings were seen as a quasi-legal process, complete with witnesses, plaintiffs, defendants, rules of evidence, legal guidelines and procedures, translators and court reporters (Colvin 2003: 8); for more details on discourse used at the Amnesty hearings, see de Klerk (2003a, 2003b).

Another framing narrative at the TRC was the political narrative of *nation building* (Wilson 1996; Harper 2000: 67; du Toit 2002). One of the overall objectives of the Commission was to strive for solidarity among South Africans and the public hearings were especially important to this project of national unity. According to Humphrey (2000: 18) individual stories of past experiences were condensed and homogenised and turned into a new nationalist narrative.

Wilson (2001a: 104) has distinguished three framing *reconciliation narratives* at the TRC: the legal-procedural narrative, the mandarin-intellectual narrative and the religious-redemptive narrative. The legal-procedural narrative was dominant among TRC lawyers, especially at the Amnesty Committee. It was a legal positivist view of reconciliation, which emerged as a result of the application of legal principles contained within the Act, and which was immune to personal emotions or values. The mandarin-intellectual narrative rejected an individually-oriented notion of reconciliation and focused on a more abstract understanding of reconciliation. Within this approach, reconciliation was situated on the level of the nation; South Africans were urged to reconcile with their past rather than with each other. The religious-redemptive narrative pursued a notion of reconciliation as a common good, defined by confession, forgiveness and redemption, and the exclusion of vengeance. This kind of reconciliation discourse was mostly expressed at the Human Rights Violations hearings and it did not so much seek the reconciliation of the nation, but the reconciliation between individuals within the nation (Wilson 2001a: 104–109).

Ross (2003b: 13) has referred to three discourses of recovery (medical, psychological and religious); Lars Buur (2000b) has written about the bureaucratic, positivist and technical discourses that underpinned the work of the TRC; and Posel & Simpson (2002: 11) have identified "science, law, global news, documentary drama, religious confessional, and the rhetoric of nation building" as some of the "distinct discursive domains" implicated in the production of the TRC's 'truth'. Finally, Leonard Praeg (2000) suggested that there are three distinct discourses constitutive of the general TRC discourse: a nationalist discourse, a Christian discourse and a discourse on *ubuntu*, or African humanism.

Clearly, the TRC's discursive complexity has been addressed by a number of researchers already, although an extensive discourse analytic investigation has not been carried out so far.

This present monograph focuses on the hearings of the Human Rights Violations Committee. These hearings did not so much concentrate on the veracity of the testimonies, and the discourse was not openly framed in a legal or quasi-judicial way. The language employed here was rather oriented towards reconciliation, forgiveness, compassion and sympathy. This HRV discourse can be regarded as a combination of psychotherapeutic discourse, religious discourse and to a lesser extent also courtroom discourse.

With regard to therapeutic discourse, for instance, the HRV commissioners often claimed that giving testimony would be positive and healing to the body. In fact, although the word 'healing' was absent in the TRC Act, the term became a very powerful and prominent metaphor amongst members of the HRVC and amongst journalists when referring to the Committee's activities. Storytelling was framed as a therapeutic exercise and feelings of anger and vengeance sometimes seemed to be signs of underlying psychological pathologies (see Allan 2000: 200; Chapman 2003b: 27; Colvin 2003).

The religious discourse mostly took shape through the religious and quasi-religious utterances and interventions of different members of the HRV Committee. Chairman Desmond Tutu in particular used to frame the HRV testimonies in theological terms, but this was also a recurring feature amongst other committee members with a religious background, such as Alex Boraine, Piet Meiring and Reverend Finca. The dramatic figure of Desmond Tutu, dressed in his purple robe, urging not only victims, but all South Africans, to put the ethic of forgiveness into practice, has been an enduring image of the TRC (Colvin 2003:9). It seemed as if the Christian doctrine of forgiveness was continually invoked, together with other religious values such as the importance of the community and the sanctity of the truth (Corry & Terre Blanche 2000:9). Also the hall where the hearings took place was usually transformed into a proto-religious setting: the tables were covered in long white cloths, flowers were displayed, and a candle was lit at the beginning of the hearings (Bozzoli 1998:170).[5]

Different examples of these types of discourse, as apparent in the testimonies of the victims, will be pointed out when analysing my data later. Of course, none of these discourses can be easily isolated from the others; many individuals and groups before the TRC used several of these discourses at once, often 'plagiarising' from one to support another (Wilson 2001a), as we will see later on.

Despite the apparent ambiguity and complexity present in the discourse used at the HRV hearings, many observers have noted how the victim hearings became 'standardised' and 'ritualised' very soon after the first ones were held in East London in April 1996 (Bozzoli 1998; Graybil 2002:82, Ross 2003a). In her ethnographic account of testifying before the HRVC, Fiona Ross (2003a:13–15) describes some of the key elements of a prototypical hearing as follows:

> Each testifier was called to the stage, sworn in, asked to describe his or her family background and … the violation about which they had made a statement … in the initial hearings, testimonies lasted from between 15 minutes to more than an hour and a half. Towards the end of the Commission's work, most testimonies lasted approximately 30 minutes … If a testifier stumbled or halted during testimony, the designated committee member asked "probing questions" … On a few occasions, when a witness cried, Archbishop Tutu led the audience in a hymn … Usually, however, a silence was preserved in the hall until the testifier's equilibrium was restored … When each testifier finished … the chairperson solicited additional questions (usually of clarification) … Testifiers were not cross-examined … When no further questions were forthcoming … the testifier was thanked, dismissed from the stage and taken for "debriefing". The next testifier was called and the process repeated.

Wilson (2001a:111–112) pursues a similar analysis in his description of the 'interpretative template' laid across individual victims' testimonies. He identifies four

---

5.   We should note that candles were not solely a religious sign in South Africa; before 1994 they had also been a characteristic of the silent protest against apartheid.

predictable chronological stages – recognising and collectivising suffering, the moral equalising of suffering, liberation and sacrifice, and redemption through forsaking revenge – that describe the routine ways commissioners took the stories of victims.

It was not only the format of the testimonies that was soon 'routinised'; a similar process of standardisation took place at the level of the stories' content. In fact, the stories at these hearings were primarily event-centred and individual accounts of physical suffering. Structural or everyday violations experienced by individuals, families and communities were not so much addressed (Colvin 2003: 3). Usually, the narrative of the victim began with the critical event itself – the phone call, the sound of an explosion, etc. When testifiers did not describe the traumatic events straight away, they were told by the commissioners to address only the violations that they had mentioned in their statements.

Very soon, therefore, according to Colvin, one could notice the emergence of an ideal-typical testimonial process in the course of the HRV hearings. This kind of storytelling as promoted by the TRC has then become the predominant model for speaking about suffering in the past in South Africa. The fact is that there were few precedents for this kind of public testimony about the apartheid past. And, especially, not a lot of other storytelling genres existed with the same kind of public recognition and legitimacy enjoyed by TRC testimonies.

Still today a number of victim-oriented organisations in South Africa make use of the storytelling format as it was developed during the HRV hearings. Let me give the example of the Khulumani Support Group (KSG). As a non-governmental organisation KSG was established in 1995 by the survivors and families of the victims of South Africa's apartheid regime. Khulumani means "Speak Out" in Zulu and was formed as an umbrella body operating under the Centre for the Study of Violence and Reconciliation (CSVR), until it de-linked itself in 1999. In its initial phase, KSG helped South Africans to gain access to the TRC process and it dedicated most of its time and resources to addressing the demands of the Truth and Reconciliation Commission. From 2000 onwards it helped victims to voice their opinions and make known their needs, amongst others by organising discussion groups where people can talk about their experiences under apartheid (http://www.khulumani.net/index.htm).

After the closing down of the TRC, voices were raised that the process should be repeated on a smaller scale. It was claimed that schools, churches, companies and private institutions, for instance, should establish their own internal truth commissions to investigate atrocities committed under apartheid. These internal mini-TRC's would provide a space for people and organisations to confront the past and they would also produce sets of recommendations. The Faculty of Health Sciences at Wits University has launched an internal reconciliation commission process and it is claimed that such an initiative could be an effective mechanism for achieving change at the local level (Goodman & Price 1999: 18).

Both these internal commissions and the discussion groups at Khulumani are examples of forums where the story-format as standardised at the HRV hearings was brought into practice. We will see that the thirty case studies used for this analysis also correspond to this testimonial standard. However, although this standard functioned as an overall template, participants still used different discourses, with different connotations and different indexicalities. These discourses were layered, combined and intertwined with each other in a highly complex manner. Trying to shed light on this discursive complexity – and especially on the reasons behind this complexity – will be one of the aims of this research.

# CHAPTER 3

# The TRC archive

## 3.1 The 'archive' as a concept

The establishment of the Truth and Reconciliation Commission, its proceedings and its final results, were seen as an attempt to reconstitute South Africa's apartheid past. The apartheid experience was to be reconstructed and then recorded and treasured to serve as a reminder of the past for future generations. Thousands of testimonies were gathered, many of them were distributed in public, a Final Report summarised the Commission's findings and many books, articles and dissertations reflected on the proceedings and the outcome of the Commission. In this way, the TRC can be considered as a place of archive; more particularly, it is a public archive (Derrida 2002: 49).

The word 'archive' derives from the Greek *arkhé,* which, according to Derrida (1996: 1), refers both to "there where things commence", "there where men and gods command" and "there where authority, social order are exercised". As a number of authors testify, the archive is a remarkable concept. It is an uncommon place, "at the intersection of [...] the place and the law, the substrate and the authority"; it "marks this institutional passage from the private to the public" (Derrida 1996: 2–32). The archive is a dual concept, which refers not only to the past, by means of repetition and remembrance, but also to the future. Derrida (1996: 68) therefore calls the archive "the affirmation of the future to come".

Although archiving is traditionally understood as an act of remembering, at a profound level it is also an act of forgetting (Derrida 2002: 54; Verne Harris 2002a: 81). The archive determines what can be forgotten or destroyed, so we can claim that destruction – Derrida (1996: 94) even calls it *archival violence* – is an inherent element of the process of archiving. The fact that archiving involves forgetting can be understood in a twofold way. Firstly, by deciding what will be included or excluded from the archive, the archivists decide what will be remembered and forgotten in the future. Because of this monopoly position, the society invests an enormous amount of power in the archivist, what Derrida (1996: 3) calls *the archontic power.* Secondly, the aspect of forgetting also works within the inclusions of the archive. The archived records are being stored away in order to be able to forget them – because you know that it will be possible to retrieve them again when needed. Or, as aptly illustrated by Derrida (2002:54): "When I handwrite something on a piece of paper, I put it in my pocket or in a safe, it's just in order to forget it, to know that I can find it again while in the meantime having forgotten it".

An archive is often not closed either; it is usually characterised by open-ended layerings of construction and deconstruction. The archive can be considered as a "quasi-infinity of layers, of archival strata that are at once superimposed, over-printed and enveloped in each other" (Derrida 1996:22). To read and investigate the archive requires an activity that Derrida equates with geological or archaeo-logical excavations. An archive is always a reconstruction and a reinterpretation of the past – which means that it is crucial for an understanding of the present and future of a society. In short, the archive is "the foundation of the production of knowledge in the present, the basis for the identities of the present and for the possible imaginings of community in the future" (Hamilton et al. 2002:9).

In this book the word 'archive' will be a key term. In essence this research can be defined as an investigation/exploration of the TRC Archive. When talk-ing about 'the TRC Archive' a distinction will be made between the prevailing, day-to-day meaning of archive as a physical record on the one hand, and the term 'archive' in a Foucaultian sense on the other. First, attention will be paid – brief-ly – to the first significance of 'the TRC Archive', by which the term archive, in ac-cordance with the Oxford Dictionary, will be defined as a "collection of historical documents or records of a government, town, etc." or a "place where such records are kept" (Oxford Advanced Learner's Dictionary 2005:67). Further on in this chapter I will also refer to this type of TRC archive by means of the words 'physi-cal TRC archive' or 'material TRC archive'.

Our understanding of the ways in which the TRC recorded and preserved its physical data will then serve as a point of departure for the construction of the 'Foucaultian TRC Archive'. Foucault's view is that an archive is not simply an in-stitution, but rather the law of what can be said, the system of statements, or rules of practice, that give shape to what can and cannot be said. In this way, archives are often both documents of exclusion and avenues to particular configurations of power (Hamilton et al. 2002:9). Therefore, an inquiry into the TRC Archive will involve an attempt to understand the conditions and circumstances of preserva-tion of the material, as well as investigating the relations of power determining inclusion and exclusion of data from the record. Since Foucault's image of the archive is central to the theoretical framework applied in this study, I will come back to it extensively later on.

## 3.2    The material TRC archive

### 3.2.1    Primary data

This physical TRC archive consists of different kinds of material. The construction of this archive already started before the inception of the Commission. Numerous articles were written in anticipation of the TRC (see for example Simpson 1993; Miller 1995; Minnaar 1995; Newham 1995), and there were some official publications on the coming into existence of the Commission as well – publications that resulted in the TRC Act as the Commission's formal starting point. Also, in preparation of the TRC, the Centre for the Study of Violence and Reconciliation in Johannesburg issued a cartoon where the objectives and working procedures of the Commission were explained. By means of uncomplicated language this cartoon tried to make the TRC concept accessible to South Africans who were beyond the reach of regular media.

The main part of the TRC archive, however, took shape after the TRC Act had been accepted by parliament in July 1995. The first component of the archive to consider should be the Truth and Reconciliation Commission of South Africa's Report. This Report consists of two separate issues: there is the Interim Report (finished in 1998) and then the Final Report (finished in 2003). The compilation of this Report was mentioned as one of the Commission's objectives in the TRC Act: "the objectives of the Commission shall be to promote national unity [...] by compiling a report providing as comprehensive an account as possible of the activities and findings of the Commission [...], and which contains recommendations of measures to prevent the future violations of human rights" (TRC Act, Chapter 2, Article 3, 1(d)). This indicates that this Report was meant to be an officialised reflection on the TRC process, as well as an authoritative archive of the apartheid past. Therefore, the TRC Report can be considered as one of the main pillars of the material TRC archive.

In addition to the TRC Report, another important element of the TRC archive is the Official TRC Website (http://www.doj.gov.za/trc/trc_frameset.htm). By making use of the World Wide Web the TRC attempted to increase the accessibility of its archive – a clear indication that transparency and accountability were cherished values in the TRC ideology. This website gives an extensive overview of the Commission and it contains many extremely valuable documents, which cannot easily be consulted in any other way. Amongst others, the site provides the transcriptions and decisions of each and every Amnesty hearing, the submissions before the TRC of the political parties, the transcriptions of all of the Human Rights Violations hearings, the special hearings and the institutional hearings, and the policy documents and workshop transcripts of the Reparation and Rehabilitation Committee. Although the site is no longer updated (the last update dates from 10th April 2003), it is still an indispensable source of information for TRC researchers.

Besides the TRC Report and the Official TRC Website, the material TRC archive also consists of a wealth of primary data that was collected during the life span of the Commission. These records include the written statements taken from the 21,290 victims, the transcripts of the workshops and in camera hearings held by the TRC, reflections on the research carried out by the Investigation Unit, etc.

Both the TRC website and the TRC Report offer an abundance of research material. There is yet another important part of the TRC archive to be considered, though, namely the original audio-visual data. With regard to audio material, all of the TRC public hearings were recorded by the radio service of the South African Broadcasting Corporation. Many hours of live recordings were transmitted over the radio and a lot of South Africans got in touch with the Commission predominantly through these radio broadcasts. The audio recordings of the TRC public hearings are available at the SABC and they can be consulted by researchers. The SABC also recorded each of the public hearings of the TRC on video and all of these tapes are in the possession of the SABC in Johannesburg.

### 3.2.2 Secondary data

So far, I have only talked about primary TRC documents. However, a large – if not the largest – part of the material TRC archive consists of secondary material. The number of articles, books, dissertations and scholarly papers produced on the South African TRC is basically immeasurable. Especially at the time of the actual TRC proceedings (mainly between April 1996 and October 1998), national – and to a lesser extent also international – newspapers devoted a lot of attention to the Commission. Certain newspapers had journalists working full-time on the TRC and the Commission appeared in many of the national newspapers on a daily basis. Giving an overview of all of the popular articles on the TRC that appeared in magazines and newspapers is an almost impossible task. This part of the TRC archive is accessible, but it is so vast that the researcher is definitely confronted with methodological problems. There is, however, research material available for many more generations to come.

Also the number of scholarly publications has increased continuously over the last couple of years. In academic circles all over the world the TRC has been reflected upon from every possible perspective, be it judicial, psychological, religious, linguistic or political – to mention but a few. In the initial phase of the TRC, these publications were merely descriptive; later on they turned out to be rather evaluative. A comprehensive bibliography of – mainly – academic TRC publications is provided by Graybill (2002).

Also the TRC Research Website (http://cas1.elis.rug.ac.be/avrug/trc.htm) gives an updated overview of the worldwide production on the South African TRC. Evidence of continued academic interest in the TRC is also to be found in the number of conferences, workshops and seminars organised almost monthly. Some of the conferences only have the TRC as topic, but even more frequently the TRC is the subject of one of the panels, lectures or discussion sessions at internationally renowned conferences. All over the world Ph.D. students are concentrating on the TRC and even special courses or semester programmes deal with the Truth Commission. All of this has resulted in a huge network of authors and researchers focussing on the TRC.

In addition to articles, books and academic research, there is also an increasing amount of audio-visual secondary material being produced. Throughout the lifetime of the TRC, special radio and television programmes were broadcast, especially by the South African Broadcasting Corporation. The most popular of these special programmes was probably the television series 'Special Report'. This programme was broadcast every Sunday evening from the 21st of April 1996 till the 29th of March 1998; altogether 87 Special Reports were transmitted.

Also special documentaries were made on the TRC, both inside South Africa and abroad. Two of the best known video documentaries are 'Long Night's Journey into Day' (1999) and 'Facing the Truth' (1999).

Finally, I should mention one facet of the TRC archive that is not always taken into consideration: artistic creations and material objects. Literature, theatre, dance and art all offer archival possibilities to release information about the past. Literature about the TRC is on the rise and already a number of novels and plays have the Truth Commission as their main topic – for instance 'Ubu and the Truth Commission' by Jane Taylor (1998) or 'Red Dust' by Gillian Slovo (2001). More recently, also the artistic Truth in Translation Project (http://www.truthintranslation.org/) has the TRC as its theme.

The preceding paragraphs have attempted to give a – definitely incomplete – impression of the existing material archive of the TRC. It should be clear that it will be impossible to ever close this TRC archive. One part of the archive, consisting of the primary records, has been closed already, when the data collection was concluded, when the hearings were over and when the Final Report was published. The largest part of the archive will never be closed, however. Everyone will be able to add something to this archive, to criticise it or to reinterpret it. This archive will be open to an infinite number of readings, interpretations and contestations, so there will never be a final closure.

This insight into the material TRC archive will now be the starting point for our investigation of the TRC archive as understood by Foucault. As hinted at in the beginning of this chapter, archiving involves a complex network of inclusion, exclusion, forgetting, remembering, construction and reconstruction, all of which being determined by power relations. It is this exploration of power relations that lies at the basis of Foucault's understanding of the archive.

## 3.3    The archive in a Foucaultian sense

The concept of the archive takes a central place in Foucault's 'L'Archéologie du Savoir' (1969) – translated as 'The Archaeology of Knowledge' (1972, 2002). In this work Foucault claims that the history of ideas predominantly consists of discontinuities, which means that historical analysis needs to consider discontinuities as a core feature of analysis. He then continues by investigating the ways in which such discontinuities can be identified and analysed. According to Foucault, the existing continuities in the history of ideas have to be deconstructed and this history has to be reduced to its raw material: statements. Therefore, the historian's project consists of "*a pure description of discursive events* as the horizon for the search for the unities that form within it" (Foucault 2002: 27). This project can be easily distinguished from an analysis of language, since it involves far more than linguistic analysis:

> The question posed by language analysis of some discursive fact or other is always: according to what rules has a particular statement been made, and consequently according to what rules could other similar statements be made? The description of the events of discourse poses a quite different question: how is it that one particular statement appeared rather than another?                    (2002: 27)

Foucault claims that an analysis of the domain of statements is the key to describing the discontinuities in the history of ideas, for:

> The domain of statements thus articulated in accordance with historical *a prioris*, (…) and divided by distinct discursive formations, no longer has that appearance of a monotonous, endless plain that I attributed to it at the outset when I spoke of 'the surface of discourse'. We are now dealing with a complex volume, in which heterogeneous regions are differentiated or deployed, in accordance with specific rules and practices that cannot be superposed.                    (2002: 145)

He continues by saying:

> (…) we have in the density of discursive practices, systems that establish statements as events (with their own conditions and domains of appearance) and

things (with their own possibility and field of use). They are all these systems of statements (whether events or things) that I propose to call *archive*.   (2002:145)

It is clear that for Foucault the archive does not refer to the material archive, as described with regard to the TRC in the previous paragraphs:

> By this term I do not mean the sum of all the texts that a culture has kept upon its person as documents attesting to its past (…); nor do I mean the institutions, which, in a given society, make it possible to record and preserve those discourses that one wishes to remember and keep in circulation.           (2002:145)

Foucault then gives a long list of definitions of what he does mean by the term archive, among which the following are especially relevant to our present theoretical framework:

> The archive is first the law of what can be said, the system that governs the appearance of statements as unique events. But the archive is also that which determines that all these things said do not accumulate endlessly in an amorphous mass (…). [I]t is that which, at the very root of the statement-event, and in that which embodies it, defines at the outset *the system of enunciability*. [I]t is that which defines the mode of occurrence of the statement-thing; it is *the system of its functioning* (…) [I]t is that which differentiates discourses in their multiple existence and specifies them in their own duration (…) [I]t reveals the rules of a practice that enables statements both to survive and to undergo regular modification. It is *the general system of the formation and transformation of statements*.
> (2002:145–146, italics in original)

The archive can only be established by contextualising the statement: "we must grasp the statement in the exact specificity of its occurrence; determine its conditions of existence, fix at least its limits, establish correlations with other statements that may be connected with it, and show what other forms of statements it excludes" (Foucault 2002:30–31). Foucault (2002:55–58) hints at three principal aspects of the archive that need to be investigated. The researcher must find out *who is speaking*, he must describe the *institutional sites* from which the discourse is produced and he should also take the *specific situation* into consideration. Since discourse is always linked to certain historical conditions and to specific periods in history, it is crucial to find out why a certain discourse took shape exactly at a specific time (Foucault 1969:61–62). Based on the principle that everything is never said, researchers have to describe why certain statements are more exceptional than others, why they are bestowed with a greater value and therefore selected to be produced.

According to Foucault, it is obvious that the archive of a society, culture or civilisation cannot be described exhaustively, nor can it be described in its totality. To the researcher, the archive emerges in fragments and levels and the greater the time distance between the object of research and the researcher, the fuller his or her understanding of the archive might be. Finally, Foucault also argues that it is "impossible for us to describe our own archive, since it is from within these rules that we speak, since it is that which gives us what we can say (…)" (Foucault 2002: 146). For the never completed, never completely achieved uncovering of the archive, Foucault uses the term *archaeology* – which is also the term Derrida uses to refer to the unlayering of the material archive (see above).

When a researcher understands how the archive has been established and why one statement appears instead of another, he or she will get an insight into the regimes of power that are operating behind the use of a certain discourse. Archivists have a tremendous amount of power, both by deciding which documents are to be included in the archive and by defining what sort of statements are allowed to be expressed. The archontic power involves the unification, identification and classification of records, and in this sense it is always determined and motivated by socio-political configurations of power. Foucault's archaeology refers to the deconstruction of these societal power relations.

In this book I will try to get an insight into the TRC archive (actually the archive of the TRC Human Rights Violations hearings) in this Foucaultian sense: why did victims talk about certain aspects of their past experience, why did the TRC commissioners only ask particular questions, how did victims relive the past by reverting to past discourses, why were certain expressions prohibited and therefore excluded from the TRC archive? The archive of the HRV hearings will be interpreted in a broader sense as well, by investigating why exactly these victims were selected to come forward, or why the hearings had a particular structure, both discursively and materially.

The deconstruction of the TRC archive will occur on the basis of the discursive analysis of a selection of Human Rights Violations testimonies. I will illustrate how these testimonies are layered, historically, ideologically, as well as on the level of identity formation. We will see how the victim's discourse was sometimes framed during the hearings, and how some of these survivors managed to get round this discursive framing, by maintaining their individual position. As a result we will get an insight into the way power relations were created in the course of the HRV hearings. I will refer to the power displayed by the TRC commissioners as a particular level of archontic power.

## 3.4    Archontic power

The guardians of an archive are invested with considerable powers by the society they serve, and this was certainly the case with the TRC. The Commission was to give an officially acknowledged and legitimised version of the apartheid past. The TRC archive was to be an institutionalised reflection of the past, a past that could no longer be disregarded, by neither the official establishment, nor South African society at large. The people who establish and guard an archive are usually called archivists. In the case of the TRC archive, the term *archons* might be more appropriate (Derrida 1996:2). 'Archons' does not simply refer to the people who collect the documents; it also encompasses the 'entities' that command and control the archived material. The archons have to unify, identify and classify the records and, according to Derrida, they also have the power to interpret the archive. It is in these latter functions that their archontic power is manifested. When considering the TRC there are a number of different layers regarding the archons of the archive.

First, there is the TRC Act, voted in July 1995 under the Government of National Unity. The TRC Act drew the outline of the TRC archive to be, so we might say that the political parties represented in the 1994 Government of National Unity composed the first layer of TRC archons.

The next level we should consider is the Human Rights Violations hearings. The archons present at the hearings were, first and foremost, the commissioners and committee members. They decided who was going to testify and for how long the victim was allowed to talk. They also decided which questions to ask and how to react to the emotions and utterances of the victims. In the first place, these decisions were made against the background of the TRC Act. The time limit of 18 months for the completion of the TRC's work, for example, was stipulated in the Act (Section 43 (1)), and this time limit obliged the commissioners to sometimes curtail the testimonies of the victims. Which victim was to appear on which day, the order of the victims and also the appointment of the committee members for each of the hearings, were aspects decided upon before the hearings took place. Preceding the hearings, commissioners, committee members and staff members of the TRC held meetings where these practical matters were discussed (Buur 2000a: Chapter 5). We could call these pre-hearing meetings a first sub-layer, while the actual hearings can be regarded as the second sub-layer of this particular archontic level. All of these decisions, taken both at the pre-hearing meetings and in the course of the HRV proceedings themselves, determined the outlook of a major aspect of the TRC archive: who was going to question which victim on which day and for how many minutes would be an inherent element of the future TRC archive. It is this layer of archons that I will discuss in detail later on.

Once the Human Rights Violations hearings were over, a next step was taken in the archiving process. Based on testimonies, submissions and investigations, findings had to be formulated. Together with a large amount of background information, these findings would be an integral part of the TRC Report. The authors of the Report were major archons of the TRC archive: they ordered part of the TRC documents, they unified and classified them in order to fit the format of the written TRC Report. The Official TRC Website was set up quite early in the TRC process, in the course of 1996. The designers of this website contributed greatly to the establishment of the TRC archive, so they can also be considered archons of the TRC archive. A next layer of archontic power lay in the hands of the people responsible for the media representations of the TRC, since during the main part of its proceedings the TRC has been inseparable from the media. TRC Deputy Chairman Alex Boraine even stated: "the TRC owes a huge debt to the media of South Africa. Without coverage in newspapers and magazines and without the account of proceedings on TV screens and without the voice of the TRC being beamed through radio across the land, its work would be disadvantaged and immeasurably poorer" (Garman 1997: 12).

Finally, the TRC archive continues to be constructed and reconstructed by authors and scholars, artists and teachers, students and researchers. All of them possess a certain amount of archontic power; all of them have the power to identify, classify and interpret the TRC records.

## 3.5   A hierarchy of archons

As shown, in the extended archive of the TRC archontic power is displayed by a large number of different actors. This power is unevenly distributed amongst these actors, however; it is related to the envisaged audience of the actors and to the action radius within which they are operating. In the present era of globalisation texts tend to move across different archives, having a different impact within each of these archival layers (Blommaert 2005: 121). Depending on the context and the available resources, people have different access to TRC texts or to the entextualisations of TRC texts. Not every context is accessible to every one and the way people interpret TRC discourse depends on who has access to which contextual space (Blommaert 2005: 66). Especially when discourses are being deterritorialised – so transferred from one cultural sphere to another – this recontextualisation can have a significantly different influence on the audience involved. Briggs (1997) has already argued that the way texts are made available across different contexts involves questions of power (Blommaert 2001a: 24). It is therefore productive to investigate how the archontic power related to the TRC archive is hierarchised. Different archons entextualise the TRC material differently, they make use of different technologies and they reach different audiences, dispersed over a wide variety of different contexts.

The political parties of the National Assembly who designed the TRC concept in 1995 had a very strong and pervasive influence on the TRC archive, just like the archons at the hearings themselves – the commissioners. Both helped to establish the outlook of the Commission and both determined to a large extent how the TRC was to be interpreted. I consider the 1995 politicians and the TRC commissioners as the most influential archons.

The writers of the TRC Report and the composers of the TRC website possessed considerably less archontic power. The TRC Report is only accessible to literate people – an aspect important to consider in a country where 14% of the population is still illiterate (see the CIA World Factbook South Africa, May 2007). Moreover, the publication was predominantly bought by large institutions and libraries, which tells us that its outreach towards South African communities must have been rather limited. Especially abroad the TRC Report is the main reference work on the TRC, so its indexical power might be more elaborate outside than inside South Africa.

These same aspects also hold for the archontic power of the TRC website. The World Wide Web has led to an archival earthquake (Derrida 1996: 16) – an earthquake that not only accelerated, but also transformed the archiving process. Because of these new archiving technologies the TRC archive took a particular structure and it influenced different strata of society differently. However, this earthquake has only had important implications for a small part of the world's population. The TRC website is an invaluable source of information, but perhaps more so in the West than in South Africa itself.

The entire network of TRC researchers and academic authors contributes greatly to the construction of the TRC archive, but again this archive is not open to the majority of the population – especially not in South Africa.

In addition to the South African political forces and the TRC commissioners, the main holders of archontic power are presumably to be found in the media. It was the media that reflected on the TRC before it came into existence; it was the media that broadcast sounds and images of the proceedings to South African families as well as to the international community. The media brought the TRC to the world, and it also brought the world to the TRC. Within South Africa the written press had only a limited impact on the way the TRC was conceptualised. The impact of television, and especially radio was more extensive. Radio and television makers determined the general understanding of the Commission, which makes them very influential archons. An analysis of the TRC should therefore include material drawn from these media sources.

After having established the hierarchy of TRC archons we should not forget that also the present researcher, Annelies Verdoolaege, has a considerable amount of archontic power. As a re-interpreter of the TRC archive my position is on top of the hierarchy of archons. I am overlooking the archontic hierarchy, analysing it and applying it to a specific field of research. My position can be described as a *post-hoc archon*, an archon who surveys and summarises the existing manifestations of archontic power and who, by deconstructing this archontic power, tries to gain insights relevant to a particular academic domain. While writing this book I am temporarily at the top of the TRC archontic hierarchy, since I interpret the TRC archive in a unique way, applying a specific theory to a specific kind of case-studies.

## 3.6   Conclusion

I have devoted a lot of attention to the TRC archive, both as a depository of material data, and as a concept referring to the rules of formation of the TRC discourse. The TRC archive has been extremely important in South Africa's transition process, since it was crucial in the construction of a collective South African memory. The TRC produced not only a new history of the new South Africa but also the archive upon which that past was constructed. It did so through inclusion, exclusion, and also occlusion – "the obstruction of the recording of, and for memory" (Brent Harris 2000: 130). The TRC presented itself as an institutionalised representative of the nation – and therefore it had the right to interpret the past. It was hoped that this interpretation of the past would herald a new, non-racial and united nation. It is quite likely that these elements of the past that were excluded (or occluded) from this archive, so parts of the past that were not consigned to the past by the TRC, would only in a very limited way be (re)read, (re)visited or (re)interpreted in the future. This is why it is so important to thoroughly investigate the ways in which the TRC archive came into existence.

This chapter has focused on the construction of the TRC archive as a whole. When talking about the data used for this research, I will elaborate on the establishment of the subarchive that consists of my research material. As I will explain, the primary data for this study are taken from two sources – the TRC website and the live video recordings of the hearings. As such, both the local and the global of the TRC archive have been taken into consideration. The TRC website is a manifestation of the international impact of the TRC archive, while the video recordings are a reflection of the TRC archive as it was experienced by a large number of South Africans at the time of happening itself. It is the conceptualisation of these specific research data that will be the topic of the next section.

CHAPTER 4

# The sample

## 4.1  Introduction

One of the theoretical domains backing this book is Critical Discourse Analysis (CDA). According to Fairclough (2003: 202), CDA can be regarded as a form of critical social research. The aim of critical social research is "a better understanding of how societies work and produce both beneficial and detrimental effects, and of how the detrimental effects can be mitigated if not eliminated" (Fairclough 2003: 203). Fairclough continues that critical social research tries to respond to the great issues and problems of today, often focussing on capitalism, globalisation, neo-liberalism, and so forth. As Wodak (2001: 3) states, the roots of CDA mainly lie in functional systemic linguistics, as well as in classical rhetoric, text linguistics, sociolinguistics, applied linguistics and pragmatics.

Basically, CDA involves the analysis of the dialectical relationships between discourse and other elements of social practices and it is particularly concerned with the function of discourse in a radically changing modern world. In addition to the key concepts of history and ideology, power, and especially institutionally reproduced power, is often considered to be central to CDA. One of the main purposes of CDA is to analyse "opaque as well as transparent structural relationships of dominance, discrimination, power and control as manifested in language" (Wodak 1995: 204). Discourse is seen as an instrument of power; "The way this instrument of power works", as Blommaert (2005: 25) claims, "is often hard to understand and CDA aims to make it more visible and transparent". CDA maintains, however, that language is not powerful on its own – "it gains power by the use powerful people make of it" (Wodak 2001: 10). According to CDA, discourse is socially constitutive as well as socially conditioned, which means that a discursive event is shaped by situations, institutions, and social structures, but it also shapes them. Therefore, CDA stresses the relevance of investigating language use in institutional settings and the necessity of a historical perspective when analysing discourse (Anthonissen 2007: 69).

CDA researchers argue that the relations between discourse patterns and social structure are problematic; moreover, they do not only want to reveal the social dimensions of language use, "these dimensions are also the object of moral and political evaluation, and analysing them should have effects in society – for instance exposing power abuse or giving voice to the voiceless" (Blommaert 2005:25). Because of the growing importance of discourse in relation to other social practices, CDA sees its own contribution as crucial to the understanding of contemporary social reality.

CDA has been liable to a number of critical reactions, for instance by Widdowson (1995, 1996, 1998), Schegloff (1997), Wetherell (1998), Slembrouck (2001); for an overview, see Blommaert (2005:35–42) or Blommaert & Bulcaen (2000) – I will also come back to this in 8.2.1. According to one of these critical debates, critical discourse analysts tend to establish power relations already before the actual analysis of discourse has taken place (see Blommaert 2001a:16). They assume the a priori relevance of aspects of context in CDA work. Instead of taking the data as a point of departure, they tend to project their own ideas onto their data and analyse them accordingly (Blommaert & Bulcaen 2000:455). In this way, interpretations are made in advance and the discursive material is only considered relevant when corresponding to these interpretations. My explicit intention has been to work inductively, so to start from the collected data in order to formulate research questions. By making use of different theoretical concepts the assembled data were then analysed, and this without adhering to one single theory, but by applying a multitude of theoretical frameworks in a creative way. In this way, the collected material was the starting point for the entire research process. Since this ethnographic approach has been my guideline throughout the research, it is important to devote a considerable amount of attention to the way in which my database took shape.

## 4.2    Textual data

Because my aim was to investigate the discourse constructed at the Human Rights Violations hearings, I needed discursive primary material. These HRV hearings came to a conclusion in 1998, which means that for this retrospective study I had to make use of data collections that had already been established. The only textual data accessible were the transcriptions of the hearings as available on the Official TRC Website.

A little over 1800 apartheid victims told their stories before the Human Rights Violations Committee, and my plan was to select between twenty and fifty case studies. Making a selection beforehand did not seem to be the appropriate method, since at that point I did not yet know what discursive features I was looking for. Bearing in mind the inductive approach discussed above, I wanted to get a general overview of the available material before deciding what would be relevant for my research.

I therefore began by reading through all of the HRV testimonies, which would then provide a sound basis for delineating a limited number of cases. Reading hundreds of gruesome stories about gross human rights violations committed under apartheid was quite a demanding task. For each of the testimonies I wrote down some key characteristics: the age, gender, ethnic background and political affiliation of the speaker, the nature of the human rights violation and the comportment of the speech participants in the course of the hearing – whether victims were emotional, angry, relieved to tell their stories, whether the audience was noisy or subdued, and whether the commissioners were sympathetic or rather harsh when talking to the testifier.

During my reading, I soon found out that the testimonies corresponded to a standardised format. I noticed that the stories usually had the same structure, that the same questions were asked by the commissioners, and that remarks of the victims were received by the commissioners in a routine way. I then started to note down other features that seemed interesting, for example how victims responded to certain questions on reconciliation or reparations, and how the commissioners reacted to emotional statements made by the victims. Since most of the 1819 testimonies were seven to fifteen pages long (so lasting between 30 minutes and one hour), it took me several months to read all of them.

It was clear, right from the start, that this textual material contained a number of limitations and deficiencies. On the TRC website the victim testimonies are grouped according to the geographical area in which they were given. Four areas are distinguished: the areas around Cape Town, East London, Johannesburg and Durban, four towns that correspond to the four regional offices established by the TRC. The way the testimonies are listed in different regions is highly inconsistent and confusing (sometimes even without mentioning the name of the victim or without stating which committee member functioned as chairperson of the hearing or as facilitator of the testifier). As the stories told by the victims are sometimes confusing or incoherent, it turned out to be quite difficult to find out what exactly had happened to the testifier.

Another problem was that a number of web pages are highly incomplete. Sometimes, the testimony breaks off in the middle of a sentence; sometimes only the first couple of sentences uttered by the testifier are given and sometimes the testimony is not accessible at all. Also other scholars have complained about the careless way in which the TRC website is maintained (see for example Brent Harris 2000). Moreover, I could only assume that the lists of testifiers given on the website did indeed include *all* of the testifiers. There is no way to check this completeness, but according to my figures it is likely that the lists on the website are complete – I counted 1819 HRV testifiers, which is also the number mentioned by other authors (Kgalema & van der Merwe 2003: 2).

Five parameters were then taken into account, namely geographical area, gender, ethnic background, political affiliation and whether or not testifiers supported the idea of interpersonal reconciliation. On the basis of these five parameters I decided to select a representative sample of thirty testimonies from the 1819 testimonies that were presented before the HRV Committee. I should stress that this selection did not take place in accordance with methods usually employed in social science research. For instance, statistical techniques such as weighing and stratification have not been applied here because the selection is too small. Since I had read over all of the testimonies I took this personal experience as the main basis for selection. It is on the basis of my knowledge of the entire corpus of HRV hearings – so on the basis of features that I noticed to be inherent to these testimonies – that I decided which parameters to choose and which concrete testifiers to select.

Although the thirty case studies are not an exact numeral representation of the different groups of HRV testifiers, every effort has been made to gather a group that, within the given limitations, is as representative as possible. This selection of thirty case studies could actually be replaced by a sample that is entirely different, but equally valid. Following the selected set of parameters I could have chosen thirty other testifiers, also at random but still meeting the same criteria. Hence, this sample is unique, but not irreplaceable. This sample is based on the same criteria of representativeness and selection as employed by the TRC itself (geographical area, gender, ethnic background and political affiliation) (TRC Report 1998, 1/6: 165–173). I have added one criterion – the testifiers' attitudes towards reconciliation –, which is based on my understanding of the very TRC process and its uniformising manner of handling the victims' narratives. Therefore, I would prefer to call this selection a *descriptive sample*. It is meant to describe the main features of HRV discourse, without pretending to have taken into account each of the possible characteristics of the testifiers or their discourse.

## 4.3   Audio-visual material

The testimonies at the HRV hearings can be considered as types of traumatic storytelling. Colvin (2003, 2004) defines traumatic storytelling as storytelling about traumatic events, whereby its form and content are guided by the psychotherapeutic language of trauma. In addition, it is a kind of storytelling that can itself be traumatising to the teller.

Understandably, affect and deep emotions were inherent aspects of these –
traumatic – HRV testimonies. Language is often inadequate, though, to deal with
intense traumatic feelings. Especially at the TRC past experiences were so horrific
that they were often simply indescribable (Gobodo-Madikizela 2003a:28; Mc-
Cormick 2003). In her analysis of the TRC testimonies, Krog (1998a:64) even
states that language ceases to exist at the moment pain begins. In this sense, extralinguistic features, such as body language, gestures, pauses, facial expressions,
tears and sobs are crucial to get an idea of the expression of affect (Biber & Finegan 1989).

Since affect was a central feature at the HRV hearings, and since not all affect can be communicated verbally, I soon realised that my textual data would be
insufficient to analyse the HRV discourse. Also, because I did not actually witness the HRV hearings myself, audio-visual material was indispensable to back
up my discursive analysis. Through contacts within the South African Broadcasting Corporation, however, I managed to buy the video recordings of the thirty
selected testimonies.

These tapes have a number of advantages when compared with the transcribed testimonies. For the first time I was able to form a real impression of the
person whose language I was analysing. I could put a face to the name and in this
way I could also closely identify with the story this person was telling. Because
of the video tapes I could check whether my assumptions regarding ethnic background of the testifiers were correct. I could also see which commissioner was
leading the testifier and which committee members posed questions – details often not given in the transcriptions. The tapes also showed when a testifier broke
down, how the audience or commissioners reacted, and how a victim regained
strength to continue (often after having been given a glass of water or a tissue by
the briefer).

The tapes also captured elements essential to the discursive situation that were
usually omitted from the transcriptions, elements such as non-verbal aspects of
the testifiers' discourse, but also background noise and certain interruptions by
the commissioners. The video recordings also provided insight into the discursive
setting of the HRV hearings: the positions of the audience, of the testifiers and
briefers and of the committee members were shown, and one could also get an
impression of the hearing hall, often decorated with banners, candles, and flowers. The camera usually focused on the person who was talking, either the testifier
or the committee member, but also the general audience, the briefers and the family members of the testifiers were regularly to be seen on the screen. In this way,
the video tapes compensated for some of the limitations inherent to the textual
material.

However, it would be an overstatement to claim that these tapes comprised some ideal research material. To begin with, it was quite a problem to get exactly the thirty tapes I asked for. Apparently, the SABC does not have a structured TRC database, according to which the tapes can be found easily. Next, not all of the tapes were complete; sometimes a tape broke off halfway, or the visual quality became very poor. Fortunately, it turned out that I did have visual images of most of the discursive fragments that were interesting for my analysis. In addition, these tapes did not always give me sufficient and unambiguous information about the language that was spoken at the hearings. On those thirty tapes the voice of the English interpreter spoke over the original language of the speech participants. Only once in a while could I catch a word of the original language.

Although not perfect as research data, the video material has been indispensable to the effect of trying to understand the ways in which this HRV discourse was constructed, as will be revealed in the discursive analyses in later chapters.

## 4.4    Translating and transcribing

Both the English transcriptions and the video data that I decided to use for this analysis are edited material. As said in 2.6 it is usually argued that discourse analysts should work with original data. Indeed, a transcription is considered to be merely "an abstraction, in which a complex phenomenon is reduced to some of its constitutive features and transformed for the purpose of further analysis" (Duranti 1997: 137). I am aware of the shortcomings of this material, but it might be useful to try to justify my decision to make use of this translated and edited data.

I decided to use these English transcriptions, first of all because they are a fairly accurate representation of the interpreters' speech. However, my main reason for choosing the English transcriptions had to do with matters of social relevance. The translated transcriptions are the only ones available, since it was only the English version of the testimonies that was transcribed and put on the TRC website. It is these English translations that are circulating throughout the world and it is predominantly through these English texts that the apartheid victims tell their stories to the world. The ideas formed by people about the TRC, especially by people who did not directly witness the proceedings of the Commission, are based to a large extent on these transcriptions.

Clearly, when taking into consideration the social impact of the TRC material, these English translations are crucial. It is also important that the transcriptions were put on the internet purposely, particularly because transparency and accessibility were highly cherished values at the TRC. Hence, by focusing on this data I was also mindful of this point of interest of the TRC.

The same holds for the audio-visual data that I used. Here also it is not the original speech of the participants that I analysed, but mainly the English translations. The original video tapes do exist, though apparently they are not open to the public and they remain hidden in the TRC or SABC archives. Also when looking at special programmes (for instance 'Special Report') or documentaries dealing with the TRC, the English-dubbed video material is always the only material used. Therefore, the way the TRC was – and still is – visualised by the outer world is almost exclusively based on the English SABC recordings.

In short, from the viewpoint of social relevance it seems to be much more appropriate to analyse data that is accessible to the international community than original material that is only available to a select group of researchers. Based on the – almost exclusive – availability and accessibility of both the English transcriptions and the English video material, I would even venture to define this material as *primary data*. Primary sources refer to original material, that has not been interpreted by anyone other than its creator (http://www.libs.uga.edu/ researchcentral/choosing/what/primary.html) and this English material is basically the most original the international researchers' community can get hold of.

## 4.5    My concrete selection

Based on my manual counting of all of the Human Rights Violations victims I selected a representative sample of thirty testifiers, taking into account the parameters of geographical area, gender, ethnic background, political affiliation and commitment to reconciliation. The result was a group of testifiers consisting of sixteen men and fourteen women; 21 of them were African, one was Indian, three were white and five were Coloured; 14 were members of the ANC or the UDF, three were members of the IFP, one of the PAC and one of APLA, three belonged to the MK and in eight testimonies the political affiliation was not mentioned; 17 of these victims supported the idea of interpersonal reconciliation, while 11 of them were opposed to reconciliation, two testifiers did not mention reconciliation at all. Regarding the geographical area, six of these people testified in the region of Cape Town, seven in the region of Durban, nine in the region of East London and eight in the region of Johannesburg.

My use of the terms 'African', 'Coloured', 'White' and 'Indian' requires further explanation. The South African population is commonly divided into these four racial categories for the purposes of research or to explain the demographic realities and/or socio-economic conditions in the country. These four racial groups are often referred to as population groups, ethnic groups or national groups.[6] I will maintain the terms 'ethnic groups' or 'population groups'.

As James and Lever (2000: 44) note: "The use of these categories is unavoidable [in South Africa] given the fixity that they have come to acquire both in popular consciousness and official businesses". Because of its strong connotation with apartheid this fourfold division has sometimes been rejected in post-1994 South Africa. However, "the political and social realities created under apartheid, now coupled with political strategies such as affirmative action, still reinforce and politicise racial consciousness involving these specific categorisations" (James & Lever 2000: 45). For almost 50 years this division in African, White, Coloured or Indian determined the existence of South Africans. There are still wide socio-economic differences between the different ethnic groups; different groups experienced apartheid differently and they still relate to apartheid in different ways (see Gibson's survey 2004: Chapter 2).

Given the individual experiences of these ethnic categorisations, the class positions, and the social-historical realities of their members, the division into these four groups seems to be justified. Gibson (2004: 26) even argues that to ignore race would be to fail to recognise that South African society continues to be shaped by its racist history. Indeed, most researchers agree that these terms are still very convenient and socially relevant, and the terms tend to be used continuously in present-day discourse. Many scholars still work with this division to characterise the South African population, although they often add a footnote stating how controversial and loaded the terms are in present-day South Africa.

By incorporating this fourfold racial division into this analysis I merely acknowledge that apartheid shaped – and continues to shape – South African reality.

In the TRC Report these ethnic categories are used without reservations. All of the people approaching the TRC were subdivided in African, Coloured, Indian or White. In the words of the TRC (TRC Report 1998, 1/6: 167–168):

> The apartheid state was fundamentally based on racial and ethnic groupings and this is still one of most important explanatory variables in any sociological and historical analysis of contemporary South Africa. Moreover, the conflicts of the past affected ethnic groups in very different ways, as did the consequences of

---

6.   In accordance with the orthography used in the TRC Report, I will write the terms 'African', 'Indian', 'Asian' and 'Coloured' – being proper names – with a capital letter. Still following the TRC Report, the words 'white' and 'black' will be written with a small letter – except when they are used in an abstract way or as a noun and thus referring to an ethnic/political category (for instance 'the Whites', 'he is a Black').

> the violations. Therefore, statement-takers asked deponents to which population group they had been allocated in terms of apartheid terminology.

and:

> The apartheid state classified people into one of four population groups, namely African, Coloured, Asian and White. Since the Commission's focus is on violations in the political context of apartheid, this terminology is retained.

In the general overview of the thirty testifiers on the following page, all of the five parameters are taken into account. I have mentioned the age of the victims as well, since age is usually also considered as a significant sociolinguistic parameter.

Considering that 1819 South Africans testified in public before the HRV Committee, a sample of thirty is rather small. However, I am confident that the case studies are fairly representative. In addition, I should stress again that this sample should be considered as a *descriptive sample*, a sample that is meant to draw the attention to certain characteristics of the testifiers' discourse, without claiming to describe this language in all of its complexities. As will become clear in the next chapters, the selected cases will be sufficient to provide insight into the ways the HRV archive was constructed in the course of these hearings.

**Table 1.** Personal selection – general overview

| Testfier | Gender | Ethnicity | Politics | Recon. | Area | Age |
|---|---|---|---|---|---|---|
| Bernadine Mwelase | Male | African | MK | Pro | Johannesburg | 39 |
| Bernice Whitfield | Female | White | No | Con | East London | ?? |
| Charity Kondile | Female | African | ANC | Con | East London | 60 |
| Emily Siko | Female | African | ANC | Con | Durban | 39 |
| Gladys Papu | Female | African | ANC | Pro | East London | 35 |
| Gregory Beck | Male | Coloured | No | Pro | Johannesburg | 43 |
| Johannah Skhosana | Female | African | ANC | Con | Johannesburg | 51 |
| Johannes van Eck | Male | White | No | Con | Johannesburg | 47 |
| Josephine Msweli | Female | African | ANC | Pro | Durban | 60 |
| Kenneth Manana | Male | African | APLA | Pro | Johannesburg | 28 |
| K.S. Mahlangu | Male | African | IFP | Pro | Johannesburg | ?? |
| Laloo Chiba | Male | Indian | MK | Pro | Johannesburg | 60 |
| Lilian Kadi | Female | African | No | Pro | Johannesburg | 26 |
| Lizzy Phike | Female | African | UDF | Pro | Cape Town | 58 |
| Manzala Dingumhlaba | Female | African | No | Pro | East London | ?? |
| Metro Bambiso | Male | African | UDF | Pro | East London | 29 |
| Mina Day | Female | African | No | Con | Cape Town | 71 |
| Muhammed Ferhelst | Male | Coloured | MK | Con | Cape Town | 27 |
| Mzothuli Maphumulo | Male | African | IFP | Pro | Durban | 75 |
| Nelson Jantjie | Male | African | ANC | Con | Cape Town | 45 |
| Nhlanhla Buthelezi | Male | African | ANC | Con | East London | 31 |
| Patrick Morake | Male | African | PAC | Con | Durban | 23 |
| Paul Williams | Male | Coloured | No | Pro | Cape Town | 40 |
| Phebel Robinson | Female | Coloured | ANC | Pro | Cape Town | 60 |
| Pralene Botha | Female | Coloured | No | Pro | East London | ?? |
| Stephanie Kemp | Female | White | UDF | Pro | Durban | 55 |
| Teddy Williams | Male | African | ANC | Pro | East London | 41 |
| Thembisile Nkabinde | Female | African | IFP | Not | Durban | 46 |
| Vusumuzi Ntuli | Male | African | ANC | Con | Durban | 31 |
| Wandile Mbathu | Male | African | ANC | Not | East London | 44 |

# CHAPTER 5

# Layering and HRV discourse

## A critical perspective

## 5.1 Introduction

In this fifth part the discourse constructed at the Human Rights Violations hearings of the TRC will be analysed on the basis of ten features. By means of these ten features I will try to provide some insight into the *archive* of the HRV hearings, and so into the "law of what [could] be said, the system that [governed] the appearance of statements as unique events" (Foucault 2002: 145). Following Foucault, as described in 3.3, the archive will here be defined as "the general system of the formation and transformation of statements" (Foucault 2002: 146). This notion of the archive corresponds to what Pêcheux (1982: 111) calls a *discursive formation*, namely that "which in a given ideological formation, i.e. from a given position in a given conjuncture determined by the state of the class struggle, determines '*what can and should be said* (articulated in the form of a speech, a sermon, a pamphlet, a report, a programme, etc.)'" (italics in the original).

Discussing these ten features and illustrating them by means of fragments from the thirty selected testimonies will shed light on which utterances were accepted, which ones were highly valued and which ones seemed to be rejected. We will arrive at a repertoire of preferred utterances – embodied by so-called 'ideal testifiers', a repertoire that will lead us to deconstruct the archive of the HRV hearings.

The ten features that will be analysed have not been chosen at random. They are based on a careful reading of all 1819 public HRV testimonies and on my interpretation of frequently occurring discursive features at the HRV hearings. It is therefore important to stress that although my descriptive sample is rather limited, each of these discussed features were prominently present throughout the HRV process.

Based on Blommaert (2005) my theoretical premise is that the HRV archive is layered, meaning that various indexicalities or meanings were established simultaneously. 'Simultaneously' here is broadly interpreted, referring to the actual time span during which the HRV process took place, from April 1996 till June 1997. These fifteen months of HRV hearings formed a crystallisation point in South African history. At these hearings a specific kind of discourse was created, what I will call *reconciliation discourse* later on. Amongst others through the features discussed here, this discourse was uniformised and it is in this standardised type of discourse that multiple indexicalities were produced 'simultaneously'.

The ten discursive features have been subdivided in three groups, depending on whether I understood them as a kind of ideological layering, historical layering, or layering on an identity level.

## 5.2    Ideological layering

### 5.2.1    Trying to define ideology

The term 'ideology' has a long and complex history, appearing in the writings of many authors and infiltrating nearly every modern discipline in the social sciences and humanities (Thompson 1984: 3). According to Eagleton (1991: 1), nobody has yet come up with a single adequate definition of ideology. To indicate this variety of meanings, Eagleton lists some definitions of ideology in circulation at the beginning of the 1990s. Let me, more or less at random, cite a couple of these definitions:

a.   the process of production of meanings, signs and values in social life;
b.   a body of ideas characteristic of a particular social group or class;
c.   ideas which help to legitimate a dominant political power;
d.   systematically distorted communication;
e.   forms of thought motivated by social interests;
f.   identity thinking;
g.   the conjuncture of discourse and power;
h.   socially necessary illusion;
i.   action-oriented set of beliefs.

Eagleton continues by arguing that it might be useful as well to get a sense of how ideology is used by 'the person-in-the-street'. What this person-in-the-street presumably means, according to Eagleton (1991: 3), when remarking that someone speaks ideologically, is that he or she sees the world through a "rigid framework of preconceived ideas which distort his or her understanding".

Some authors do use a specific definition when dealing with the term ideology, although out of necessity this definition is often a very broad one. For Therborn (1980: 2), for instance, ideology refers to "that aspect of the human condition under which human beings live their lives as conscious actors in a world that makes sense to them to varying degrees". According to Hawkins (2001: 8) an ideology is "a system of ideas that shapes experiences and expectations regarding those experiences". Hodge & Kress (1993:6) define ideology as "a systematic body of ideas, organised from a particular point of view". Van Dijk (1998b:21) presents a socio-cognitive view on ideology, breaking it down into a cognitive, a social and a discursive element. He defines ideologies as a shared framework of social beliefs, which organise the social interpretations and actions of people, mainly with regard to power relations between groups.

A different approach is taken by Jones & Wareing (1999:34), who define ideology as "any set of beliefs which, to the people who hold them, appear to be logical and 'natural'". Wodak (1989:59) employs a more confined, Marxist inspired definition, assuming that ideology is "a system of ideas based on value judgements and attitudes, which aids certain forces within a society to further their interests or to stabilise their power". Finally, there are O'Barr & Conley (1996:114) who say that the definition of ideology is elusive, although "most definitions share the core element of ideology as a system of beliefs by which people interpret and impart meaning to events".

This limited number of examples should suffice to illustrate what a complex task it is to try to define the term ideology. Also, it is important to realise that strictly defining ideology is not always necessary – definitely not in this case, where I will rather employ the term *ideological master narrative*, as explained later. For a comprehensive overview of the ways in which ideology has been defined and conceptualised in recent history I refer to Blommaert (2005: Chapter 7).

### 5.2.2 Ideology through discourse

Ideology has been thoroughly investigated in Critical Discourse Analysis, since most CDA scholars have identified discourse as a major site of ideology. A large number of authors, both belonging to CDA and to a number of other academic disciplines, have discussed the relationship between discourse and ideology (Kress & Hodge 1979; Therborn 1980; Thompson 1984; Fowler 1985; Wodak 1989; Gardiner 1992; Fairclough 1995a; Gee 1996; Van Dijk 1998b; Silverstein 1998; Kroskrity 2000 and Cameron 2001 to mention but a few). These scholars recognise that ideology operates through language; hence a discursive analysis can reveal the ideological foundations of various speech participants (whether it be persons or more abstract entities such as the press, government institutions or educational systems).

It is not my intention to explore the vast domain of research focusing on the connection between ideology and discourse. I will only, for the sake of comprehensiveness and because certain concepts and terminologies will prove useful for the remainder of this chapter, deal with a couple of perceptions on the relation between discourse and ideology.

Bakhtin is one of the authors who claim that ideology functions symbolically – usually through language. If we accept the inter-dependence of discourse and mind we should study language in order to understand ideology (in Gardiner 1992:67). According to Bakhtin, ideology is perpetually recreated through social practices – an assertion also held by Althusser and Gramsci. Since language is regarded as a social practice, ideology is constantly created in language. Following Volshinov, Bakhtin talks about *behavioural ideology*, referring to the fact that ideology is constructed through linguistic behaviour (see Steward 1986:52–54). Also Lukes (1974) proposes that instead of thinking of ideology as a state of mind, one would better regard it as "a set of practices, primarily of a discursive provenance" (cited in Clegg 1993:26).

According to Hodge, Kress & Jones (1979:81) "ideologies are sets of ideas involved in the ordering of experience, making sense of the world". It is these systems of ideas which constitute ideologies that are expressed through language. "In speaking", they continue, "we establish, maintain, confirm and often challenge the categorisations of language, and of the ideologies which language expresses. The analysis of language is in fact a necessary part of any attempt to study ideological processes: through language ideologies become observable". Speakers select certain words and structures on the basis of their ideology, which implies that discursive items always carry – various – ideological meanings (Kress 1985:31). Fowler & Kress (1979:186) are convinced that linguistic meaning is inseparable from ideology. As a result "linguistic analysis ought to be a powerful tool for the study of ideological processes", a linguistic discipline they define as *critical linguistics*.

Norman Fairclough has been considered as one of the prominent voices in the domain of Critical Discourse Analysis. His research on the relation between discourse and ideology is extensive. According to him, social groups try to impose their ideology through naturalising their ideologically coloured discourse – making it seemingly self-evident. A lot of ideas that go without saying and that are expressed through language are ideologically constructed. It is the aim of CDA to 'denaturalise' this discourse by revealing the connection between what can or cannot be said and the ideological background (Fairclough 1995a, 2001b). Also the ever-present ideological struggle and ideological variation are expressed in language, according to Fairclough (2001a:71–72). Form, content and style of discourse are always ideologically determined, and vice versa, ideological formations are also constructed through discourse. When bringing his theory into practice Fairclough (1995a:72) tells us that ideology can be expressed linguistically through elements such as turn-taking, lexical choices or forms of address.

Although I will analyse the concrete discourse of the HRV hearings, my analysis will not involve a narrow linguistic description. Due to the fact that my data consist of translated material, items such as passivisation, nominalisation and word choice will only briefly be discussed. Instead, the main weight of attention will be paid to intended meanings and interaction patterns, and to the socio-political and contextual features underlying this HRV discourse.

### 5.2.3 The TRC ideological master narrative

When dealing with the concept of ideological layering at the HRV hearings, I will use ideology in a very specific way. Ideology will refer to the set of beliefs as presented by the TRC, the values and principles that seemed to be inherent features of the TRC concept and its practices, the ideas the TRC was associated with by the outside world and which the Commission also deliberately identified with. The aim is to investigate how this institutionalised ideology was expressed through concrete discursive practices.

This TRC ideology can be discerned on a number of different discursive levels, ranging from a very explicit master narrative to implicit interaction patterns. When discussing these different discursive levels and also the issue of ideological layering later on, I will use the term *ideological master narrative* (IMN) instead of 'TRC ideology'. This master narrative took shape on the basis of a number of discursive practices and it embodied the TRC's main ideological values. The most explicit level of this master narrative predominantly manifested itself through the TRC Act. It is on the basis of this most explicit level of the master narrative that I decided which features to classify under the heading 'ideological layering'. This explicit narrative was then converted to implicit interaction patterns at the actual TRC proceedings – it is these concrete patterns that will be the focus of my research.

Based on the TRC Act and subsequently on the TRC mandate we can conclude that striving for reconciliation and national unity were essential within the objectives and intentions of the Commission. The TRC Act stipulated that the objectives of the Commission were "to promote national unity and reconciliation in a spirit of understanding which transcends the conflicts and divisions of the past" (TRC Act 1995, 3(1)). On the basis of this Act the TRC was conceived as "part of the bridge-building process designed to help lead the nation away from a deeply divided past to a future founded on the recognition of human rights and democracy" (TRC Report 1998, 1/4:47). We can therefore argue that both reconciliation and national unity were two values cherished by the TRC. For this reason

I will consider *reconciliation* and *national unity* as the two main pillars of the TRC ideological master narrative.

The TRC Act (3 (c)) also stated that one of the other objectives of the Commission was to "establish and make known the fate or whereabouts of victims", to "restore the human and civil dignity of such victims by granting them an opportunity to relate their own accounts of the violations of which they are the victims" and to "recommend reparation measures in respect of them". In addition, when dealing with the victims, the Commission was to be guided by the following principles (TRC Act, 11 (a)–(f)):

> *Victims shall be treated with compassion and respect for their dignity; victims shall be treated equally and without discrimination of any kind*, including race, colour, gender, sex, sexual orientation, age, language, religion, nationality, political or other opinion, cultural beliefs or practices, property, birth or family status, ethnic or social origin or disability; (…) *appropriate measures shall be taken in order to minimize inconvenience to victims* and, when necessary, to protect their privacy, to ensure their safety as well as that of their families and of witnesses testifying on their behalf, and to protect them from intimidation; *appropriate measures shall be taken to allow victims to communicate in the language of their choice.*
>
> (any italics are mine)

Not only was it the duty of the Commission to restore the human dignity of apartheid victims on a general level – and to extend this human dignity to the future, it was also the Commission's duty to ensure that during the actual TRC process victims be treated with respect and dignity. Inconvenience to the victims had to be minimised at the hearings and victims were to be allowed to testify in the language of their choice. On the basis of these assertions, I have decided to consider *respect for the victims* as another inherent element of the TRC ideological master narrative.

Finally, I have also defined the *emphasis on emotional discourse* at the HRV hearings, such as relating in detail how someone was tortured, or elaborating on the physical and psychological effects of a particular human rights violation, as an aspect of the TRC ideological master narrative. This is a feature that seemed to be prominent throughout the victim testimonies. A number of authors have tried to find an explanation for the emphasis on emotional and personal details during the HRV hearings – I will come back to these explanations later. For now, we can say that, according to my understanding, this feature could be connected to the image the TRC wanted to spread to the world. The more emotional the hearings, the more the TRC would be perceived as an indispensable institution to help South Africans deal with the apartheid past.

Except for the last one, all of these ideological features are based on the founding legislation of the TRC – the TRC Act and subsequently the TRC mandate. Both the Act and the mandate constituted the frame of reference by which the TRC process – so also the HRV hearings – were to be conducted. In addition to what was stipulated in this founding legislation, the TRC ideological master narrative also took shape at the actual HRV hearings, meaning that the HRV commissioners regularly referred to these features as key components of the TRC's set of beliefs and values. It is on the IMN as manifested through this concrete discourse that I will concentrate in this chapter.

Having established my interpretation of the TRC ideological master narrative, attention will now be directed to *ideological layering* – so the layering of this IMN. The ideological master narrative forms the frame by which each of the thirty selected testimonies was ideologically influenced in highly divergent manners. Each of the four established elements of the TRC ideological master narrative was layered, meaning that they were stratified and contained various dimensions and indexicalities. In each of the HRV testimonies these four ideological features were expressed and applied. However, the way in which these features were given shape varied greatly from one testimony to another. The ideological foundations of the TRC as expressed in the mandate, so the ideological position from which the commissioners framed their discourse, remained constant throughout the proceedings. As I will show later on, though, these foundations shifted in practice. This means that depending on the profile of the testifier, on the way he or she reacted to the commissioner's discourse, or on the way he or she had already been committed to these ideological values beforehand, this ideological position changed. It could be challenged, accepted or rejected by the testifier; it could be voiced explicitly or tempered by the commissioners; it could be adapted to the personal background, the mentality or the individual beliefs of the victim. I speak here about ideological layering in a discursive way, about the manner in which this TRC IMN took a different shape through the discourse constructed at the HRV hearings.

### 5.2.4  Feature One: Introducing reconciliation

According to the founding legislation of the Truth and Reconciliation Commission, the objectives of the Commission were "to promote national unity and reconciliation in a spirit of understanding which transcends the conflicts and divisions of the past...". As mentioned before, this indicates that the concept of reconciliation was very important in the ideology of the TRC.

A number of scholars claim that the TRC was definitely supposed to start a process of reconciliation (see amongst others Parlevliet 1998a; Villa-Vicencio & Verwoerd 2000). Indeed, it is quite likely that many people, both in South Africa and abroad, saw the TRC as an important symbolic instrument to enhance reconciliation. However, while the concept of reconciliation took such a prominent position in the proceedings of the Commission, the TRC mandate gave very little direction as to how the Commission was to pursue the goal of promoting reconciliation. According to Chapman (2003b: 2): "this mandate to promote reconciliation was heavy on rhetoric and lean on specifics". It did not stipulate the activities intended to contribute to the process of reconciliation; it did not identify who was to be reconciled with whom; and it did not offer guidelines to evaluate the contribution of the TRC to reconciliation (Borer 2001; Chapman 2003a). According to the TRC Report (1998, 1/5: 109), the Commission must:

> not only lay the foundation for a society in which physical needs will be met; [it] must also create a home for all South Africans. The road to reconciliation, therefore, means both material reconstruction and the restoration of dignity. It involves the redress of gross inequalities and the nurturing of respect for our common humanity. It entails sustainable growth and development of the spirit of ubuntu. It implies wide-ranging structural and institutional transformation and the healing of broken human relationships. It demands guarantees that the past will not be repeated. It requires restitution and the restoration of our humanity – as individuals, as communities and as a nation.

Later on (TRC Report 1998, 1/5: 106), reconciliation is defined as both a goal and a process, and different levels of reconciliation are mentioned. Reconciliation, according to the TRC Report, is about "coming to terms with painful truths"; it involves "reconciliation between victims and perpetrators", "reconciliation at a community level" and "reconciliation and redistribution". However, clear guidelines on how reconciliation is to be brought into practice concretely are lacking.

The TRC was convinced that aspects such as the democratic, transparent and inclusive process of the Commission, the establishment of "as complete and reliable a picture as possible of past violations", facilitating the acknowledgement of these violations, and making recommendations aimed at preventing future violations, had indeed contributed to the promotion of national unity and reconciliation (TRC Report 1998, 1/5: 107–108). No directions were given, though, on how this supposed contribution of the TRC to reconciliation had taken place.

Because of the failure of the TRC to convey a clear and well-developed view of reconciliation, Commissioners and staff often pursued different approaches to reconciliation. Some of the Commissioners were looking at reconciliation from a religious perspective, mainly linking reconciliation with repentance and forgiveness. Others put forward a more political or judicial concept of reconciliation (Chapman 2003b: 3). Very rarely, also national reconciliation was raised or there were discussions on the need for reconciliation between the different South African population groups. As we will see, also the testifiers interpreted reconciliation in a wide variety of different ways.

For all these reasons it is difficult to clarify exactly how to define reconciliation when analysing the HRV testimonies. Therefore, when discussing my data I will not limit myself to one interpretation of the term reconciliation. The interpersonal definition of reconciliation is only one of the conceptualisations that will emerge. In what follows, this interpersonal reconciliation could be seen as a point of departure, but it will definitely not be the only interpretation referred to. Other understandings of the notion reconciliation will gradually be revealed, demonstrating the highly complex nature of the HRV hearings with regard to this feature. Initially, attention will be paid to the explicit and concrete voicing of reconciliation-related terms. Later we will see that reconciliation could also be referred to in a much more implicit and subtle manner. In accordance with for example Yandell (1998: 45) and Shriver (1998: 136) I will consider individual forgiveness as a necessary – though not sufficient – condition for reconciliation. Therefore, references to forgiveness will also be seen as inherent elements of the TRC reconciliation discourse. The richness of the term reconciliation will be illustrated throughout this work and gradually its semantic multiplicity will be revealed.

The aim of this section is to illustrate how the testifiers' discourse was directed towards reconciliation, and this by means of illustrations taken from the thirty selected case studies. This will provide insight into the rules of formation – the HRV archive, since we will arrive at a set of utterances that seemed preferred at the HRV hearings, while another set of utterances seemed rather unacceptable. Throughout the HRV hearings, we notice, indeed, that the commissioners tried their best to construct a specific type of *reconciliation discourse*. This kind of discourse took shape on the basis of a number of discursive practices.

First of all, one notices that reconciliation itself tended to be strongly emphasised by the TRC commissioners. They sometimes urged the victims to speak out in favour of reconciliation – in particular having the testifiers *pronounce* terms such as 'reconciliation' or 'forgiveness' appeared to be of the utmost concern. In some instances, victims were explicitly asked whether they would be prepared to meet their perpetrators, whether they would be prepared to talk to the perpetrator, or, very straightforwardly, whether they would be willing to actually reconcile with the wrongdoer. These are some examples of this discursive method, whereby commissioners explicitly asked the testifier to reconcile.[7]

The first example comes from Mrs. Gladys Papu, whose husband was killed by a rival political group. After she has told her story and answered the additional questions, commissioner Xundu concludes the testimony. He raises the question of reconciliation in this way:

> REV XUNDU: Thank you Mr Chairperson. Mam, I heard your story. *I only have one question. According to you what can be done so that there can be peace? Is there a conflict between yourself and this other group?*
>
> MRS PAPU: What I want is for them to come forward to tell the truth.
>
> REV XUNDU: *You are saying that reconciliation can be built if they can come forward?*
>
> MRS PAPU: Yes, if they can come and tell the truth.
>
> REV XUNDU: *If they can come forward you will forgive them?*
>
> MRS PAPU: Yes.
>
> REV XUNDU: Thank you.

In this example it seems as if commissioner Xundu literally puts the words of forgiveness and reconciliation in the mouth of the testifier. It then became almost impossible for the victim to react against this reconciling atmosphere or to even try to modify the language of the commissioners. Commissioner Xundu keeps repeating the terms reconciliation and forgiveness, until the testifier admits that she fully agrees with what he says. The commissioner is posing leading questions and it seems to be a question of actually pronouncing these terms out loud – in this way the attention of the TRC audience would be focussed on the importance of establishing interpersonal reconciliation.

The following example comes from Kedu Mahlangu, who was set alight and almost died from his injuries by ANC 'comrades'. The questions are posed by commissioner Manthata and by the chairperson:[8]

---

7. All of the fragments cited in this text are literally taken from the TRC website. Spelling mistakes and grammatical errors have not been corrected. The italics in the cited fragments are always my own.

8. The transcriptions of the HRV hearings did not always give me sufficient details on who was participating; therefore, I do not have the name of this chairperson.

> MR MANTHATA: But what would you say today with the call made by King Mayisha *that he desires reconciliation and peace in the whole region of Moutse, KwaNdebele?*
>
> MR MAHLANGU: We share the same sentiments as the King, even though our hearts are sore because we are broke as now. There is nothing that we can do. That is a most disturbing first factor. If he can compensate us, maybe, or help us in any way, we can accept that and go back.
>
> CHAIRPERSON: We thank you Mr Mahlangu. We have listened to your story and how you were troubled. We so wish that the people of this province can listen to the King's wish that let there be unity. *Let the nation be one, so that the past can be forgotten and people reconcile and be one thing. Thank you.*
>
> MR MAHLANGU: I will also be happy that when we reconcile the truth has to be put on the table, so that we can see that this person really wants reconciliation, but if someone is avoiding the truth then, I am sorry.

After Mr. Manthata's question Mr. Mahlangu follows the commissioner's suggestion by not speaking out against reconciliation. However, he immediately adds that reconciliation will be made easier if some material compensation will be granted first. The chair then concludes by expressing his hope for future forgiveness and reconciliation in the region. Mr. Mahlangu is not supposed to start talking again, but without a question being asked he takes the floor once more. He stresses again that he and his companions do want to reconcile, but that these reconciliatory feelings must be reciprocal. The enemies should also come forward with the truth, otherwise reconciliation will be put at risk. He clearly blames the enemies: if they will tell the truth and if they are willing to compensate them, he is prepared to reconcile – this is their responsibility. By answering the commissioners' questions in such a way, Mr. Mahlangu finds a balance between being on the one hand a reconciliation-oriented victim, and on the other hand expressing his personal opinion – a personal opinion that is largely incompatible with the unconditional kind of reconciliation that is promoted by the TRC commissioners.

Also Lizzy Phike is openly asked to reconcile, and just like Kedu Mahlangu, she only wants to reconcile under certain conditions. Lizzy Phike was arrested by the South African police and while in detention, her son was shot dead. She is questioned by commissioner Xundu:

> REV XUNDU: You've told us the story that shows that in your community there was a conflict. *Are there efforts now that could lead you to reconciliation?*

MS PHIKE: No efforts – there were no efforts, but we – during the elections I raised the point that the people who were oppressing us, who never apologized will never be our leaders.

REV XUNDU: *You mean you have a wish that something should be done so that it could bring about reconciliation?*

MS PHIKE: My wish is that the people just before they – the people who are going to be our leaders, they must first talk to the people who are oppressing us as we were fighting for freedom.

REV XUNDU: Are you talking about the AZAPO organisation and UDF?

MS PHIKE: I'm talking about the AZAPO people who never came to apologize and who are also enjoying the results of our freedom. We just want them to come and apologize so that we could be at peace.

Rev. Xundu starts by explicitly asking Ms. Phike whether she is prepared to reconcile. Her answer is not very straightforward, so he asks again whether she has a wish to establish reconciliation. Through a number of fairly leading questions the commissioner tries to get this testifier to actually pronounce the term reconciliation – Ms. Phike does not follow him however. Finally, she seems to be prepared to reconcile, but only if the enemies come forward to apologise. Also here reconciliation is conditional, and although Rev. Xundu insists on expressing reconciliation, Ms. Phike continues to divide society in two groups – reconciliation between those two groups ("we" and "they") does not seem to be unproblematic. In this example we see how the lexical frame offered by the leading commissioner is not necessarily or automatically adopted by the victim. There could be attempts at resistance, often carefully dealt with by the commissioner. In these illustrations we get the first signs of the intricate manner by which this HRV reconciliation discourse was constructed. While it is clear that the entire discourse was framed by the commissioners, it was not void of power exertion from the side of the testifiers either.

The mere fact that commissioners explicitly requested to reconcile could be seen as a subtle way of imposing the concept of reconciliation. Considering the context of the TRC, which supported the idea of forgiveness and interpersonal reconciliation – testifiers were aware of this fact, even before they appeared before the HRV Committee, victims had to be decisive and strong-minded to refuse to reconcile with the perpetrator. Some testifiers did have this psychological power, for example Emily Siko, whose family was attacked by the Afrikaner Weerstandsbeweging (AWB), an extreme right-wing organisation. Dr. Randera is the facilitator leading Mrs. Siko in her testimony. At the end of the testimony the floor is given to Mr. Manthata who poses a number of additional questions. It is also commissioner Manthata who inquires about possible reconciliation between Emily Siko and the perpetrators:

> MR MANTHATA: Do you think there is a possibility of reconciliation with these people?
>
> MRS SIKO: No, I don't think so.
>
> (...)
>
> MR MANTHATA: I will ask you this question again. Do you think these people are Christians, the AWB?
>
> MRS SIKO: They have their own church, they built it in Ventersdorp.
>
> MR MANTHATA: Are you Christians?
>
> MRS SIKO: Yes, I am a Christian. I attend the Anglican Church.
>
> MR MANTHATA: Is there any communication between your ministers and their ministers?
>
> MRS SIKO: No.
>
> MR MANTHATA: Are you saying no or you do not know?
>
> MRS SIKO: No, the AWB people don't mix with other ministers from other churches.
>
> MR MANTHATA: I thank you.
>
> DR RANDERA: Mrs Siko, in there anything else you would like to say?
>
> MRS SIKO: I just have a problem with my child. I would like them to pay for what they did to my son. The child is going to be cripple for a lifetime.
>
> DR RANDERA: Mrs Siko, thank you very much for sharing your story with us.

In this testimony committee member Manthata introduces the issue of reconciliation gradually by first trying to find a common point of interest between Mrs. Siko and the AWB people. Both of them appear to be Christians, which could enhance mutual feelings of sympathy. Mr. Manthata then tries to find out whether there is any communication between the victims and the perpetrators. Even after he intrusively repeats the questions, Mrs. Siko denies any contact categorically and Mr. Manthata concludes by simply thanking her.

Next, commissioner Randera takes over by asking what Mrs. Siko's requests are from the Commission. Straight away, the testifier elaborates on the physical condition of her son. The child has been severely injured as a result of the AWB attack and Mrs. Siko wants the perpetrators to compensate him for these physical problems. The distance between her son on the one hand and the AWB people on the other hand is emphasised by putting "them" and "they" in direct opposition with "my son". She stresses the contrast between "us" and "they", and this distance seems to be in contradiction with feelings of mutual understanding and reconciliation.

As is clear from this fragment, Emily Siko is able to resist the insistent tone of commissioner Manthata. She keeps to her conviction that personal reconciliation with the perpetrators seems impossible even though this is insisted upon by some HRV committee members.

A different way of reacting to the commissioners' framing of the testifier's discourse is to be found in the testimony of Bernice Whitfield. Mrs. Whitfield testified about the killing of her husband during an APLA bomb attack in 1993. Throughout her testimony Mrs. Whitfield self-identifies as devoutly religious and she reverts to her faith in order to by-pass the reconciliation-oriented questions of the commissioners. Mrs. Whitfield is guided in her testimony by committee member Maya and also commissioner Sandi poses some questions:

> MISS MAYA: Mrs Whitfield, *if you were to come face to face to this person or if you were given an opportunity to convey a certain message to him or to them, what would you like to convey to them?*
>
> MRS WHITFIELD: As the Lord said to me when he gave me this word, he can walk away from us with the deeds that he's done but one day, when he comes face to face with Jesus he will have to answer because when the Lord deals with you it hurts, if I deal with him he won't feel anything and that is my hope.
>
> (…)
>
> MR SANDI: Thank you Mr Chairman. Mrs Whitfield, I may be asking you the same question, but maybe in a different way. I don't seem to get you attitude too clear as to how you would relate to those who perpetrated this gross human rights violation. *Let us suppose the people who did this to your husband and other victims of the tragedy were to come to you and say to you they are asking for forgiveness, how would you respond to such a request?*
>
> MRS WHITFIELD: I've got no grudge against anybody; I feel if I have then I cannot call myself a child of God, because if God forgives us, we can forgive others. (…) Here on earth there is no justice. I've never seen justice in this world, but when he comes face to face with the Lord, that is the day he is going to get judged and that is my only hope.
>
> MR SANDI: Thank you very much Mrs Whitfield. Thank you Mr Chairman.

By reverting to her faith, Mrs. Whitfield succeeds in expressing her desire for vengeance, without contradicting the message of reconciliation the TRC wanted to convey. It seems as if she only wants to forgive because she is a believer – it is an obligation that does not correspond to her sincere feelings. In addition, she seems to perceive the amnesty process of the TRC as unjust. Justice will take place when the perpetrators have to appear before God, and then she hopes they will be punished. This is a creative way of getting round the persistent questions of the commissioners. In a subtle way Mrs. Whitfield indicates what her personal opinions are, while still keeping in line with the TRC ideological master narrative. Hence, in a more sophisticated way than Emily Siko, Bernice Whitfield refused to openly comply with the commissioners when they insist on expressing forgiveness or reconciliation.

Committee members frequently concluded testimonies by using reconciliation-oriented phrases. Testifiers were praised if they had displayed reconciling attitudes in the course of their testimonies or if they were prepared to forgive their perpetrators. If victims had been resentful, committee members sometimes attempted to temper these feelings. They kept emphasising that reconciliation was the only way to build a new South African society. If testimonies were concluded by creating such a reconciliation-oriented atmosphere, it could become extremely hard for the next testifier to talk in a spirit of vengeance or retaliation. In fact, the next testifier would often hear the previous testimony and he or she would be aware of the reconciliation-oriented atmosphere that was built up in the hall. These are some illustrations:

Kenneth Manana, a former APLA member who was arrested and tortured by the South African Police, openly expressed feelings of forgiveness in the course of his testimony. This is picked up by commissioner Mkhize in her final statement:

> MR MANANA: This was mentioned to show that in all that had happened I now realise that some of those things were mistakes and that those people who do something bad to me at the present moment that I think *I do have the heart to receive them and forgive them. Just to show before the Commission that I do have the heart to forgive.*
> (…)
> MS MKHIZE: We would like to thank you for having been able to come. *We also thank you for having started a new life. Also being ready to reconcile and forgive. As you have already said that you are a new man, you have repented.* We pity you for having suffered under the hands of the police. We also believe that you work with us to add any information that we might need in your statement. Thank you very much.

When asked about his relationship to other people, specifically to the perpetrators who attacked him, also Mr. Beck speaks out in favour of forgiveness quite spontaneously. Mr. Beck was attacked by members of the UDF while patrolling through Soweto as a policeman:

> DR MAGWAZA: Mr Beck it is obvious that your life changed after the attack, *I would like to ask in what way did your life change in your relationship with other people or relationship with liberation movements?* How did your life change in relation to your work? And how did your life change generally because something did change?

> MR BECK: Yes more than likely. If all these things didn't come to the fore of what happened, then maybe I would still bear a grudge. *The reason why my life changed is that I've now learnt from all the stories I've learned from and the example that our State President has brought us for forgiving after he went through all these atrocities as well, and he can forgive, and I became more tolerant now and more understanding, which before I wasn't. I can understand now from both sides,* and people's problems daily in my job as well.
> (…)
> MR TUTU: (…) Now the Commission is in fact being charged with telling this story, not so that we should be masochists who enjoy pain, our pain, the pain of others, that we should in fact then, as the Act says, transcend, rise above the conflicts of the past and ultimately if we are going to have the change then *it is clear that forgiveness, reconciliation, are quite central to that process.* And justice is an element of it as well. But forgiveness ultimately is to say you give people the chance to change. (…) We pray that that process will be accelerated and that we, all of us, because all of us need to change, all of us are wounded people, all of us are traumatised people, *all of us are people who need to forgive and who also need to be forgiven.*

Note that Mr. Beck seems especially prepared to forgive after the example of Mr. Mandela – indeed, HRV testifiers often referred to the fact that following the role model of Nelson Mandela was their main motivation behind reconciliation-oriented attitudes. In his closing statement chairperson Tutu explicitly comes back to Mr. Beck's commitment to reconciliation, labelling it not only as an individual necessity, but also as a national prerequisite for a peaceful future.

Finally, I will give the example of Mrs. Kemp's testimony. Stephanie Kemp was detained and maltreated by the South African Police. She is absolutely committed to reconciliation in South Africa, as is clear from the following extract:

> MS MKHIZE: On the other hand we have the victims, on the other hand we have the alleged and in some instances now the identified perpetrators. And as you can see, the whole predominantly black, *what is your suggestion in terms of moving towards national reconciliation.*

> MRS KEMP: *Without question reconciliation is necessary for the survival of our country*. And I think if it wasn't for our president, it would have perhaps been harder for me and many people like me, to even contemplate the possibility of reconciliation.

This awareness of the need for reconciliation is highlighted by chairlady Sooka in her closing statement:

> MRS SOOKA: (…) I think part of the struggle in this country is to find the solution to what gives people the ability to make those choices. *Because that is going to make the difference to salvaging this nation, because some times reconciliation seems to be very cheap*, and the price is often the cost of the victims, and I think that what we are really struggling with is what you have said in your last few remarks. That we need for people to say more than it was a mistake. *We need for them to really come forward and repent, because only in that repentance will the rest of us be able to find some kind of solace that the reconciliation on which we are building this country will not be a cheap one.* Thank you for coming forward and for sharing your testimony. I think for many of us who have heard your story before, you have always been a shining example. We do salute your courage in coming forward. Thank you.

Mrs. Kemp's expression of reconciliation-oriented emotions seems to be highly valued, which turns the testifier into a respected victim – note the formal "We do salute your courage in coming forward". Again, such a level of attributed respect and appreciation in the closing statement made it almost impossible for the next testifier to refuse to reconcile. The atmosphere was further steered in the direction of reconciliation, a direction that was very hard to ignore or to try to break through.

Another discursive method of directing the testifiers towards reconciliation has to do with the written fragment. The questions and remarks raised at the public hearings were based on the written statement victims had submitted before appearing before the Commission. Sometimes, the commissioner read parts from these statements, to remind the testifier of what he or she had stated before. In some cases, the commissioners emphasised that reconciliation had been expressed in the written statement and they explicitly read the appropriate fragment to the victim. In this way, people had to confirm that they had been in favour of forgiveness and reconciliation, at least at the time when they gave their statements. It was then very difficult for the testifier to retract these words by proclaiming vengeance or hatred instead.

An example of such explicit reference to a written statement comes from the testimony of Mrs. Manzala Dingumhlaba. She spoke about the torture of her father. The concept of reconciliation is introduced by commissioner Crichton:

> MS CRICHTON: I want to ask you a question, because in your statement you said something that has interested me deeply and I want not only the Commission to hear this, I want the people that are listening to this across South Africa to hear it as well, because there is a need for them to hear it. *May I quote from what you said in your statement about the perpetrators? In your statement you said:*
>
> > "I wish that the perpetrators would ask for forgiveness and compensate me for the loss of my father and the humiliation that they caused."
>
> Do you remember saying that?
>
> MS DINGUMHLABA: Yes I remember.
>
> MS CRICHTON: *Is that still your wish?*
>
> MS DINGUMHLABA: *Yes, I want them to ask for forgiveness, because we are left as orphans.*
>
> MS CRICHTON: Thank you very much. Thank you Mr Chairman.

Also Lilian Kadi expressed a willingness to meet the perpetrators after being explicitly asked by commissioner Meiring. In this case also the written statement forms the point of departure for raising the reconciliation concept. Mrs. Kadi testified about her father and uncle who were both necklaced by members of the ANC. At the end of the testimony commissioner Meiring inquires about the possibility of coming to terms with the perpetrators; note the repetition of "Are you willing to meet with the perpetrators?" – whereby meeting the perpetrators could be seen as a first step in the reconciliation process:

> PROF. MEIRING: Thank you. There's a last thing that I would just like to mention. *You say in your statement that you are prepared to meet with the perpetrators of this deed*, if they are willing to meet with you and explain what happened., is that still the case ? *Are you still willing to meet with the perpetrators?*
>
> MRS KADI: *Yes, I'm prepared to meet with them.*
>
> PROF. MEIRING: Thank you very much.

Initially, Mrs. Kadi seems to be in favour of reconciling with the ANC members who attacked her father and uncle. However, when the chair, Mr. Randera, poses a final question on her current state of mind vis à vis the incident, Mrs. Kadi expresses grief and anger instead. She does not continue her explicitly reconciliation-oriented discourse, and she seems to be more concerned with the disastrous results of the incident on her everyday life:

> MR RANDERA: After all these years, *how do you actually feel about what happened?*
>
> MRS KADI: They disturbed our lives, because we could have gone to school. Now we don't have somebody responsible who can help us further our studies. I was, I could have been working, I could have been at school now.

In this last extract we notice that Mrs. Kadi frames reconciliation differently than in the beginning of her testimony. Mrs. Kadi implies that the perpetrators have not only destroyed the past, but also her present life and her future. Her father and uncle were the breadwinners of the family and their killing resulted in the end of her studies – not only her studies, but also the studies of her siblings as indicated by the inclusive "our". In these phrases, the testifier interprets reconciliation in a slightly divergent way, indicating that such a reconciliatory attitude can also be accompanied by feelings of bitterness and rage. Within one and the same testimony we therefore see that the notion of reconciliation could be conceptualised quite distinctly. Initially, the testifier complied openly with the TRC's reconciliatory ideology – possibly also because Mr. Meiring explicitly asked about meeting the perpetrator. In the final sentences, however, Mrs. Kadi takes a different stance: she emphasises that the perpetrators "disturbed our lives", an expression by which forgiveness or reconciliation are framed in a new and rather unexpected manner. This multiplicity of interpretations regarding the term reconciliation will be elaborated on in a later section.

To conclude this chapter on reconciliation we can say that, on a personal level, individual testifiers probably covered a wide range of attitudes, veering between supporting and rejecting the concept of reconciliation. Through interaction with the commissioners, though, these personal attitudes were homogenised. Only a minority of victims made unsolicited remarks about reconciling with the perpetrators; also a minority was straightforwardly opposed to reconciliation. In a number of victim testimonies the notion of reconciliation was raised by the commissioners and to a greater or lesser extent it was also accepted by the testifiers. When watching or listening to these testimonies it may look as if the majority of the victims embrace reconciliation. A closer analysis tells us that the TRC commissioners were often the driving force behind this commitment to reconciliation, but that testifiers could also challenge or transform this proposed frame.

As a result of the persuasive voice of the commissioners it appeared as if some of the testifiers displayed contradictory attitudes towards reconciliation in the course of their testimonies. In the beginning of their testimonies they could express a willingness to reconcile, which then gradually or abruptly changed to a rejection of reconciliation – as we have seen in the testimony of Mrs. Kadi. These seemingly ambiguous attitudes tell us a lot about the pressure to forgive that might have surrounded the Human Rights Violations hearings. Initially, testifiers could subscribe to the reconciliation discourse, but depending on the response they received from the commissioners, they could refuse to further participate. In addition, these seemingly ambiguous attitudes also give us an early indication of the multilayeredness of the term reconciliation before the HRV Committee.

I would suggest that a reconciliation-oriented atmosphere was deliberately created at the HRV hearings. The term reconciliation was given a vague, but at the same time very broad meaning. At the hearings the commissioners allowed for a wide interpretation of the term, thus having the word associated with a large variety of divergent opinions. This lack of a clear definition of reconciliation could have been a conscious policy on the part of the TRC – I will return to this point later. Testifiers with different attitudes vis à vis reconciliation were united before the HRV Committee, making the term acceptable to a large group of apartheid victims.

I see this commitment to reconciliation as one of the crucial aspects of the *reconciliation discourse* that was constructed during the victim testimonies. Not only do I consider this commitment as one of the most important features of the reconciliation discourse; I also see it as an all-embracing feature of the entire discourse. The adherence to reconciliation can be seen as a superstructure, as a co-ordinating feature of the other features and of the whole reconciliation discourse. When trying to gain insight into the rules of formation of this HRV discourse, we shall see that this commitment to reconciliation was crucial. This feature will therefore take a central place when trying to build the Foucaultian archive of this HRV discourse.

### 5.2.5  Feature Two: Stressing national unity/community spirit

According to the TRC Act, the objectives of the Commission were not only "to promote reconciliation", but also to "promote national unity in a spirit of understanding which transcends the conflicts and divisions of the past…" (TRC Act, Chapter 2, 3 (1)). Based on this legislative text we can consider national unity as one of the other ideals closely associated with the TRC. Already in the build up to the TRC process, at the conference organised by the Institute for a Democratic Alternative for South Africa (IDASA) in July 1994, it was pointed out that working towards a unified South Africa would be one of the key objectives of the TRC.

In the publication 'The Healing of a Nation' (1995), which was the report of this conference, it is stated that:

> The Commission should be used to promote and foster coexistence and community between all South Africans, but particularly between the oppressed and the oppressors collectively and between the privileged and the disadvantaged. (…) Then, as a nation, we can begin to foster massive and collective trust, honestly, openness, understanding, forgiveness, acknowledgement, tolerance and respect. (…) With [the TRC], national reconciliation, coexistence and community become possible. The aim is to heal the nation and to fulfil the ideals of our new Constitution.                        (Boraine & Levy 1995: 82–83)

In the same way as with reconciliation, the TRC also had to try *to contribute to the process* of nation building; it was not supposed to establish national unity right away. Also in this case, the role of the TRC was dual. On a concrete level, the drive for nation building was directed towards the testifiers. Both the amnesty applicants and the victims had to feel accepted and respected in the new South Africa. Ideally, they should feel a desire to reach out to fellow South Africans, perpetrators as well as victims, in order to establish a united future. On the other hand, with regard to national unity, the TRC also had a symbolic function, aimed at the South African public at large. In essence, people had to be shown explicitly that there was a desire to build a nation among South Africans, meaning that the testifiers were urged to express their commitment towards a unified country.

In addition to establishing a national identity among apartheid victims, the commissioners also tried to enhance community spirit among the HRV testifiers. What I have labelled *community spirit* can be seen as an aspect of national unity and national solidarity. Community spirit, as I understand it here, refers to showing consideration for other community members and wanting to live together peacefully at the level of the local community. Throughout the hearings this aspect of community spirit was frequently stressed. Caring about other members of one's community could indicate a willingness to build a society together – an awareness of communal solidarity. At the TRC, this communal solidarity tended to be extended to a national level; the willingness to build a community together was expanded to a willingness to build a nation together.

The master narrative of national unity took shape in ways similar to the establishment of the master narrative of reconciliation. Sometimes, the spirit of national unity was already referred to in the opening statement of the testimony, thus setting the stage for the narrative to come. In these statements victims were reminded of the necessity to build a new South African nation, and this together with other victims, with perpetrators, with members of their communities, and with members of the entire nation. One example is taken from the testimony of

Mzothuli Maphumulo, who had three of his children killed by members of the ANC. In his opening statement, Mr. Dlamini evokes a few aspects of the master narrative of national unity:

> MR DLAMINI: Mr Maphumulo and Mrs Maphumulo, I welcome you. Mr Maphumulo, you are here because three of your children were killed and one person who was a tenant at your house. You are staying in a township. *Your case is one of the saddest cases we've heard, and people who are coming from townships and other settlements they know how you are feeling because some of them have experienced that.* When I am looking at this testimony I realise that organisations were used just because people wanted to. We understand that your wife also got injured in this attack.

In this statement, commissioner Dlamini refers to a level of local community spirit and to a level of national solidarity. By stressing how fellow-township dwellers might empathise with the story the testifier is about to tell, the commissioner refers to a possible feeling of togetherness among the inhabitants of these townships. In addition, by highlighting that other people might have experienced the same traumatic events, individual suffering is lifted to a nation-wide level. The message is that all South Africans have been victimised, they should all sympathise with each other and strive for a peaceful future.

The ideological value of nation building was especially enhanced by emphasising the need for national unity and through proclaiming equality of all victims in the closing statements of the testimonies. The closing statements of Mrs. Nkabinde's testimony, for instance, were clearly oriented towards national unity – both the final words of leading commissioner Dlamini and the actual closing statement of chairperson Lax. Mrs. Nkabinde was a supporter of the IFP and she was attacked by members of the ANC. As is obvious from the words of commissioner Dlamini, Mrs. Nkabinde is one of the rare IFP victims who came forward to the TRC – the IFP officially boycotted the Commission. Her courage is praised, but her political affiliation turns her into an a-typical victim. Therefore, her testimony is used by two of the commissioners to stress that victims from different sides of the apartheid conflict suffered equally:

> COMMISSIONER DLAMINI: Again I will also like to say from all these places where we've been in most cases ANC people are the ones who are coming forward to give evidence, and that thing makes it difficult to find evidence, and I'll also like to thank you for your courage as an IFP member to come forward and give evidence so that we can see that it wasn't just IFP fighting alone, they were fighting with someone. *It's not just IFP, it was IFP/ANC. No one came out innocent.* ANC people thought they were the ones who were just

being killed and no one else, and women and children died. This picture that you just gave us, I am sure that even the ANC will realise that they were not the ones who just lost children and wives, but also Inkatha people.

(…)

COMMISSIONER LAX: You heard – you must have heard the evidence of the lady before you, Mrs Khumalo. She told a similar story to you about being attacked in her own house, the house being set alight, and in her case she said it was members of the IFP who did that. In your case you said it was members of the ANC. *And our view is that from wherever this violence comes it's wrong, and that you and Mrs Khumalo are sitting here together, you are members of different parties, but you have both been victims of violence.* And what has that violence brought to you? Nothing except sadness, fear, misery. And we hope that the message will go out from this Commission that violence doesn't help anything.

Also the testimonies of Pralene Botha and her daughter Rosaline Parrot were used by the commissioners to add an extra dimension to the TRC narrative of national unity. These testifiers belonged to the Coloured community, a community where identifying with the new nation was not always obvious (Frost 1998: 106–107). Mrs. Botha's husband was killed in prison by the security police. The closing statement of commissioner Finca is an illustration of the efforts the Commission put in to include the Coloured population in the nation-building story. First, I will give a fragment from the testimony of the daughter, Mrs. Parrot, in which she expresses how much also her late father struggled for a new nation – an indication of how intensely this family (as a representative of the Coloured community) wants to belong to the new South Africa and how committed they are towards national unity:

> MRS PARROT: When my father passed away he was like a father to us and he was like a husband to my mother and I would like to add that he wasn't the type of person that would take his own life because he was looking forward to the future. *He was the type of person that wanted to build a nation, a good nation.* That's all I want to say.
>
> (…)
>
> REV FINA: You've told your story with dignity and with grace indeed the dignity that belongs to a person like George who gave his life for the liberation of *our land.* We convey to you our respect, we convey to your mother our respect and we just want you to know that to-day we salute George and *we appreciate the fact that in the so-called coloured community there are people who even at that stage took the position that something wrong was happening*

*in this land* and it is to be corrected even if it cost them their lives. Thank you very much.

Mrs. Parrot's words clearly seem to fit in the TRC nation-building discourse, as she also stresses that her father was striving for a new nation, where people from different ethnic backgrounds would be treated equally. Rev. Finca highlights these ideas explicitly when talking about the father as someone "who gave his life for the liberation of our land". Strikingly, he talks about "our land", interpreted inclusively as belonging to all South Africans. In fact, in all of these illustrations, the HRV commissioners regularly used the inclusive terms 'us' and 'our', to emphasise that all South Africans were united as apartheid victims and that they all belonged to the post-apartheid nation.

Commissioner Finca continues by openly praising the Coloured community. He emphasises again that also Coloured people took part in the struggle; they also felt that things were going the wrong way in the country, and they also gave their lives to liberate it.

Just as with the feature of introducing reconciliation, the idea of community spirit was sometimes hinted at by the commissioners by referring to the written statement of the testifier. One example comes from Wandile Mbathu, who was injured at the Bisho massacre. At the end of his testimony commissioner Sandi inquires about Mr. Mbathu's requests before the Commission:

ADV SANDI: Do you have a request to put forward to the Commission?

MR MBATHU: I request that as I am injured, that I could get my money because it's quite problematic. I need pension.

ADV SANDI: *I notice here that there is another request that you have made, that has nothing to do with you personally. Do you remember that request?*

MR MBATHU: Yes I do.

ADV SANDI: Can you tell us Mr Mbathu?

MR MBATHU: I said I wanted a house.

ADV SANDI: *Did you not say that this Commission should ascertain or make a request to the government to build houses for victims like you?*

MR MBATHU: Yes I did say.

ADV SANDI: Do you have another request that you would like to make Mr Mbathu?

MR MBATHU: No I do not but I just need my money because I was injured.

It looks as if commissioner Sandi urges the testifier to admit what was expressed in the written statement – the request to the government to build houses for apartheid victims. Requesting houses for fellow-victims was a typical example of community awareness. It indicated that the victim was concerned about the well-being of the community as a whole, and not solely about his or her own problems. The first request spontaneously expressed by this testifier talks about a pension: Mr. Mbathu has been injured, so he wants financial compensation. Adv. Sandi then refers to the written statement, hinting at another request "that has nothing to do with you personally". Apparently, he wants to hear the communal request from the mouth of the testifier himself. But still, Mr. Mbathu seems only to be concerned with his personal request: he wants a house – a typical individual and material request, so one of the requests probably less preferred by the TRC. Finally, Adv. Sandi has to take the initiative by reading aloud what he wants the testifier to express. Mr. Mbathu can only admit that he is indeed concerned about his community – the written text is a piece of evidence that cannot be dismissed. It soon becomes clear, though, that his real concern lies elsewhere: he stresses again that he needs money first and foremost. Commissioner Sandi does not elaborate on this request and jumps to another topic.

In all of these cases an atmosphere of national solidarity and communal awareness was established. In such a context, testifiers were urged to commit themselves to communal values. It became very hard to stress personal requests for instance, and *not* to voice an individual desire towards national unity. One of the messages thus spread to the TRC audience might be that, since the victims seemed to be committed towards community spirit and national unity, also the nation at large should put in an effort to strive for nationwide togetherness.

By discussing this feature we have noticed that the HRV commissioners made ample use of collective terminology; they also tended to categorise apartheid victims collectively. For instance, testifiers were said to belong to a specific group (population group, community, generation) and as a result of this membership they had experienced great suffering. In this way, South African society seemed to be subdivided in a wide variety of different groups – creating a colourful, mosaic-like image of post-apartheid South Africa. Although all of these groups had their own particularities, they had all undergone the disastrous effects of the apartheid regime. Therefore, with all their different shades, experiences and backgrounds, they now formed one coherent whole, namely this multilayered and highly diversified new nation. This presentation of the new South Africa complied with the metaphor of the *rainbow nation*, an element of the reconciliation discourse that became in vogue in post-TRC South Africa.

Similar to the findings in the previous chapter, I would suggest that stressing the issues of community spirit and nation building was a preferred discursive feature for victims who appeared before the TRC. I would therefore also consider this commitment to national unity as a crucial element of the *reconciliation discourse* constructed at the HRV hearings. Later on, this emphasis on nation building and community spirit will be considered as a prominent feature when trying to gain insight into the rules of formation of this HRV discourse.

### 5.2.6 Feature Three: Respecting testifiers

One of the reasons why South Africa opted for a truth and reconciliation commission instead of a criminal justice procedure revolved around the concern for apartheid victims. It was claimed that in a court case attention primarily focussed on the perpetrators, while victims tended to be largely ignored (see for instance Rakate 1999; Shea 2000:6). After the transition to democracy the negotiating parties decided that in post-apartheid South Africa the victims should be the centre of interest. The victims should not only be given a voice at the HRV Committee, they should also be explicitly honoured and respected in compensation for what they had endured.

The TRC Act defined guiding principles for the Commission when dealing with victims. These included treating victims "with compassion and respect for their dignity", treating them "equally and without discrimination of any kind", taking appropriate measures to "minimise inconvenience to victims" and to "ensure their safety" (Picker 2003:2). Based on this mandate the Human Rights Violations hearings were to achieve several goals: amongst others, the hearings had to restore the victims' "human and civil dignity" and they had to try to contribute to "the healing of a traumatised and wounded people (...)" (TRC Report 1998, 1/5:127). It was also with regard to respect for the victims that the HRV Committee decided to limit the number of public testimonies: "We wanted to ensure that people felt they had had ample time to tell their story and that they had been duly acknowledged", according to chairperson Tutu (1999b:84).

There clearly existed a dominant culture at the TRC "of being sensitive to the needs of victims and survivors (...)" (Harris 2000:77–78). This respect for victims tended to be related to the search for reconciliation, which was embedded in the TRC process. Honouring and respecting victims would make them feel valued in South African society, a sentiment that could be the first step towards building a reconciled and united society.

When analysing the HRV hearings the considerable respect attributed to the testifiers is quite striking. Special attention was paid to their requests, to their needs and to their expectations. Testifiers were praised and characteristics that were less praiseworthy were ignored or justified. Many times, the victims were honoured explicitly, especially in the opening and closing statements of the commissioners. Sometimes, respect could be inferred indirectly from the discourse of the commissioners. Clearly, it was crucial that the victims would feel at ease and that they would leave the TRC with a positive inclination towards the whole process.

Before testifiers were asked to tell their stories at the HRV Committee they always had to take the oath or make an affirmation (to swear that they would tell the truth) (TRC Act 1995, 29 (4)). Usually, the request to take the oath was formulated very carefully. One example comes from Gregory Beck; as a police officer he was shot at by members of the UDF. This is how commissioner Boraine requests him to take the oath and then introduces the testifier:

> DR BORAINE: (…) *I'd be very grateful* if you would stand *please* for the taking of the oath.
>
> GREGORY EDMUND BECK: (sworn states)
>
> DR BORAINE: Mr Beck you are or were a policeman, I am not sure if you still are.
>
> MR BECK: I am a detective.
>
> DR BORAINE: *Thank you very much Detective Beck.* The story that you are going to tell took place in 1988 and you will remember it very vividly, but in order that someone can help you and guide you and direct you in this a fellow Commissioner Hlengiwe Mkhize will lead the discussion. *Thank you.*

Note the abundance of the expression "Thank you" and also the attention paid to Mr. Beck's title. The testifier explicitly says that he is a detective and Mr. Boraine immediately uses this title as the form of address.

In the course of his testimony Mr. Beck attests to a change of attitude via à vis the liberation movement. He explicitly states that he did not understand the viewpoint of the liberation movement in earlier days, while he does so now. He is also critical about the liberation movement when he accuses them of having killed many policemen. This attitude is accepted by the commissioners – a sign that the TRC respected various viewpoints of testifiers, among which also criticism towards the liberation movement:

> MR BECK: But as you mentioned there that it was well-known that the liberation movements had an armed struggle against the State and we, as the police, were the first targets of that armed struggle. In that year a lot of policemen were killed.
>
> MS MKHIZE: *Well I must thank you for your openness about your understanding of what was going on.*

Next, commissioner Ally poses a question about the relation between the police forces and the apartheid state. This sensitive topic is introduced most circumspectly, by first of all praising the victim. After having answered, Mr. Beck is thanked for his honest reply:

> DR ALLY: *Mr Beck I don't want you to take the question that I am going to ask as any indication of any insensitivity to what you have experienced. I am sure that everybody here round the table is moved by what actually happened to you and sympathises.* But I would like to know what your opinions are on the – it is well-known that during the period that you are speaking about the police and the army and all other such structures were seen as an extension of the apartheid state which was oppressing people, and therefore as legitimate targets, how do you feel about that position and in the context of what actually happened to you?

> MR BECK: Okay. Before 1990 *I can say that we as ordinary policeman didn't know much about these covert operations. We didn't know anything about it.* It was mostly the specialist policemen, the Security Police, Murder and Robbery and all those kind of guys who knew about these type of operations, and as we are now in the transparent and new South Africa more of these incidents are now revealed.

> DR ALLY: *Thank you for that honest answer.*

The next example comes from Bernice Whitfield, whose husband was killed by an APLA bomb attack in 1993. This lady is highly critical about the South African government and about the TRC process itself. It might have been on purpose that the TRC treated her with a lot of respect – to stress that the Commission was unbiased, that it wanted to include all apartheid victims and also that it stood open for vehement criticism. Especially Miss. Maya, the leading commissioner, is extremely understanding and respectful. Her questions are always formulated very cautiously and note the abundant use of softeners ("just", "thank you", "are you able to") and modal expressions ("would you like", "would you"):

> MISS MAYA: *Thank you Mrs Whitfield, I would like to ask you just a few questions as I said earlier.*
> (…)
> MISS MAYA: *I would like you to share with us* the effect that his death has had on you and especially your children and also tell us how many children you have, their ages and whether they are schooling or not.
> (…)
> MISS MAYA: *Thank you. Are you able to tell us at all* what the nature and the extent of injuries your husband sustained in the shooting?

(…)

MISS MAYA: *Thank you. Would you like to place a request* or a recommendation before us so that we can convey that to the State President?

(…)

MISS MAYA: *Thank you very much.* I'm going to hand you back to the Chairperson but there could be other questions from the rest of the panel. *Thank you Mrs Whitfield.*

In his closing statement commissioner Finca explicitly emphasises the Commission's respect for Mrs. Whitfield:

> REV FINCA: Reverend Xundu? Okay the question is withdrawn. Just one question from me Mrs Whitfield. You have painted a very gloomy picture of our future and even your coming to the Commission has been put in a context which has a lot of pain and doubt about the validity of doing that and *I've got very serious respect for that in that you have been honest, you have been forthright in talking to us and that is very helpful.* It reminds us that we are a Truth Commission and if people come to us in truth although it may be painful to listen to that truth but it's also very helpful (…).

Also Mzothuli Maphumulo, whose three children were killed by the ANC, is treated with a lot of respect in commissioner Lax's closing statement. Based on the video images we see that Mr. Maphumulo is an elderly gentleman. According to his physical appearance he seems to be committed to traditional Zulu values. Maybe, his old age and his status in the community command the commissioners' respect – an attitude clearly expressed in this closing statement:

> MR LAX: (…) *We know that this incident will leave you sad, it will leave you with sadness that won't leave you, but we hope that you are able to progress, and to use your age and your stature and your maturity to continue working to bring both sides together,* because, as you know, political violence of this nature brings nothing to people except misery and grief, and we hope that if anything is learnt from this that it is that people should – despite their differences they should live and work together. *So again thank you very much for coming in and sharing your story with us. Thank you.*

Finally, these are the opening and closing statements of the testimony by Josephine Msweli – the respect for this victim is striking:

> MR LYSTER: It's Mrs Josephina Msweli. Good afternoon, Mrs Msweli. *Thank you very much for coming in.* You've come to tell us about the death of your son, Simon Msweli, and also Michael Mthetwa. Before you tell us that story *please can you stand up and take the oath.*

(...)

MR LYSTER: *Mrs Msweli, thank you very much for coming in and we know it has been very difficult for you to relive all those terrible experiences that you have gone through* but you have volunteered to come here and *it's very important for us that you have come here*, to have told us what it was like for you and your family to have lived through those times, to have given us a detailed description of how the police harassed you perpetually, continuously harassed you, and killed two of your sons. (...) So thank you for giving us your story. *It's a very important story. Thank you very much.*

I should also mention that many of these testimonies were highly emotional and more than once, testifiers broke down while talking about their traumatic experiences. In these difficult instances a great deal of respect was always shown for the victim: the commissioners often repeated that the testifier could take time to recover, they asked whether the testifier felt all right and they requested to offer water or a tissue. I will list a few of these interventions by the commissioners – no further explanation is needed.

At a certain point, Emily Siko bursts into tears when she tells how members of the AWB hit her with a brick. Commissioner Randera immediately intervenes:

DR RANDERA: *Take your time, all right. Can you please give the lady some water to drink, please.*

And this is the example of Mrs. Nkabinde:

MR DLAMINI: And what happened about the case?

MRS NKABINDE: There was not enough evidence so the case never proceeded up until today.

MR DLAMINI: *Take your time. We understand that this is very sad. It's not easy for one to relate such a sad story. (Pause) You can continue if you're ready.*

MRS NKABINDE: I was confused because I never quarrelled with anyone. I was never involved in any conflict. I heard that people were fighting, IFP/ ANC were fighting, but I was never involved.

In this chapter I have illustrated the different ways in which testifiers before the HRV Committee were honoured and respected. As set out in the TRC Act, respect for the victims was an inherent feature of the HRV proceedings; in fact, it was obvious that testifiers should be welcomed, comforted, praised and admired while giving their testimonies before the TRC. And indeed, in each of the victim testimonies commissioners tried their best to honour victims: they honoured their past experiences, their present situations and also their courage to build a better future.

Although saying something respectfully does not always guarantee that respect is shown, I hope to have demonstrated that the TRC commissioners were sincere in wanting to show respect towards the victims. Through all kinds of implicit and explicit statements they made sure that this indispensable and highly valued *culture of respect* took shape. Not only were their statements and expressions respectful, their facial expressions and their gestures also indicated sympathy and concern for the testifier. This happened time and again, at every HRV hearing and vis à vis all kinds of testifiers, hence also demonstrating the inclusive nature of the TRC. Respect for the victims was part and parcel of the reconciliation discourse created at the HRV hearings, so it has been important to give a few examples of the different methods employed by the commissioners to reach this end.

### 5.2.7  Feature Four: Emphasising emotional discourse

The TRC has been labelled the 'Kleenex Commission' by a number of critics (Tutu 1999b: 83). This was due to the fact that a lot of emotions tended to be displayed at the hearings: testifiers started to cry spontaneously when reliving their traumatic experiences and sometimes the commissioners themselves wept and broke down. In these highly emotional moments the briefers, who were assisting the victims while testifying, often handed a Kleenex tissue to the speaker – hence the term 'Kleenex Commission'.

The content of the HRV narratives was often very emotional, since it was an explicit reliving of traumatic incidents from the past. Therefore, we could define the HRV testimonies as *narratives of trauma* (Rogers et al. 1999). Not only was the content emotionally loaded, other trauma signals were also displayed at the hearings, such as long silences, a sudden loss of control over emotions, repetitive reporting or changes in voice and body language (Benezer 1999: 34–36). In addition, a feature also apparent at the HRV hearings, traumatic narratives tend to be very incoherent and fragmented (Leydesdorff 1999: 15).

The point I want to make here is that testifiers were sometimes stimulated by the TRC panel to express emotions. This stimulating of emotions mostly happened by referring to personal – often physical or medical – details during the hearings. Testifiers were explicitly asked to elaborate on torture experiences, to give details about their physical condition since the time of the incident, or to explain what kind of psychological treatment they were getting. A number of commentators, such as Ross (1996) and Franz (1997) have argued that the TRC's primary focus has been on violations of the body, although "by focusing too closely on bodily experience other aspects of the testifiers' sufferings could be left unnoticed" (Ross 1996:27). Recalling medical details or reliving torture incidents could be highly emotional to the testifiers, in the same way as listening to these issues could be highly emotional for the audience and for the HRV panel members. This could clearly be seen therefore as a way to create an extremely dramatic and emotional atmosphere.

Indeed, on the basis of my reading, the commissioners at times prompted testifiers to talk about these personal experiences, even if the testifiers were not inclined to do so. Metro Bambiso, for instance, was a testifier who was very reluctant to talk about his torture experiences. Commissioner Sandi, however, insists on hearing details about the way Mr. Bambiso was tortured. Mr. Bambiso was arrested and severely tortured by the South African security forces:

> ADV SANDI: What did they do after they handcuffed you?
>
> MR BAMBISO: They tortured me.
>
> ADV SANDI: *Please explain to us the ways in which they tortured you.*
>
> MR BAMBISO: Firstly, Mr Chairperson, *it is very painful for me to say or to explain to you what was happening.* They were kicking me. Even in the township before they took me to the van they were assaulting me, kicking me in the township and they took me to the police van, took me to town. They did not take me to the police station. There was a place which was used as a rent office in town in the BAAB offices. They took me there. It was quarter past nine at that time, because there was a watch there. From quarter past nine till quarter to three they were assaulting us. They would squeeze our private parts and they would close them to a drawer. That is when I got injured.
>
> ADV SANDI: *When you say that you were being tortured and everything was done to you, what do you mean?*
>
> MR BAMBISO: There are many ways, there are many things they did to us. The police would take a cigarette to our noses and they would take needles and put them under our nails.
>
> ADV SANDI: For how long did this last?
>
> MR BAMBISO: We arrived in this building at quarter past nine and we were released at quarter to three in the morning when we were taken to the charge office.
>
> ADV SANDI: *Were you injured in any way?*
>
> MR BAMBISO: Yes.
>
> ADV SANDI: *Please tell us how were you injured?*

> MR BAMBISO: I was injured in my private parts, because after all this my private parts were swollen up, because of the Boers.
>
> ADV SANDI: Did you receive any medical treatment or are you receiving treatment now?
>
> MR BAMBISO: I am not receiving any treatment.

We see that this dialogue about the personal physical experiences of Mr. Bambiso takes quite a long time. When Adv. Sandi's first question is briefly answered by "They tortured me", it seems to be obvious that Mr. Bambiso does not want to elaborate on this traumatic incident. Adv. Sandi insists, whereupon Mr. Bambiso tells him in a polite, but very affirmative way how difficult it is to relive this torture practice by talking about it. Nevertheless, he gives some details, but this does not seem to satisfy the commissioner. Throughout this fragment Adv. Sandi insists on hearing the personal details of the victim's experience, although Mr. Bambiso clearly feels uncomfortable.

Not all testifiers were unwilling to talk about their torture experiences. Mr. Laloo Chiba, for instance, gives detailed information about the ways in which he was tortured by the apartheid security services. Even so, the commissioners demand more details, especially commissioner Sooka. Mr. Chiba was severely tortured and detained for eighteen years. I first give a fragment to illustrate how, unsolicited, he elaborates on the torture details:

> MR CHIBA: They started assaulting me, punched me, kicked me and in the process my face was badly bruised. My left ear-drum had been punctured. They wanted to know who my contact was in MK. They wanted to know the next link in the chain of command. I pleaded ignorance. I told them that I didn't know anything. I told them that actually there must be some sort of a serious mistake that they were making on their part.
> The assault must have lasted half-an-hour or so. It is very, very difficult for me to assess the passage of time under these circumstances. But what was to follow was far more serious than the assault that had taken place.
> From behind someone threw a sack, a wet hessian sack over my body so that half my body was covered and I was partially strait-jacketed. I was then flung onto the floor. My shoes and socks were removed and I could feel electric wires being tied to my toes, to my fingers, my knuckles and so on.
> They wanted to know who my contact was. To them that was a very crucial issue. I pleaded ignorance. I told them that I did not know. Every time I resisted answering the questions, they turned on the dynamo and of course, violent electric shocks started passing through my body. They did so every time I refused to answer. All I could do was to scream out in pain. I could only scream and scream and plead ignorance.

(…)

MS SOOKA: Thank you very much. *I am just going to take you back to a few issues, just for clarity.* We have had the evidence of Abdulla Jassat, and he was quite detailed, in fact, about his own torture. He detailed the question the wet bag treatment and it seems that that was quite common. It was done to you as well. *But he also described a particular form of torture where you were held by two policemen and dropped by the one standing in front of a window and then the other person grabbed the other leg.* For me it seems that it would point to the fact of how a number of people were killed, in falling from different floors. *I wonder with you, was that done to you as well?*

MR CHIBA: Thank you. No, that was not done to me.

(…)

MS SOOKA: *It is also important for the Commission to document the kind of torture that took place. It is very important for our records.* Particularly in the different periods during our history, because there was a definite change after a certain period. But you talk about the Stockholm Syndrome, and I would be grateful if you could just deal with that briefly.

Mr. Chiba does not appear to be uncomfortable talking about the torture methods that were used on him. He is very emotional, though, when reliving these experiences. A number of times he breaks down, he starts to cry or he has to stop talking. However, Mrs. Sooka is interested in more details on these torture methods. She urges how important it is to get insight into the torture methods under apartheid, in order to obtain a clear picture of the past – revealing apartheid atrocities was indeed one of the main objectives of the TRC. By reverting to the historical relevance of torture information this commissioner tries to justify her questions. She might have felt uncomfortable confronting Mr. Chiba so explicitly with his torture experiences. By framing the questions in this particular way she might have indicated that it was not her desire to extract a description of the torture methods – it was her *duty* as a TRC commissioner.

The next testifier I would like to refer to is Phebel Robinson. She talked about the detention, torture and killing of her husband. On two occasions commissioners Wildschut and Potgieter make reference to the way he was gruesomely murdered:

MS WILDSCHUT: Ms Robinson *I have before me some really gruesome photographs of your husbands body. I know it's very terrible for you to go through this experience.* You did say that you were not allowed to see your husband's body at the time of the funeral. *Where you able at any point to – to get to know how badly he was hurt?*

MS ROBINSON: (…) Because he was fair but he did not have any color in his face because it looked like burn marks and candle marks the way they tortured him. That is why I doubt it because if the police weren't after him for all these years, I wouldn't have had such strong doubts and reservations in my mind.

(…)

ADV POTGIETER: Apart from the stab wounds, which other injuries were inflicted on the body – *which other injuries could you see?*

MS ROBINSON: [indistinct] marks as they dragged him along and I don't know what else they did with him. But it was – it's a long report and I cannot say – I cannot mention everything because the report is far to long. Because every part of his hand, his fingers had marks, stab marks, scuff wound – scuff marks from being dragged. *I just cannot mention everything.*

Ms. Wildschut starts by referring to the "really gruesome photographs of your husband's body", words that emphasise the dramatic nature of Ms. Robinson's experience. Cruelty is visualised by incorporating these pictures in the testimony. This dramatic atmosphere is even intensified by the following words: "I know it's very terrible for you to go through this experience".

Mr. Potgieter continues along this emotional line. He also wants to know what kinds of injuries were inflicted on Ms. Robinson's husband. In this way, Ms. Robinson is forced to relive the traumatic moment of identification, probably the most traumatic instance of the entire incident. Ms. Robinson gives a few details, but then she says twice that she just cannot mention everything. She might not be able to remember the details from the medical report, or she might be unwilling to re-experience this physical confrontation with her husband's mutilated body.

These illustrations show that at the HRV hearings the stress on emotional and personal details in the victims' testimonies was a recurring feature. A number of explanations for the emphasis on emotional details during the HRV hearings have been formulated. First, eliciting details on torture methods or on the physical consequences of being imprisoned could be seen as part of the Commission's task of establishing the apartheid truth. This factual knowledge about the methods of the police could then become part of the official TRC record. Another explanation could be that talking about these personal aspects was healing for the victims. Elaborating on past traumas could be a cathartic experience, an appropriate way of dealing with these traumatic incidents. It has been claimed many times indeed, that for most of the victims who came forward to the HRV Committee testifying was a healing experience (see for instance Boroughs 1997; Minow 1998:66; Fourie 1999; Meiring 1999:371). Talking about past traumas is not always healing, though; not all victims are prepared to relive the traumatic past

(Rigby 2001: 2). Sometimes, narratives of trauma stir up memories, which victims have fought hard to keep out of their consciousness in order to get on with their lives (Leydesdorff et al. 1999: 17).

In my opinion, stressing emotional, physical and dramatic issues in the victims' testimonies could also have been a way of highlighting the necessity of the truth commission. If a lot of emotions were shown at the TRC, the devastating effect of apartheid was emphasised and in this way the necessity of the TRC as a healing instrument became more apparent. At the same time, dramatic language and emotional detail could also enhance the nation-wide compassion for the victims of apartheid. As a result, the more shocking the system of apartheid seemed to be, the more people could be convinced that the reoccurrence of such a system has to be prevented at all costs – a conviction the TRC wanted to communicate to the entire world. Also, paying detailed attention to emotional matters could be a means to try to meet the appeal for spectacle that might have existed among the TRC audience – especially the media producers. Indeed, the HRV hearings were designed to have a powerful public effect. They were not merely meant to be representative, but also to be demonstrative, hence the attention paid to particularly graphic narratives.

When trying to understand the rules of formation of the HRV *reconciliation discourse* the emphasis on emotional discourse will be a prominent feature. Torture details, and descriptions of physical or psychological injuries were valued statements at the HRV hearings. The fact that these statements were preferred might have had a purpose: they could have served the testifiers themselves, the TRC as an institution, or the wider audience (media included). Creating an emotional atmosphere also seemed to be an element of the master narrative the TRC sought to construct.

## 5.3    Historical layering

### 5.3.1    Introduction

Three out of the ten features discussed in this work will be categorised under the label of historical layering. As stated by Blommaert (2005: 135), discourse is always firmly anchored in history – it is always intrinsically historical. Every discourse is a discourse *on* history, since it always refers to a variety of historical time frames. At the same time, every discourse is a discourse *from* history, since it articulates a particular position – or different positions – in history. Discourse analysis is a way to elucidate how discourse relates to time and one possibility is to investigate how people position themselves and their discursive practices vis à vis particular time frames (Blommaert 2003: 177). People can speak from various positions in history, so from within various layers of historicity. At the same time, they can also orient their discourse to these different historical frames. During one and the same discursive event people often shift back and forth between various historical layers, identifying themselves differently vis à vis the past, the present and the future.

This historical positioning can have a tremendous impact on the continuity of meaning and on the coherence and incoherence in discourse (Blommaert 2005: 130). Moving back and forth in time while engaging in discourse can add an extra layer of significance to this particular discourse. However, without the necessary background knowledge, such a historical layering can also be a heavy burden on the overall interpretation of the discursive event. Clearly, for a full understanding of a discursive event one always has to take into account the historical position from which a person speaks.

At the Human Rights Violation hearings testifiers spoke from different historical positions and oriented their discourse to various historical time frames. What I will illustrate here is how testifiers moved between a variety of different time frames while testifying before the HRV Committee. While telling their stories at the TRC, they alternately spoke from a past – apartheid – position, they addressed the audience in a deliberate attempt to impact on the future, or they reacted to the questions posed by the commissioners, thus directing their discourse to the present TRC moment. In one testimony, victims could relive the past by reverting to so-called *apartheid-talk*; immediately thereafter they could consciously focus on the present or offer a vision towards the future.

All this will tell us that, even within one testimony – so also 'simultaneously', the HRV discourse was historically layered. The past was brought to the present TRC moment and at the same time, the present experience of testifying before the HRV Committee was extended to the future. People moved between these time frames by employing various discursive techniques, thus creating a kind of discourse that was prototypical for one specific historical moment (the transition from apartheid to post-apartheid South Africa), but that at the same time radiated to the past and the future. Hence, in HRV discourse the past was relived and the future was reflected upon; in this way, the historical bridging position of the TRC was symbolised. The full complexity and the significance of this reconciliation discourse in present-day South Africa can only be grasped if insight is provided into its connections with the past and its implications towards the future.

### 5.3.2  Feature Five: Apartheid-talk

In any discursive event, people refer to the past and reflect on the future by using specific linguistic registers (different styles, different words, different grammar or different language varieties). In the course of their testimonies before the HRV Committee, victims constantly went back and forth, shifting between present-day discursive registers, connotations and indexicalities, on the one hand, and associations with the past or reflections on the future, on the other hand. In their discourse we mainly notice an interaction between two historical layers: the current day time frame belonging to the liberated South Africa, and the time frame of the apartheid past, with terms and connotations linked to the pre-1994 era of repression and terror.

I have labelled the discursive elements that clearly refer to the apartheid era as *apartheid-talk*; apartheid-talk involves emblematic discourse where apartheid as such is thematised. It refers to a set of apartheid frames that are being activated by means of various discursive practices – and this usually retrospectively. This term includes a range of linguistic features: mostly involving non-Afrikaans speakers employing Afrikaans words or phrases in the course of their testimonies, and the use of certain terms – usually judicial, military or racial terms – that had an emblematic apartheid connotation. According to my interpretation, when non-Afrikaans speakers made use of the language Afrikaans, they explicitly wanted to relive certain instances from the apartheid past, or they used Afrikaans to convey a certain metapragmatic impression about individuals or experiences from the past. Through Afrikaans the apartheid past was evoked, the traumatic event was re-experienced and the testimony was given an extra dimension – this often happened by quoting someone in Afrikaans, or by using the Afrikaans terms for certain specific words.

Although in the new South Africa Afrikaans is one of the eleven official languages, it can still be stigmatised as 'the language of the apartheid oppressors'. The National Party's ruthless apartheid regime and simultaneous promotion of the language forged a link between the language and the political system that remains to this day (http://nc.essortment.com/historyafrikaan rqrs.htm). According to the 2001 census, 13.3% of South Africans have Afrikaans as their mother tongue (http://www.info.gov.za/yearbook/2004/landpeople.htm). It is the first language of approximately 60% of South Africa's Whites, and over 90% of the Coloured population. Nowadays, and in spite of the fact that a large number of non-white South Africans have Afrikaans as their mother tongue, the language still carries certain apartheid-related connotations, also internationally – which is one of the reasons for my use of the term apartheid-talk.

In cases where Afrikaans was not transcribed in the HRV testimonies, or in cases where only single words were used, I could not find out whether this Afrikaans was a standard version or rather a more subcultural variety (for instance Tsotsitaal, see Gilbert & Makhudu 1984) or a dialect used by black and Coloured people. In other cases, it seemed to me that the Afrikaans reproduced was a more standard version, as used my most white Afrikaners – and carrying white/apartheid connotations.

Afrikaans was not regularly used by victims who appeared before the HRV Committee. Some white and Coloured victims did speak Afrikaans when testifying – among my thirty case studies there are only two people who testified in Afrikaans: the Coloured lady Phebel Robinson and the white Afrikaner Johannes van Eck. When discussing apartheid-talk the testimonies of these native Afrikaans speakers will not be taken into account. In what follows I will give a number of examples of testifiers who relived the past experience by using apartheid-talk. These examples will clarify my understanding of the term in question.

The first example comes from Emily Siko, who talked about an attack by the Afrikaner Weerstandsbeweging (AWB). Mrs. Siko testifies in an African language, most likely in one of the nine official African languages of South Africa – more research definitely needs to be done on the linguistic context of the TRC testimonies, because for an outsider it is now almost impossible to find out in which language exactly these people testified. Mrs. Siko tells her story in the African language throughout, but when she gets to the actual attack she quotes some of the AWB people in Afrikaans. In the transcription only the English translation is given, but on the video one can clearly hear how Mrs. Siko speaks Afrikaans. In the following fragments it is the italicised words that are pronounced in Afrikaans, though transcribed in English:

> <u>MRS SIKO</u>: They were axing the door. They were saying AWB, we have no place here, *this is our place, this is our place for our nation*. Then I said, *please "baas", I didn't put myself here, but somebody sent me to stay here*. Then they hit me with a brick.
>
> <u>DR RANDERA</u>: Take your time, all right. Can you please give the lady some water to drink, please.

Both of the phrases "this is our place, this is our place for our nation" and "please, baas, I didn't put myself here, but somebody sent me to stay here" are pronounced in Afrikaans. Apparently, this is a highly traumatic recollection to Mrs. Siko, since she starts to cry after the sentence "They hit me with a brick".

Switching to another code is sometimes a *marked language choice* (according to Susan Gal 1979 and Myers-Scotton 1993, for example), and also in this case this passage is very interesting. It looks like an instance in which Mrs. Siko attempts to evoke the past by literally quoting the AWB members. In the literature on code switching it is argued that people are often quoted in the original language. Quoting is even said to be one of the reasons for code switching (Auer 1984; McClure & McClure 1988; Alvarez-Caccamo 1998). In the course of her testimony, though, Emily Siko quotes the AWB people a couple of times, and she usually does so in the African language she is testifying in.

In view of Mrs. Siko's emotional reaction afterwards, it might be that this was one of the most traumatic moments of the entire experience. Possibly, it is these exact words that are branded onto her memory. The experience might have been so traumatic that the only way to relive it is by literally quoting the AWB people. In addition, the attackers are clearly identified as apartheid suppressors by quoting them in Afrikaans. A stereotype inherent to many of the HRV narratives was that the apartheid perpetrators were white Afrikaners, while the victims were black, Coloured or Indian South Africans. By quoting the attackers in Afrikaans, and by identifying them explicitly as white Afrikaners, the stereotype is confirmed.

Very interesting in this fragment is the use of the term "baas". 'Baas' can be literally translated as 'chief, master, boss'. Under apartheid 'baas' was the term whereby non-Whites were supposed to address white men, even if they were not the chief or master (http://roepstem2.tripod.com/snaaks.html). This term expresses the inferiority of the person who uses the term and the superiority of the one who is addressed. By using this term when telling her story before the HRV Committee, these same attitudes and emotions are evoked and brought back from the past to the present. Mrs. Siko is about 30 years old when testifying before the HRVC, which means that she grew up under apartheid. For her, addressing a white man with 'baas' might be natural. And although life changed in South Africa after 1994, it is possible that these apartheid discursive patterns are still dominant in the minds of many non-white South Africans.

Muhammad Ferhelst is a victim who told the main part of his story in English. In the course of this English narrative he also quoted some people in Afrikaans, just like Mrs. Siko. Mr. Ferhelst was imprisoned by the South African police and severely tortured. These are some fragments from his testimony:

> MR FERHELST: There was approximately 20 to 30 'cops' in the dining room and this Captain burst into the room where I was laying, I was till in a shorts. He pulled me up, he said can I use the exact words because like it's hard for me to forget what that man said today and like I tried to forget, but it's always there, this Captain his name is Van Brakel. He came into that room, he and about 4 or 5 other SB's, he said to me, **jou slym etter gemors, ons het jou, ons**

**gaan jou nou vrek maak** you piece of trash, we have you now, now we going to kill you.

(…)

<u>MR FERHELST</u>: From there they took me to Bracenfell police station, they booked me in, threw me in a cell. At about seven or eight Van Brakel came, he started asking me questions, smacking me around what and then he left again and he said **ons maak jou nog vrek, voor jy uit die tronk uit kom** they told me they would kill me.

(…)

<u>MR FERHELST</u>: Ja, they took me to a doctor once, I can still remember the doctor was somewhere in Bellville, my whole body was bruised. I had marks on my face and I came to the doctor, the doctor just took out a stethoscope, put it against my heart and he reckons to the SB, **die donner makeer fok all, vat hom hier weg**.

In the first two fragments, Mr. Ferhelst quotes a white policeman. Although he often quotes white policemen in the course of his testimony, he usually does so in English. These quotes in Afrikaans could have a special significance. Possibly, when interrogated by the police, it is these exact words that are branded onto Mr. Ferhelst's memory. Quoting the policeman in Afrikaans might have been the only way to relive this extremely traumatic experience. In the transcription the Afrikaans words as well as the English translation are given, but on the video tape you mainly hear the voice of the interpreter who translates these words into English.

These Afrikaans words are extremely harsh, impolite and rude. Using them in front of the TRC makes one re-experience the apartheid era, but it could also have another specific purpose. Perhaps, Mr. Ferhelst wants to describe this policeman as a rude and uncivilised person, a barbarian who uses very insulting words. Quoting him in English would not have made the same impression on the audience and it is possible that this victim purposely wants to shock the audience.

As in most of the previous examples this code switching is a *metaphorical code switching* (Gumperz 1982), as it concerns communicative effects and is not related to any kind of situational change. The people who transcribed and edited this text also noticed that these words have a special – pragmatic – connotation: it either emphasises the highly traumatic nature of the experience, or it specifically identifies the apartheid police in a negative way. That is why the transcribers highlighted them in the transcription (in bold letter type). Usually, no other language than English was used in the transcriptions, so the mere fact that the Afrikaans is transcribed already indicates that the transcribers noticed something peculiar about these words.

Finally, Mr. Ferhelst also quotes the doctor he was taken to by the police after they had tortured him. This appointment with the doctor was probably traumatic as well, which could be one reason for reliving the past by quoting this doctor literally. Another possibility is that Mr. Ferhelst wants to present this doctor as an accomplice of the police, by quoting him in the same vulgar Afrikaans.

In each of these three cases, the code switching to Afrikaans projects the present-day TRC reality back to the apartheid era. The terror of a police interrogation and the humiliation by apartheid doctors are re-experienced in the event-time of the TRC moment, taking the listeners back in time and sharply drawing the difference between the apartheid and the post-apartheid eras.

Another interesting victim with regard to the use of apartheid-talk is Nelson Jantjie. He testified about his sister who was shot by the police and about his own imprisonment. Mr. Jantjie testifies in Xhosa, but he switches to Afrikaans on a number of specific moments in his testimony. It seems as if he wants to highlight certain words in his testimony by pronouncing them in Afrikaans. Later on he also quotes some policemen in Afrikaans:

> MR JANTJIE: These policeman were trying cover up their filth, it is Silingo who had killed this – who had killed this man. Because they were covering up their filth, they were accusing me. They are filthy people these **gemorse** – I don't know anything about anything, I worked in Cape Town, I don't know anything, the nonsense that went on, the petty stuff I had just arrived, I was from Cape Town, they ruined my life because I was going to marry a woman. But I had to part from here, because of them – *these bastards.*
> (...)
> MR JANTJIE: I did not get bail, they refused, our advocates tried to get bail for us. They even requested if I could go to my sister's funeral, they refused. They said that *I am dangerous – they are the one's who are dangerous not me.*

In the first fragment, Mr. Jantjie only pronounces the word "gemorse" ('shits') in Afrikaans. This Afrikaans term is retained in the transcription and even highlighted in bold letter type. Mr. Jantjie is very angry when testifying. Pronouncing 'shits' in Afrikaans adds to the sense of Mr. Jantjie's fury. "Gemorse" is a negative and very insulting word. By identifying the policemen as 'gemorse', the testifier wants to point up their negative image. By applying this word to these policemen, Mr. Jantjie might be recontextualising the apartheid term in a way appropriate for the new South African situation – the policemen can be called bastards now, and not solely the black people as was the case in the apartheid era.

Towards the end of his testimony, Mr. Jantjie quotes the policemen in Afrikaans: "They said that *I am dangerous*", and then he pronounces the rest of the sentence in Afrikaans as well, although this is no longer a quote. He imitates the policemen by reversing the roles that were established by the police: "hulle is gevaarlik, ék is nie gevaarlik nie." Through these words he evokes the apartheid past, where policemen used to insult and humiliate people in Afrikaans. In addition, he also seems to ridicule the police – something that is very well understood by the audience as they react by laughing.

In all of these cases, the reported speech of the testifiers reproduces the language of the police in a congruent or *isomorphic* way, that is, according to observed behaviours or typifications (Alvarez-Caccamo 1996: 34). By doing so, the speakers are reconstructing a specific sociolinguistic reality, which means that they are aware of the socio-indexical potential of language. They use the code of Afrikaans on the basis of underlying linguistic ideologies, telling them which language is appropriate for a given character under certain circumstances. In fact, the testifiers not only convey a representational meaning (what language the police actually used), but also an evaluative meaning (indicating their alignment with the speaker they quote). As Alvarez-Caccamo (1996: 56) argues, "selective language choices for reported speech are an act of power". Through this reported speech, the testifying victims try to impose an order in the interpretation of the events being retold – focussing the hearers' attention on the unequal human relations that existed during the apartheid era.

Another important example of apartheid-talk is when testifiers manifestly used apartheid racial categories, such as 'White', 'Black', 'Coloured', 'Indian', especially when these terms were used in combination with other identifying words in order to form a stereotypical category – for instance "white perpetrator", "black victim", "white soldier". Combinations like these recalled apartheid oppositions. It was known that the majority of perpetrators was white and the majority of victims was black, so there was no need to explicitly mention this. By still doing so, the testifying victims – perhaps unconsciously – relived apartheid categorisations. They brought pre-1994 social stratifications to the present TRC moment.

One testifier who used racial terminology explicitly was Josephine Msweli. She testified about her sons who had been killed by the KwaZulu/Natal police:

> MRS MSWELI: We were branded as ANC criminals, that's how they called the police to come and attack us. And when I sat down and spoke to the police telling them that there was nothing of the sort, *they said I was a criminal myself – the white police.*
> (...)
> MRS MSWELI: (...) and there were *certain white people* who came who were building the gum-trees. They said we should move to another place but Msweli at that time refused to move from that place because he was self-employed. That was his sole source of living. He said that he was going to fix the land for himself because he wanted to use it later and he went to the chief's father. And the chief asked him as to what he was going to do with gum-tree.

> He asked what were *the white man* doing with gum-tree. He was going to do the very same thing that *the white men* were doing with the gum-tree and he went to *the very same white people* and they gave him permission that he should plant the gum-trees.

In the first fragment Mrs. Msweli is describing an interaction with policemen. The police are explicitly labelled as 'white', a term which identifies them negatively. The 'white police', as an inextricable unit, are presented as the evil ones, as a highly condemnable group, thus clearly evoking apartheid stereotypes. In the second fragment Mrs. Msweli is talking about white people who came to plant gum-trees and her husband who wanted to have the same land rights as these white people. She manifestly identifies the people who planted the gum-trees as "white". Through using the indefinite identifier "certain" in the beginning of the fragment Mrs. Msweli negatively categorises the white people. By putting her family, her husband and the chief in one camp (the 'good ones') and the white people in the other (the 'bad ones'), she recalls the racialised apartheid oppositions, again projecting past associations to the present TRC moment.

Another example comes from Lizzy Phike. This lady also made use of what I call apartheid-talk – she also testified in an African language, most likely Xhosa. She was arrested and while in detention her son Ntemi was killed by the police. When talking about policemen, Ms. Phike consistently identifies them by means of racial categorisations (for instance: "the police came, the whites came to fetch me at home"). She also uses the Afrikaans term 'boer' to refer to the Afrikaner policemen:

> MS PHIKE: She also told me about what was happening in the township, about the AZAPO, the PAC's and *the Boers* who were – who wanted the youth – were collecting the youth. And they also wanted Ntemi. I was worried because even my husband was once harassed by *this white boers*. They even said that my husband was lying it he says he doesn't know anything about them. They said they had the right to ask for whatever they want. I told them to take Ntemi to – to – I told them to take Ntemi to Gugulethu. My cousin took Ntemi to Gugulethu so that the police couldn't find her.

The Dutch word 'boer' originally meant farmer, but in the South African context the significance of the word has been narrowed down, referring now specifically to Afrikaners or Afrikaner policemen (http://dictionaries.travlang.com/Afrikaans-English/). When used by non-Afrikaners it is sometimes perceived as a term of insult to refer to white South Africans. 'Boer' is a typical South African word, associated with white Afrikaners as they lived their lives under apartheid. Identifying white South Africans by means of this term brings the addressees back to the apartheid past, to a different historical layer.

Through these examples we come to understand how discourse used by the HRV victims was still partly anchored in apartheid era connotations and indexicalities. Typical Afrikaans or English apartheid terminology was recontextualised and the apartheid experience was relived. By doing so, past emotions and conceptualisations were projected to the TRC discourse. Through HRV discourse the apartheid regime was re-experienced, and in this way the post-apartheid era was vividly opposed to the era preceding the 1994-transformations. This historical layering turned HRV discourse into a multivoiced phenomenon. Testifiers relived the past in order to construct a certain kind of discourse appropriate for their present position as a HRV testifier. By doing so, they constructed a multidimensional identity, an identity that was in transition between the old and the new South Africa.

Another method through which the testifiers indicated that they were still reliving the apartheid past had nothing to do with their formal discourse, but rather with the content of their narratives. Namely, in these traumatic stories victims regularly expressed a sense of continuity between their lives under apartheid and their lives in the present post-apartheid moment. Illustrating this feature will be the purpose of the next section.

### 5.3.3 Feature Six: Continuity between the past and the present

The Truth and Reconciliation Commission stood as a symbol of the transition to post-apartheid South Africa. Apartheid roles were reversed, recommendations were formulated with an eye to a peaceful future and the past was remembered in order to be able to gradually forget it. Throughout the testimonies, however, victims indicated that although the post-apartheid era might have been heralded symbolically, in practice nothing had changed in their lives. They continued to relive the apartheid terror and humiliations, often not as starkly as in the past, but still significant enough to mention before the HRV Committee.

I will give a few examples of the ways in which testifiers discursively stressed the continuity between the past and the present. This is an aspect of historical layering, since it involves a shift between different time frames, bringing the apartheid past to the present and projecting it to the future. The first example comes from Laloo Chiba, a victim who was very emotional in connecting the past experience to the present. He talked about his detention and torture by the South African security services. Through his discourse one can understand that he still relives the traumatic incident, on a personal and emotional level, as well as when thinking about his friends. Also on a political level Mr. Chiba connects the past to the present, thus indicating continuity in the policy of the ANC:

> MR CHIBA: At this point in time I think it is necessary for me to say that I was rather pleased with myself at the fact that I had not divulged any information whatsoever. *I feel proud* of that fact. To deny the enemy the information that they so dearly wanted, was something that I felt good about.
> (…)
> MR CHIBA: Yes. At the same time I think I must say something. I had screamed out in pain, I had pleaded for mercy from an enemy, a people's enemy, I had asked them to stop torturing me. I had given them the pleasure of listening to my screams and it is something *that haunts me up till today.* As I repeat this here, *I feel a deep sense of shame for the shortcoming.* I don't think that a revolutionary should actually give the enemy the pleasure of listening to one's screams. I think I failed in that respect. I hope that you people understand that. *It haunts me up until today, and I don't think that I can ever come to terms with that.* Anyway ...
> (…)
> MR CHIBA: Thank you. No, that was not done to me. I know that Comrade Abdulla Jassat was very, very severely tortured. It had been done to him. I wasn't an eyewitness to that, but that he described to me, he described that to me later. But I want to state this, that he was so severely tortured that *up to today he suffers* from epileptic fits, if I remember correctly, and *he is unable to lead a normal life.* I have witnessed, I have seen that myself.
> (…)
> MR CHIBA: So what I can say here, that was very, very unfortunate. I myself am not happy with that and those people, the undisciplined elements have to be dealt with, they need to be dealt with. But *it is not the policy and it was not the policy of the African National Congress.* Sometimes accidents do take place but I want to stress it was certainly not the policy of the African National Congress.

The first two fragments deal with Mr. Chiba's emotional self. He expresses an ambiguous attitude: on the one hand he still feels proud about the fact that he did not divulge any information to his torturers, on the other hand he feels ashamed because he screamed when being tortured. By using present tenses and by saying "up until today" the witness indicates that these ambiguous feelings are still pursuing him to the present moment. Also this victim has not been able to return to a normal life. There is even a connection with the future, since Mr. Chiba thinks that he will never be able to come to terms with these emotions. The traumatic incident will have repercussions for the rest of his life, again an idea that stresses the dramatic nature of the narrative.

The same link between the past and the present is expressed with regard to the torture of a friend of Mr. Chiba. The experiences of this friend are incorporated in Mr. Chiba's story and it is stressed that this person also still suffers from the consequences of the apartheid atrocities. Finally, Mr. Chiba moves to a political level and also on this level the past and the present are connected. By using the present tense he claims that there is continuity between the policy of the ANC under apartheid and its current policy. Although South Africa has been transformed following 1994, the past still reverberates in the present, and this on a number of different levels.

Vusumuzi Ntuli is a young man who was attacked by members of the IFP. Throughout his testimony he links the past to the present, both to indicate that a lot of conflict situations from the past still remain unresolved and that even today he suffers from the effects of the attack:

> MR NTULI: This went on until in 1993 one day, it was late at night, I think it was about half past eight – comrades at that time, ANC comrades, never used to sleep home because they were scared, so they used to run away. *Up until today there are a lot of cases which were opened and they were never investigated.*
> (…)
> MR NTULI: In 1994 Inkatha came to my house. They attacked my house, they broke windows, and the ZPs were there. I even know the KwaZulu Police who shot me, because one of them told me that he's Bravusi, and he's from Durban to kill me. *Now they aren't driving that Golf, they are driving other cars, but they are still around.* That Golf disappeared. Even that Cressida, that white Cressida, disappeared. We don't know where they took those cars to.
> (…)
> COMMISSIONER LAX: It was because of this hand?
>
> MR NTULI: Yes. I can hold with my hand, but *I have difficulties in doing so because I have cramps.*
>
> COMMISSIONER LAX: Did they tell you to stop working or you decided to stop because of your problem?
>
> MR NTULI: Yes, i"s me. I decided to stop because I could tell that I can't handle. *Even when the weather is cold I have a problem.*

In the first extract Mr. Ntuli expresses criticism with regard to the present government: some of the cases remain uninvestigated today, which means that these cases are still not closed and that the victims have not received any compensation for their suffering. When talking about the IFP attackers, Mr. Ntuli explains that these perpetrators are still around. He means that the situation as it existed under apartheid still persists – it is perhaps also the case that his emotions of fear and terror have not lessened since the 1994-transition. The effects of the human rights violation still continue in his daily life, which is made clear when he tells the TRC panel how he had to leave his job because of medical problems. By linking the past and the present Mr. Ntuli conveys a straightforward message: conditions of life have not really changed in the new South Africa – from day to day the past is relived.

Also Thembisile Rita Nkabinde explicitly linked the past to the present, both when she states that the case has not been brought to court up till today, and when she claims that life has not really changed since 1994. As a supporter of the IFP she was attacked by members of the ANC:

> MR DLAMINI: And what happened about the case?
>
> MRS NKABINDE: There was not enough evidence so the case never proceeded *up until today.*
> (…)
> MRS NKABINDE: And another thing as well is that people used to come and break our windows, harass us. In 1994 as well our house was attacked. ANC attacked our house. At home there was no one who was active, who was an Inkatha member who was active, except for me. My brothers aren't like that. *Even now I can't walk alone at street. I am scared.* Even though I know I have never fought with anyone, but *I am scared walking alone in the street. Even now I don't know what to do.*
>
> MR DLAMINI: This harassment that you are receiving, is it words people are swearing at you, or people are breaking something?
>
> MRS NKABINDE: No, *people are harassing me,* swearing at me.
>
> MR DLAMINI: These people who are doing this thing to you, do you see them, do you know them, can you identify them?
>
> MRS NKABINDE: Yes, I can.

In the first fragment Mrs. Nkabinde implicitly complains about the fact that the perpetrators have not been punished so far. Further on, she gets very emotional when talking about the present-day situation in her neighbourhood. She is still afraid to walk the streets, people are still harassing her and she can even identify these current day attackers. Clearly, the apartheid past continues well into the present for this victim. Misery and terror are still experienced on a daily basis and the atmosphere of conflict has not been transformed to peace and security.

As we have seen, for many HRV testifiers there seemed to exist a level of continuity between the apartheid past and the present. Often the human rights violation they came to talk about still affected their lives and many of the apartheid conflicts still remained the same. Post-apartheid South Africa was very similar to apartheid South Africa to many of these people.

When constructing the archive of the HRV discourse I will suggest that expressing continuity between the present and the past was an inherent feature of the HRV hearings. Through the links between past and present time frames, the past incident could be vividly relived, both by the testifiers and the commissioners, and by the TRC audience. The result could be an increased level of empathy vis à vis the testifier. The audience and the commissioners could imagine the emotions and sufferings the testifier had experienced and the dramatic atmosphere at the hearings was enhanced. Emphasising how strong the past incident still affected victims' present lives – medically, socially and emotionally, and stressing how the apartheid past was re-experienced by those victims on a daily basis, could turn the TRC into an indispensable transitional instrument. It is possible as well that this historical layering contained an aspect of social relevance. When testifiers indicated that their lives had not really changed since the end of apartheid – that they still felt threatened, or that they still experienced the same poverty – the Commission could send a clear message of social criticism to the present government.

### 5.3.4 Feature Seven: Audience as actor

In this chapter I want to illustrate how some of the testifiers were capable of taking advantage of the public space provided by the HRV hearings. Obviously, this public space was created on behalf of the testifying victims, so it was their right to make use of the audience in a manner they deemed suitable. Some of them, though, very explicitly addressed the audience and clearly considered the audience as participants to the HRV hearings.

What I will call the *immediate audience* – the people actually present at the hearings – usually consisted of friends and relatives of the testifiers, of members of their communities, of people from the press and also of a limited number of 'foreigners', in addition to the HRV Committee itself. Besides this immediate audience we should also take into account the *wider audience*, consisting of TV watchers, radio listeners and readers in South Africa and beyond. When using the term *audience* here it will mainly refer to the people present at the hearings: the actual public and – to a lesser extent – the TRC commissioners.

At this TRC moment, unique in history, most of the testifiers wanted to project a specific identity – a feature that will be discussed more elaborately later on. By interacting with the audience these testifiers tried to confirm or boost this desired identity. In this way they used the TRC moment not only to deal with the past, but also to project a specific identity. In the following examples I will not deal with the identity formation of the victims, since this will be the topic of other chapters. I will merely illustrate which discursive techniques were used to establish this dialogue with the audience. I have categorised this chapter under the heading of *historical layering* because it actually focuses on how a certain discursive moment was used with an eye to the future. This interaction with the audience was aimed at the future, because it was the audience (friends, family, community – also media) the victim was going back to when stepping down from the TRC stage.

HRV testifiers oriented their discourse towards the audience by means of all kinds of different linguistic devices, some of them verbal (vocabulary, grammar or morphology), some of them paralinguistic (facial expressions, gestures, eye contact). In what follows I will mainly pay attention to vocabulary, terminology and to verbal expressions. I will discuss how the testifiers tried to catch the attention of the audience, how they referred to the audience or how they manifestly directed their discourse to the audience, thus engaging in a subtle kind of dialogue with the members of the extended TRC public.

One of the most assertive, proud and also angry testifiers from my selection is Mr. John Buthelezi, who related a story about detention, torture and betrayal. In the beginning of this testimony the audience is noisy, which was often the case when the next testifier came to the stage. This is how chair Manthata tries to calm down the public:

> MR MANTHATA: (…) Sorry, sorry, Mr Buthelezi, come, I am sorry. *Please, please, let there be order, please.* Mr Buthelezi, who is, who is accompanying you?

Mr. Buthelezi immediately starts to talk about the torture and the harassment he suffered at the hands of the police. Right from the start it looks as if he wants to show off and to make an impression on the audience. In fact, Mr. Buthelezi proposes to demonstrate how he was tortured, this probably with the audience and the TV cameras in mind. He might feel that words are not adequate enough to express his harrowing experiences; acting out these experiences will have more of an effect on the audience:

> MR BUTHELEZI: I was handcuffed to the pole, the flagpole, at the police station. I was handcuffed, *maybe I should demonstrate how I was handcuffed to the pole.*
>
> MR LEWIN: Please do.
>
> MR BUTHELEZI: *Yes, I was standing like this* and they tied my, the rope around my legs to the pole and my hands were handcuffed to the pole and

I was tortured until I started to bleed. I was bleeding profusely through my mouth and my nose and they continued to torture me.

A little later on we see that Mr. Buthelezi is angry and that he explicitly mentions that he is unwilling to reconcile. According to the reaction of commissioner Lewin, the public reacts fiercely to these words:

MR BUTHELEZI: I will explicitly emphasise the fact that I will never reconcile until I mention those who wanted to attack me and kill me.

MR LEWIN: *Could we have quiet please.*

MR BUTHELEZI: I will only reconcile if I will be given opportunity to see those people who called me informers, (…)

Exactly the same happens a couple of minutes later. Every time Mr. Buthelezi raises the topic of reconciliation, either by stressing that he will only reconcile after he has met the traitors and informers, or by maintaining that he refuses to reconcile, the audience reacts fiercely:

MR BUTHELEZI: (…) I want to tell you that I will only reconcile when only I could be given opportunity to see those people who were painting others black and yet they were the evil ones, the traitors and the informers. That is when I will reconcile.

MR MANTHATA: *Order please. Order, order please. We are asking you could you please be quiet.* Go on.
(…)
MR BUTHELEZI: (…) I know all of those people and I am prepared to make mention of their names **right here**. People are here to reconcile.

MR LEWIN: *Could we please have quiet. Do you want to read the Riot Act and I will...*

MRS SEROKE: Sorry.

MR LEWIN: *Read the Riot Act. Just ask them, explain that we have to have quiet.*

MR MANTHATA: *Please we are expected to be quiet. If you want to hear the truth and let everybody here hear the truth, please, let us be quiet.*

MR BUTHELEZI: What I will say is that I was so much assaulted, harassed and I was going through sufferings and people would point fingers at me saying I am a traitor, an informer, calling me a sell-out.
(…)
MR BUTHELEZI: So, I am not going to, I am not going to reconcile, I am not about to.

MRS SEROKE: *Order please, order.*

MR MANTHATA: Buthelezi, could you, I think you have come to the end, could you please take questions. Thank you.

MR LEWIN: Thank you, Mr Buthelezi, *and could we please give the witness a chance to have his say.*

Mr. Lewin, Mr. Manthata and Mrs. Seroke take turns trying to calm down the audience. According to the reactions of the committee members the noise is very disturbing. The public could be noisy because Mr. Buthelezi does not fulfil the role of a docile, reconciliation-oriented testifier. In addition, Mr. Buthelezi talks about traitors and informers. He implies that these informers belong to the community and that they are even present in the hall – note the "right here" in the fragment. It looks as if he wants to mention these traitors in front of the Commission. Therefore, people in the audience might feel threatened or they might disagree with his accusations, both of which could lead to commotion.

The public then seems to be silent for a couple of minutes; towards the end of the testimony, though, there is uproar once again:

MRS SEROKE: Nhlanhla, you have said in your statement you were tortured because you were manufacturing petrol bombs at home, you opened your own factory of petrol bombs. Is that true?

MR BUTHELEZI: Yes, that is true. Not alone.

CHAIRPERSON: *Order please.*

MR BUTHELEZI: With other Comrades.

MRS SEROKE: Were you alone or you had some company in this manufacturing?

MR BUTHELEZI: As I have said, we were many, except that the venue was my home.

MR MANTHATA: *Please, people, we are here to listen to each and every word that comes from the witness.*
(…)
MRS SEROKE: You say you launched an operation after they injured you at your private, on your private parts. How are you fairing now?

MR BUTHELEZI: No, I feel good, I feel good about myself. I, that is what I will say.

MRS SEROKE: *Okay. Order please. Order.* Thank you.

MR MANTHATA: Mr Buthelezi, we are very grateful for you to come and share with us today.

It looks as if the people in the audience are enjoying themselves. The victim re-fuses to comply with the typical HRV victim profile: he is showing off and he seems to be proud of himself as a victim. At the end of his testimony Mr. Buthelezi even seems to ridicule the Commission. The utterance "As I have said, we were many, except that the venue was my home" must be phrased in an ironic fashion, since the audience bursts into laughter (only audible on the video). The chair then intervenes to calm down the audience. Finally, Mrs. Seroke inquires about Mr. Buthelezi's injuries at his private parts. Here again, the testifier projects the im-age of a boasting young man – especially since Mr. Buthelezi smiles after having pronounced the words "I feel good about myself".

To conclude, it should also be emphasised that throughout his testimony, Mr. Buthelezi makes sure to mention some of the names of people who tortured him. He might do so with an eye to the audience as well: these torturers were probably known in the community and mentioning their names was a way of taking his revenge. This extract, taken from the end of his testimony, will serve as an illus-tration:

> MR BUTHELEZI: When I was tortured at Denota Police Station I was kicked at my private parts and the person who kicked me was *a police Templeton Sibaka*, who is late now, and another one who use to torture a lot was *Bushlong*. I have forgotten his surname, also I have forgotten to make mention of his name when I was telling you the whole story.

In this testimony we notice two ways in which the audience became involved in the hearing. First, the public is noisy in reaction to Mr. Buthelezi's words: they might feel threatened by his accusations, they might enjoy his boasting manner of challenging the commissioners or they might like his showing off and his mani-fest self-confidence. In addition, it also looks as if Mr. Buthelezi enjoys the atten-tion paid to him by members of the audience. His proud way of talking about his experiences and about his personality, his threats aimed at the audience and his explicit refusal to reconcile seem to be consciously directed towards the public. Hence, it appears as if Mr. Buthelezi's construction of the interaction with the public has a lot to do with his self-legitimation.

Sometimes, testifiers explicitly mentioned gruesome details of the incident they came to talk about, with the specific intention, it seems, of impressing or shocking the audience. This could be the case with Phebel Robinson, whose hus-band was tortured and killed in prison. Obviously, each testimony of these HRV victims was aimed at the audience. All of them wanted to tell the world about what they had endured. Sometimes, however, a certain change of intonation, a certain gaze, or a certain gesture could indicate that a specific phrase or descrip-tion was directly aimed at the audience.

After having related her story, Ms. Robinson comes back to the fact that her husband was "gruesomely murdered". In great detail she describes how his body was mutilated – she even brought pictures to show, which indicates that the idea of impressing the audience might have been prepared beforehand. These shocking utterances are pronounced with a different intonation, with a louder and more explicit voice. Such an expressive intonation was likely to attract the attention of the audience. While pronouncing these words Ms. Robinson also gesticulates to demonstrate where her husband was stabbed and how his arms were slit open. Maybe, this effort to make the trauma more visible was also aimed at the audience:

> MS ROBINSON: I would like the truth. Who is behind this whole thing or who was in on the murder *because my husband gruesomely murdered. It wasn't just one stab wound, his arms was slit open, he had several stab wounds on his body and marks from where they had tortured him.* That is not one persons work, the report is laying there. I brought it with me who ever wants to read it can read it so that they can see what happened to him.

Later on, Ms. Robinson explicitly presents her husband as an activist who stood for his community. It is quite likely that this projected identification is oriented towards the audience, where many people from the community were present:

> MS ROBINSON: My husband wasn't scared, he was not afraid of anyone and he fought for human rights. *He was a man for his community.* He supported the poor, and the people that were battling.
> (…)
> MS ROBINSON: So once again I say that he was not afraid of anybody and he stood for what he believed in and for his community. *There are many people here that can bear testimony to that – to the fact that he stood for his community.*

During these utterances there is manifest interaction with the audience. After the phrase "He was a man for his community" the public applauds, indicating that they endorse Ms. Robinson's assertion. The testifier also emphasises the word "community", meaning that she does not only talk *about* the community, but also *to* the community. Also in the next sentence Ms. Robinson incorporates the audience into her testimony: she addresses the audience by claiming that many people in the audience can bear testimony to her husband's community spirit.

Throughout this testimony Ms. Robinson is openly valued and acknowledged by the audience. The testifier takes advantage of this situation by manifestly adding to the interaction with members of the public, mainly through gestures, facial expressions and intonation. Strikingly, this interaction with the audience – and the noise produced by the audience – is not constrained in any way by the TRC commissioners, this in contrast with Mr. Buthelezi for instance. Apparently, certain testifiers were permitted more of an opportunity to take advantage of the public space than others.

A testifier who explicitly established an interaction with the audience in order to arouse compassion is Bernice Whitfield. Mrs. Whitfield's husband was killed in an APLA bomb attack. Her testimony is full of self-pity, for which she tries to arouse sympathy from the audience. This self-pity is evident from Mrs. Whitfield's detailed and repeated explanation of her financial problems and from the dramatic ways in which she relates many different kinds of misfortunes that befell her family; some of which having nothing to do with the APLA bomb attack, such as the fact that her daughter was killed in a car accident. She also gives a gruesome description of the way her husband died – a description that might have raised the attention and sympathy of the audience:

> MRS WHITFIELD: I think it was either three or four bullet wounds in the chest. He was alive for a while but he drowned in his own blood. That's when he died.

A number of discursive constructions as well are directed towards the audience:

> MRS WHITFIELD: In the end that building was sold and I had to move again. *Just bear in mind that* the first time I had Seven Hundred Rand plus Seven Hundred Rand maintenance deposit plus lights and water which was Five Hundred and something Rand at that stage. It came to over a Thousand Rand which I had to have spot on to move into Baysville from the house.
> (…)
> MRS WHITFIELD: Yes, fourteen years suspended for thirteen years. They had a picture of the gentleman in the paper and they said that they managed to catch this guy and it was a Black gentleman and they said that he got fourteen years suspended for thirteen years. I just tore the paper up and I said *you know* this is justice and I'm not even interested.
> (…)
> MRS WHITFIELD: Yes, I do have a lot of hope and because I don't put my hope in people I put my hope in the Lord I see a lot of hope in the world. As I said if we focus on God because it's only God that can give you inner peace … *you know* I help and encourage so many people who come to me with broken heart and I say to them the world might reject you but Jesus will always love you and *you know* that gives us so much hope.

In the first fragment, "Just bear in mind" focuses the attention of the audience on the financial difficulties Mrs. Whitfield encountered, in the same way as "you know" in the second fragment stresses the injustice in present-day South Africa.

Indeed, as indicated by Schiffrin (1987:290) "you know" leads a hearer to focus attention on a piece of information being presented by the speaker. "You know" "creates an interactive focus on speaker-provided information". The speaker is marked as information provider, but the successful fulfilment of that role is dependent upon hearer attention. Schiffrin suggests that "you know" functions this way because it is an expression which is reduced from a "do you know" question. The fragment on Mrs. Whitfield's faith is especially aimed at the audience. It seems as if this lady wants to persuade the audience of her religious beliefs. It almost sounds as if she tries to convert the listeners by convincing them of the overall blessing of Christianity.

To sum up, in the course of this chapter we have noticed that quite a number of times the commissioners tried to calm the audience. It looks as if they wanted to stay in control and constrain the participatory power of the audience. In this way the commissioners stressed that the HRV hearings consisted of two main participants: the testifiers and the HRV Committee. The audience was considered as a third rank participant: it was necessary for the public character of the TRC, and sometimes – as in the case of Mr. Buthelezi demonstrating how he was tortured – the interaction with the audience was encouraged to enhance the dramatic effect of the hearings. However, the audience was not supposed to actually participate in the conversation. It was never allowed to actively interact with the main participants – for instance by posing questions or by openly reacting to the expressions of the victims or the commissioners.

A second conclusion we can draw deals with the extent to which the testifiers took advantage of the presence of the audience. When going over the illustrations, it looks as if it was mainly a specific kind of testifier that addressed the audience. Testifiers who consciously oriented their discourse towards the audience were usually self-assured victims, victims who presented a well-defined identity at the hearing. Often, self-esteem, self-pity, pride or anger were incentives to address the audience explicitly. All of these people tried to attract the attention of the audience and they all tried to raise understanding for their projected identity. They all wanted to be explicitly acknowledged and they incorporated the audience in their efforts to create a distinct profile for themselves.

To conclude, the audience present at the hearings was definitely an actor at the HRV hearings. We cannot really talk about 'co-authorship', since the dialogue between the victims and the commissioners dominated the testimonies. There did exist a kind of 'dialogic monologue', in which the testifiers addressed the audience, without expecting a reaction in return. Apparently, each of the three discourse participants at the HRV hearings used the present interaction between testifier and audience with an eye to the future. At the actual TRC moment the range of discursive opportunities was explored, developed and manipulated with specific future-oriented purposes. The victims tried to project a certain identity into the future, the commissioners tried to present a certain image of the HRV hearings into the future, and the audience wanted to preserve a unique experience for future generations.

## 5.4   Identity layering

### 5.4.1   Introduction

This chapter will discuss three features labelled as layering on an identity level. As with the term ideology, the concept of identity is anything but self-evident. It is an extremely complex construct; simple definitions of the term are difficult to find, as there is no neutral way to characterise it. In a very broad way, identity could be described as "an individual's self-concept" (De Fina 2003: 15). Among most authors working in the field of identity studies it is accepted that people do not possess an identity, but rather that identities are constructed, produced or performed. Identities are never fixed, they are constantly created and self-created in different circumstances, different times, different places and different situations. People's identification changes all the time and this change takes place in close cooperation with a large number of external factors.

In discourse-oriented studies identity is often seen as established through discourse. Philips & Hardy (2002: 29) even argue that together with social control and social differences, identity production is one of the key research domains of discourse analysis. According to Edley (2001: 210) identity and the self are constructed through language and they are also evoked by means of language. Or, as Kerby (1991: 112) claims, the identity of a person only exists through language and conversation – it is through discourse that a body is given an identity.

In the domain of narratology it is suggested that narrative is a key element in a person's identity. Stories are crucial to our identities as individuals; stories are how we give our lives meaning (Johnstone 1990: 127). According to Kerby (1991: 4), self-narration is creative as well as receptive and by telling stories in the present, the self – in the present, but also in the past and in the future – is constantly reconstructed. Life stories show how people would like to be, what roles they would like to play; life stories are "presentations of self", according to Goffman (1959, quoted in Johnstone 1990: 129). Relating life stories always involves the individual activity of remembering and it is through remembering that people construct their own identities (Gilmore 2001: 34).

Brockmeier & Carbaugh (2001: 8) argue that when telling a story, people constantly re-create their identities – each time in a different manner. But, as Johnstone stresses, stories do not arise in an individual vacuum. They shed light on the individual self of the narrator, but they are also a key to the communal existence of groups of people. Through stories, people demonstrate their membership of a social, political or economic group, partly on the basis of their own identity construction, partly based on shared ways of storytelling and shared values (see also Thornborrow 1999b: 142). The form and content of stories and storytelling behaviour are all "sensitive indices, not just of personal selves, but also of social and cultural identities" (Schiffrin 1996: 170). In addition, Bruner (2001: 35) states that by telling a story, people take a certain position in the world, they construct themselves as part of reality and they usually identify as an in-group, as opposed to the out-group. In this way, through his or her story, the narrator constructs a world that seems *right* – not necessarily a world that is *true*.

We will see that at the HRV hearings various discursively constructed identities were often established by the testifiers in the course of one and the same testimony. The victims shifted between different identifying indexicalities; hence, the testifiers' identities emerging from their discursive performances were often shifting, ambiguous and interpretively open. In the same narrative event, they spoke from different positions; they "spoke as different subjects, enacting different 'roles'" (Blommaert 2005: 209). It is this constant restructuring and reframing of the HRV testifiers' narrative identities that I have classified as *identity layering*.

Three types of identity layering will be dealt with: a very intense type of identity layering was established when testifiers struggled with their Afrikaner/white identity. Further, I will illustrate how, in the course of one and the same testimony, testifiers were alternately identified as victims or perpetrators, and finally I will explain how the testifiers' identification sometimes shifted back and forth when it came to opposing or associating with the African National Congress. Through these kinds of layering, insight will be provided into the complex identity of apartheid victims in their process of testifying before the HRV Committee.

### 5.4.2 Feature Eight: Struggling with an Afrikaner/white identity

In my corpus of thirty HRV testifiers I have selected three white South Africans: Johannes van Eck and Stephanie Kemp are Afrikaners; Bernice Whitfield is an English-speaking white South African. All three of them are a-typical victims, since the overwhelming majority of victims who came to the TRC were non-white – only 1.1% of the people who gave written statements to the TRC were white (TRC Report 1998, 1/6: 167). The profile of Stephanie Kemp approaches the stereotypical HRV victim profile to a certain extent. Mrs. Kemp had been an active member of the South African Communist Party, she was detained and maltreated in prison, and she lived in exile for a large number of years. Strikingly, she testifies in English. Mr. van Eck corresponds to the image of a typical Afrikaner man: he speaks Afrikaans, he is very critical about the present government, about the ANC and about the Truth Commission itself, and he manifestly proclaims his Christian faith. Mrs. Whitfield speaks English, she is very negative about the current situation in South Africa and she also seems to be a strong believer. Both Mr. van Eck and Mrs. Whitfield have suffered from human rights violations committed by the liberation forces.

What we notice is that each of the three white victims seemed to struggle with his or her identity. This was mainly the case for Mr. van Eck and Mrs. Kemp, since they were Afrikaners – the population group that was most targeted before the TRC. Although Mrs. Whitfield is not an Afrikaner, I did include her in this chapter, since she too seems to have troubles identifying herself as a white woman before the HRV Committee. In my understanding, 'struggling with an Afrikaner/white identity' can be interpreted twofold with regard to these three victims. In the case of Mr. van Eck and Mrs. Whitfield there appeared to be a tension between accepting their position as a victim before the HRV Committee – hence participating in the TRC process – on the one hand, and defending themselves as a white South African, at this TRC site that was attended mostly by Blacks, on the other hand. Both of these testifiers were categorised as *TRC victims*, so they belonged to a specific group in post-apartheid South Africa. This was an uncomfortable identifying label, as will become clear in the illustrating fragments.

Mrs. Kemp, on the other hand, is also struggling with her identity, but on a more fundamental level. She does accept her identity as a TRC victim, but it looks as if she is rejecting a particular aspect of her identity as a member of the Afrikaner community. This is not a struggle that is taking shape at the TRC moment itself, as is the case with the two other white victims, but a struggle that has been developed and fostered throughout Mrs. Kemp's life. I will first discuss the testimonies of Johannes van Eck and Bernice Whitfield.

Mr. van Eck testified in Nelspruit, in September 1996. In December 1985 his car hit an ANC landmine, which resulted in the death of his wife and two children. The 'identity struggle' I am distinguishing here refers to the opposition between Mr. van Eck's participation in/collaboration with the TRC on the one hand and his implicit condemnation of the Commission on the other hand. Hence, we are talking about a struggle between a well-defined macro-identification on the one hand and implicit micro-indexicalities on the other.

Although Mr. van Eck never explicitly shows his aversion to the TRC, this attitude becomes clear when scrutinising the construction of his discourse. While reading his statement, Mr. van Eck expresses strong resentment vis à vis the ANC, and this right from the start. He is shocked that the ANC members who were responsible for planting the landmine have been released from prison and he is especially embittered about the fact that they were rewarded by Nelson Mandela later on. He then continues:

> MR VAN ECK: *I'm expecting from the ANC, through this Commission,* to answer the following questions:
> Is it actually the way of doing things to kill innocent peoples, women and children to show that you're a hero? *Is this actually your way of doing things* to kill children of ten years and younger in order to obtain your objectives?
> Is this your way of doing things to kill innocent women or anyone who is just an ordinary citizen to achieve your objectives? Is this your way to perform in a cowardly fashion by planting landmines on isolated private properties where you know innocent citizens are moving about? Is this your way of doing things to eliminate the families of citizens?
> Is this your way of doing things to citizens and families and friends, to give them this pain by killing their loved ones? Is this your way of doing things that you justify all your murderous acts by linking it to a struggle against a regime? Is this actually habit or your or policy to differentiate between just and unjust, murder? Is this your way of doing things or policy to call a killer of innocent women and children a freedom fighter? Is it your policy to honour the murder of innocent women and children? Is it your policy to honour cowardice? *Mr Chairman I must ask you if it is your policy or practice* to condemn bomb attacks like those at the Olympic Games but to revere the murder of women on our own soil as acts of bravery?

In these lines Mr. van Eck accuses the ANC of cowardice, of inconsequence and of injustice. These are very strong accusations, which indicate that Mr. van Eck opposes the new ANC government. Interestingly, this accusation is formulated in direct speech, and seems to be aimed at the Commission itself. By voicing his criticism of the ANC in this particular way, Mr. van Eck gives shape to the idea living in the minds of some white South Africans, that the TRC was merely a political instrument in the hands of the ANC. The TRC and the ANC are closely associated in Mr. van Eck's statement, which could involve an implicit condemnation of the Commission's work.

The story of Mr. van Eck is disturbing in the extreme: he recounts the state in which he found his family members after the landmine explosion and this story clearly makes a huge impression on the commissioners. At the end of his story Mr. van Eck again associates the TRC with the ANC, by addressing – and accusing – the Commission directly:

> MR VAN ECK: And the question I have is this? *What are you going to do? What is the ANC going to do about this?* Are we going to overlook this evil deed and let sleeping dogs lie, so to speak?
> Mr Chairman I appreciate the fact that there was an opportunity like this one that I could speak about this. *You have responsibility, I say, you have responsibility.*
> The question is, *are you going to take this up or are you going to turn a blind eye?* Thank you very much *Mr Boraine.*

Although his accusation of the ANC is more explicit than his accusation of the TRC, Mr. van Eck strongly associates the two and he blames the Commission by addressing them directly – "*you* have a responsibility", "are *you* going to turn a blind eye". Also by mentioning chairperson Boraine at the end of this extract it looks as if the previous questions were aimed at the Commission. The testifier then continues:

> MR VAN ECK: Mr Chairman, I think it was very clear in my submission, *all I'm asking, my only request is that it (the Commission, sic) should be consequent,* I said, leave those people as they are, leave them where they are, but then we should look at who we are hunting for in vain. *In other words, the Commission stands for equality and justice. That's all I'm asking for, for justice and nothing more.*

In this fragment Mr. van Eck implies that the TRC is inconsistent, that it is hunting people in vain and that it does not live up to its promises of equality and justice. Although he completely complies with the formal requirements of the Commission, he utters critique vis à vis the Commission throughout his testimony.

The identity struggle I am discussing here is in fact a conflict between Mr. van Eck's self-identification as an Afrikaner and the way he is identified as a TRC victim by the outer world. Mr. van Eck does not forsake his Afrikaner identity in front of the TRC: on an implicit level he shows the audience that he is still a very proud and faithful Afrikaner, that he resents the ANC government, and that he is also highly critical about the objectivity and the consistency of the TRC. When looking at this testimony from a macro-perspective, though, Mr. van Eck does collaborate with the TRC. He aligns with a large number of black apartheid victims. Therefore, there is clearly a contradiction between Mr. van Eck's discourse (which is probably a reflection of his self-identification) and his practice (which results in him being identified as a cooperative HRV victim in the TRC records).

Mrs. Bernice Whitfield testified towards the end of the TRC proceedings. She is a white lady, probably a member of the English-speaking white South African group. Her husband was killed in the APLA attack on the Highgate Hotel in East

London in May 1993. Throughout her testimony, Mrs. Whitfield displays an extremely negative attitude. She complains about the lack of justice in the new South Africa and she is vehement about the salaries of government people – whom she identifies as renegades and criminals. She is negative about South African society in general and in the same fashion she does not hesitate to strongly criticise the TRC. I will only give a few illustrations of this attitude:

> MRS WHITFIELD: I just say to myself the renegades that were responsible for various attacks are being paid by the Government. At the moment they're sitting in high positions like big heroes and we've got to face a financial battle. *Why do we waste our time in listening to what everybody has to say and opening up our wounds here.* Nobody feels anything for us. I'm speaking for all races not because I'm White and this one is Pink, Yellow and Green. I'm speaking for all of us. There's a lot of people that are in the same position that I find myself in …. All these renegades who've completed their murders and brutal violence are being looked after in high positions in the Government earning fat salaries and we the victims sit with a financial battle to make ends meet. *The Truth Commission too I'm sure you get compensated for what you are doing.*
> (…)
> MRS WHITFIELD: *As I said before in East London nothing has been done and nothing will be done and I really don't expect anything to be done because nothing will be done.*

In this testimony of Mrs. Whitfield we find the same struggle as in the testimony of Mr. van Eck. By appearing before the HRV Committee she inscribed herself in the TRC process and she is also identified as a *TRC victim*. On the other hand, though, the whole TRC concept is a pointless and money-wasting initiative to her.

Compared to the testimony of Mr. van Eck, the expressed negativity, also with regard to the Commission, is much stronger. Mrs. Whitfield explicitly voices her aversion to the TRC, an aversion not only aimed at her present performance for the TRC, but also aimed at the possible achievements of the TRC in terms of the future.

Finally, Mrs. Whitfield's testimony is also concluded in a very negative way:

> MRS WHITFIELD: As far as I'm concerned *I'm wasting my time.* I'm here for Jesus. As I said to June Crichton when she phoned me I said *I'm not interested in coming here because you don't get anywhere here, you won't get anywhere here* but I'm here because God has told me to be me here and say these words to everybody.

Apparently, the TRC means nothing positive to Mrs. Whitfield. She entirely rejects the concept, with God as the only driving force behind her testifying before the HRV Committee. Personally, she is not interested in coming to the TRC – obviously because she resents the whole concept which is defined as a "money-consuming witch hunt". Since it is the will of God, though, to tell the world about her experiences, she is prepared to appear before the HRV Committee. In fact, the struggle that is apparent throughout Mrs. Whitfield's testimony – cooperation with the TRC versus aversion to the Commission – is transcended. The identity struggle between the micro- and the macro-level is given a rationale: personally, Mrs. Whitfield is opposed to the Commission, but her faith urges her to make a sacrifice and to testify before this much-resented institution.

Stephanie Kemp, the third white victim from my selection, displays a completely different attitude towards the TRC. She has been an anti-apartheid activist and she talks about her detention and the ill-treatment she suffered in prison. During her study period at the University of Cape Town she became politically involved and from then on she started to reject her Afrikaner identity:

> MRS KEMP: So, I had an Afrikaans upbringing with the Dutch Reformed Church dominating the town, with cousins in the Broederbond who for the 30 years after I became political severed all ties with my family.
> (…)
> MRS KEMP: By the early 1960s when I was at the University of Cape Town, studying physiotherapy I had come to the painful realization that the poverty, that Sharpeville and detention without trial were ways in which my own people were trying to claw their way into white privilege in our country. *I never spoke Afrikaans again* until my return from exile in 1990.

At this point in the testimony we can detect the first signs of Mrs. Kemp's identity struggle: on the one hand she still identifies as a white Afrikaner, but on the other hand she refuses to totally incorporate this identity, for instance by adopting the language. In the following part of her testimony, Mrs. Kemp emphasises her Afrikaner identity a number of times:

> MRS KEMP: *But I was born an Afrikaner*, and from childhood we were fed, force fed if I might say on the glory of our people in the Anglo Boer War.
> (…)
> MRS KEMP: Through the truth and reconciliation commission, *and as an Afrikaner*, I call on the Broederbond, the Dutch Reformed Church, EW de Klerk, and the National Party to do more than say sorry, it was a mistake, I call on them to confess and repent their seminal role in nurturing murder and mayhem in our country, based on an ideology of race superiority.

Gradually, this testifier also expresses how she is torn apart by this identity struggle, how embittered she is by the fact that the apartheid regime has forced her to abandon her identity:

> MRS KEMP: For me the horror of the apartheid years is compounded by the loss to me through *its prostitution of my language and my culture.* The direction that Afrikaner nationalism took into obliterating all in its wake now, no matter how murderously, I lay at the feet of the Broederbond, the Dutch Reformed Church and the National Party.
> (...)
> MRS KEMP: I think I feel particularly bitter because once I came back into the country I found that it did matter to me that I wanted my culture back. I did feel – *I do feel very bitter and angry that these people took my language, they took my being,* and they turned it into this machine.

Clearly, Mrs. Kemp's identity struggle has been going on for many years. As she explains herself, it was especially after 1990, when she came back from exile, that this struggle became openly manifested to her. She then realised how strongly the Afrikaner culture and language were associated with the apartheid regime – and she understood how difficult it would be to reclaim this Afrikaner identity.

For Mr. van Eck and Mrs. Whitfield the identity struggle I discussed involves the juxtaposition between being a white South African who is opposed to the TRC on the one hand, and cooperating with the Commission on the other. This struggle is a result of the very TRC concept; it takes shape in the course of their involvement with the Commission. This is in contrast with Mrs. Kemp, whose identity struggle has a different foundation. In her case, the struggle is a psychological issue she has been dealing with for thirty years. It is in front of the TRC that Stephanie Kemp tries to resolve this struggle. By openly emphasising her Afrikaner background, it looks as if she tries to reclaim her Afrikaner heritage. Mrs. Kemp's appearance before the TRC can be seen as an attempt to reconcile the two parts of her torn identity – hence, the TRC is not the result of the identity struggle, but a way of healing it.

To conclude, we have seen that each of these three a-typical victims expressed some kind of identity struggle while testifying before the IIRV Committee. I would like to define this struggle as a type of layering on an identity level. With Mrs. Whitfield and Mr. van Eck one layer refers to the macro-level of identification – their cooperation with the TRC and their identification as a TRC victim. The other layer can be distinguished on a micro-level – their opposition to the TRC by means of concrete language practices. This micro-level is indexicalised in an implicit manner by Mr. van Eck and in a much more explicit manner by Mrs. Whitfield.

In Mrs. Kemp's testimony, both layers are manifest on a micro-level (so on the level of the actual discourse). She explicitly voices the struggle between her Afrikaner and anti-Afrikaner identities and she clearly tries to find a way of bridging the gap between these two layers.

Each of these three testifiers offers an example of the way in which the TRC was a key site of identity construction. In different ways it forced white South Africans to reconsider their identities. All of these people testifying had to try to find a compromise between conflicting identities. Both implicit and explicit identifying layers had to be merged together to construct an identity that was acceptable before the TRC. It was these constructed identities that were presented to the world; these constructed identities created the public image of the Truth Commission.

Finally, when considering these three victims we see an interesting variety of constructed identities, ranging differently on the scale of *HRV acceptability*. Keeping the theoretical concept of the archive in mind, we should try to indicate which identities were more likely to be permitted at the TRC site. The identity constructed by Mrs. Kemp could be regarded as an ideal TRC identity. Stephanie Kemp is an illustration of a white Afrikaner who has been active in the liberation struggle and who would now like to reclaim her Afrikaner identity. She embodies national unity and reconciliation in the new South Africa. Mrs. Kemp is also positive about the achievements of the new government and she openly cherishes the prospect of a united and reconciled country.

Next on the scale of acceptability is Johannes van Eck. Although he belongs to the population group most targeted by the TRC and although he is negative about the new government, his criticism of the Commission is implied. Finally, there is the negatively-oriented testimony of Mrs. Whitfield. She is highly critical of the TRC, of the government and of South African society in general. She does not appear before the TRC because she supports the initiative, but because it is her Christian duty; she even ridicules the entire TRC concept. Therefore, the identity Mrs. Whitfield presents during her testimony is probably the least accepted.

When trying to deconstruct the archive of the HRV hearings, we will be able to propose that although each of the three expressed identities was tolerated, and although each of the three was important for a specific aspect of the TRC image, there seemed to be a preference – so a scale of acceptability.

### 5.4.3 Feature Nine: Victim-perpetrator identity

The people who appeared before the Human Rights Violations Committee were identified first and foremost as victims of gross human rights violations that had taken place under apartheid. They had all suffered from maltreatment, detention, torture or abduction, or a loved one had been killed or abused. All of them told horrifying stories, arousing compassion from both the audience and the commissioners.

However, a number of victims had also committed human rights violations themselves. Some of them had done so as a member of the liberation forces, which meant that the violation was politically motivated. Some of the victims had also committed crimes that were not politically motivated, but that were the result of social strife or historical circumstances.

In my selection of thirty victims, a number of testifiers presented such a double identity. Quite understandably, they seldom referred to the perpetrator identity themselves. Instead, this identity was often introduced by the leading committee members, although they usually indicated that the victim identity was acknowledged as the dominant one. Sometimes, victims accepted this double identity and they were prepared to give more information about the committed violation. In other cases, victims tried to get round this particular identification: they either ignored the reference to the perpetrator identity or they tried to justify their criminal behaviour.

In these testimonies we clearly notice an interesting shifting back and forth between these two identifications. This results in a fascinating combination of re-fusing, accepting, ignoring and stressing either of these two identities. This layering was usually co-constructed through interaction with the commissioners, the commissioners who were committed to prioritise the victim identity of the testifiers, but who were unprepared to dismiss the flip side of their personalities – and who sometimes even emphasised this flip side deliberately.

The first testifier who presented a double identity is Kenneth Manana. He was arrested and subsequently tortured by the South African Police. Mr. Manana is one of the victims who personally identifies himself as a perpetrator in the course of his testimony. He talks about the committed robbery right from the start of his testimony, so in fact this crime forms the departure point of his narrative:

> MR MANANA: At the present moment I am working. I am working at Queue. I am also saved, I am a Christian and I was so happy to get a subpoena to come before the Commission and explain as to what have happened to my friends and others. *From the time we were detained after we robbed some premises at Savoy* there were some people from Soweto and others were from Alexandra.

Although Mr. Manana's story is rather incoherent, we do understand that he talks about a robbery, which then resulted in his detention. Mr. Manana's narrative is intense but short, and soon commissioners Manthata and Mkhize take over to ask clarifying questions. Strikingly, already in the first question, commissioner Manthata only stresses the perpetrator identity of the testifier:

> MR MANTHATA: Kenny please forgive me, *I will try to find out as to your arrest. Was it to do with your robbery at Savoy?*
>
> MR MANANA: I would say it was connected with that matter.
>
> MR MANTHATA: Because the others were killed there was no one who witnessed that your issue was political.
> (…)
> MR MANTHATA: *What I want to find out is whether you were sure that there wasn't anyone, we know that you were an APLA member,* that all that you were doing you were involved in politics and did you only (indistinct) a story. I would say that up to the time when the case came to an end you were the only person who knew that you were an APLA member. Your involvement or your contact with police, it wasn't anything connected with politics. It was only the robbery issue which came into the focus.
>
> MR MANANA: I would say that the police knew about the issues of guns. While they were investigating they also assured me – they were telling us that the particular organisations they were using these arms in their struggle. Police knew that but in court they used it – they called it as a criminal case.
> (…)
> MS MKHIZE: *From the beginning you said you a person you have changed or repented.* When you say that why do you think it is necessary to mention that?
>
> MR MANANA: This was mentioned to show that in all that had happened I now realise that some of those things were mistakes and that those people who do something bad to me at the present moment that think *I do have a heart to receive them and forgive them.* Just to show before the Commission that I do have that heart to forgive.
>
> MS MKHIZE: That repentant heart of yours, if there other things that you have done while you were an APLA member, something that was against the law, *will you be prepared as a changed person to go before the amnesty committee to ask for forgiveness?*
>
> MR MANANA: *I will say since I was charged for the criminal act that I have committed the case is over.*

Commissioner Manthata highlights the perpetrator identity of the victim, because he wants to find out whether this robbery was politically motivated. This was an important aspect, since a politically motivated crime was more or less justified in the TRC context. It is not obvious to find out what Mr. Manana tries to say. In the end we understand that the robbery is connected to his APLA activism, although the police called it a criminal case.

Throughout this testimony Mr. Manana is manifestly projected as a perpetrator – initially by himself, although only briefly, but later on more explicitly by different commissioners. When referred to by the commissioners, Mr. Manana refuses to adopt this identity. He accepts that a criminal act has been committed, but he was punished and he should now be considered as an apartheid victim in the first place. Only to a limited extent is this victim identity addressed by the commissioners, although Mr. Manana has obviously suffered greatly at the hands of the security services.

Metro Bambiso is a victim who was also detained and tortured by the police. In the victim findings of the TRC Report (2002, 7:18) it is stated that Mr. Bambiso was detained and tortured by the police in 1986. The Report also says that Mr. Bambiso was arrested because of the attempted 'necklacing' of the girlfriends of Municipal Policemen, which indicates that Mr. Bambiso can be identified as a perpetrator as well.

Mr. Bambiso starts off by explaining what led to the necklacing, so he actually presents himself as a perpetrator right from the start. He does not seem to be ashamed of the fact that they cold-bloodedly decided to "burn" the informers. According to his discourse Comrades had the right to punish informers:

> MR BAMBISO: As we were this group of Comrades we wanted to get rid of the people who were known as the stumbling blocks. In other words, people who were informers. There were three ladies who were staying in Masikane area in Bedford. They were Rooibot Chain, Selina Lange and Thembeka Sikasi. They were together with the police. They were having affairs with the police. *We sent certain Comrades to go and call these ladies, because a decision was taken that we will deal with them.* At that time it was half past four during the day. They came to hear what they were called for. We wanted to know about their position in the struggle in our community. They did not give us an answer. They told us they will shoot us. They would get guns from their boyfriends and shoot us. We must leave them alone. *Because they answered the way they did we decided to burn them. We tried to organise things that we were going to use in order to burn these people.* The police were phoned by certain people informing this.

After this explicit self-identification as a perpetrator, the perspective is shifted and Mr. Bambiso is identified as a victim in the following part of the testimony. Commissioner Sandi asks about the way this victim was tortured and how he was physically affected by his detainment. Clearly, in this middle part of the testimony, Mr. Bambiso is explicitly framed as a victim.

It is only towards the end of the interview that the perspective is shifted again to Mr. Bambiso's perpetrator identity:

> CHAIRPERSON MANTHATA: Mr Bambiso, you explained to us about your involvement in necklacing the three ladies in Bedford. You have told us what happened. You told us that you were involved in this incident. I have also noted that according, to your statement, *you were charged and you were sentenced because of this incident.* I want you to look back, maybe if you can, *I want you to tell the Commission how you feel today when you look back at your plans for burning these three ladies.* How do you feel today?

> MR BAMBISO: When looking back, Mr Chairperson, firstly, *I would like the Commission, on my behalf, to ask forgiveness for the victims,* although I was forced by the political situation to act the way I did. I want them to forgive me about the plan that I made although I was sentenced.

Since he openly asks for forgiveness from the victims, Mr. Bambiso seems to be prepared to accept this perpetrator identity. Nevertheless, this acceptance is conditional: he is a perpetrator and he asks for forgiveness, *but* he stresses that he was forced to commit human rights violations as a result of the political situation. And further, he wants the victims to forgive him for the plans he made, *but* he stresses that we was already sentenced for this crime. These phrases indicate that Mr. Bambiso still predominantly identifies as a victim. It is especially here, at the end of the testimony, that he is urged by the commissioners to address this perpetrator identity – apparently this is not an identity he is prepared to fully incorporate.

An interesting case of a constructed double identity can be found in the testimony of Bernadine Mwelase. He was an MK operative who was captured by members of the South African Police. He was severely tortured and was forced to become an *askari*.[9] As an askari Mr. Mwelase had to infiltrate in the liberation movement to try to eliminate activists.

In the main part of this testimony Mr. Mwelase is identified as a victim. He is asked about the circumstances of his arrest and about the way he was ill-treated in detention. This is clearly the part in which a victim identity is projected onto the testifier. Gradually, the questions move in a different direction when the commissioner asks how he became an askari and what his job was as an askari. These expressions regarding Mr. Mwelase's askari identity can be seen as a transitional micro-narrative. In this micro-narrative the two identities have merged into one expression, the askari. By definition, an askari was both a victim and a perpetra-

---

9.  Askari is an Arabic-derived East African name for soldiers or policemen. In Africa it denoted former ANC or PAC members working for the South African Police (de Kock 1998: 305).

tor. Askaris had usually been severely tortured in order to force them to cooperate with the apartheid regime. As an apartheid operative they often had to carry out the dirty jobs, which meant that they often had to kill activists (sometimes their former colleagues).

After this intermediate micro-narrative the leading commissioner poses a final question. From then onwards Mr. Mwelase is characterised as merely a perpetrator:

> MR DLAMINI: I think we have heard, or perhaps we've seen this picture you've laid to this Commission, but my last question. As I am listening to your evidence you are a person who we may refer to as one that was tortured, and whose human rights were violated as an askari as well, *but what I would like to ask is that are you prepared to admit an application to the Amnesty Committee?*
>
> MR MWELASE: *No, I only have to ask for amnesty from the community or the people of South Africa,* because even now I can't be employed.
>
> MR DLAMINI: No, that's – here we are just looking at how your human rights were violated, but when you go beyond us now, as you also were an askari, *and violating other people's rights, now that falls under the Amnesty Committee. It may be wise for you to apply for amnesty, and be careful now because there is a D-day on the 10th of May this year. After the 10th of May they won't be accepting any applications thereafter.* Now, you want to be careful about that, especially if you want to take that decision as a former askari, because after that time your application won't be accepted if you want to apply for amnesty.
> (...)
>
> MR MWELASE: *Let me turn this thing around.* I would like to see this traitor, as to how much was he paid and how many did he sell or spy on? I know that there was a traitor behind me, and how much was he paid for that and how many did he lead into this? And the last thing I would like to say this .... I want you to investigate also how they used me.

In these phrases the testifier is categorised as a perpetrator, since the initial question solely belongs to the perpetrator oriented discourse of the Amnesty Committee. Mr. Mwelase reacts fiercely and he totally refuses this identification. He is prepared to apologise to the community, but he does not want to formally apply for amnesty. He even wants to turn Mr. Dlamini's question around – it is not *he* who is the perpetrator, but the people who betrayed him.

In these three examples the layering on the level of the victim's identity takes various forms. In each of the three cases a double identity is openly manifested in the course of the testimony. On a macro-level, all of these testifiers were categorised as 'victims of gross human rights violations committed under apartheid' –

this will be their permanent label in the archive of South Africa's apartheid history. When analysing the actual discourse, we notice that different identities were constructed, sometimes by the testifiers themselves, and sometimes by the commissioners. Sometimes, testifiers accepted to be labelled as perpetrators, and they even talked about their committed crimes spontaneously. Sometimes, testifiers tried to reject this perpetrator identity, for instance by justifying their behaviour and by rejecting the proposal to apply for amnesty.

In trying to find a compromise between these two conflicting identities, the commissioners had a huge responsibility. For the future coexistence of South Africans it was crucial to identify past victims and perpetrators. Stressing that some victims had also been perpetrators could be advantageous for reconciliation on a national level – national unity and reconciliation might be stimulated when people realised that some of them had this double identity. As a producer of historical knowledge the TRC had to construct identities with an eye to a peaceful future for South Africa. Simplifying the apartheid past by dividing people in either victims or perpetrators would probably not advance the aim of a unified South Africa. It was in fact very useful to have a number of testifiers with mixed identities. In addition, this element also demonstrated the inclusive nature of the TRC: it proved that even victims with a history as a perpetrator were welcome at the HRV Committee. That is why this particular identity layering was an inherent feature of the HRV discourse.

### 5.4.4 Feature Ten: Pro-con ANC identity

A number of victims who appeared before the HRV Committee strongly identified with one particular political party. For many it was the ANC, but there were also supporters of the IFP, the PAC, APLA or MK. For some of the victims this projected political identity was their dominant identity while testifying before the HRVC. Sometimes, however, testifiers shifted between different political identifications. They did not so much move from one particular political affiliation to another, but rather constructed different identifying indexicalities vis à vis one and the same party – so that in the course of their testimonies they ranged from strongly supporting a political party to totally despising this same party. I will illustrate this identity layering by means of attitudes towards the ANC. I have chosen the ANC because a majority of testifiers in my selection identified with the ANC and because it could be challenging for the victims to resist the ANC in the context of the TRC proceedings.

The first case is the testimony of Charity Kondile. Mrs. Kondile talked about her son Sizwe, an MK operative who was killed by the apartheid security services in 1981. Throughout her testimony Mrs. Kondile seems to display an ambiguous attitude towards the ANC. On a macro-level she supports the ANC, its policy and its liberation struggle. In some instances, this support of the ANC can also be detected on a micro-level, so on the level of the actual discourse. More often, however, Mrs. Kondile seems at this concrete micro-level to be highly critical towards the ANC.

We might first of all observe that Mrs. Kondile is proud of her son's activism and about the fact that he was prepared to give his life for the liberation. The extralinguistic manner (only visible on the video tape) in which she pronounces the following words underlines this sense of her pride:

> MR NTSEBEZA: What did he tell you about the ANC, if anything when you found him here?
>
> MRS KONDILE: Well Sizwe reassured me that he had joined the struggle and there was no way of turning back. When I spoke to him about coming home *he told me that there was no ways he could come back home before he had achieved his mission in the struggle.*

Mrs. Kondile then continues her story. She elaborates at length on the fact that Sizwe was abducted from Lesotho by the security forces, while some of his ANC comrades had the impression that Sizwe had turned traitor. It is at this stage of her testimony that she is highly critical about the ANC and some ANC officials:

> MRS KONDILE: Well I must explain to this Commission that even on that day, when I greeted one of Sizwe's friends in the street, to my disappointment, this girl shouted at me and said that Sizwe had stolen their car. I immediately realised that there was some trouble. If I went to one friend where I was staying, a certain Dolly Mabusela, and immediately I came to Dolly's house, Dolly phoned some people and Dolly told me that *these people* were saying, *some ANC officials* were saying that I should get out of Maseru immediately.
> (...)
> MRS KONDILE: As I say, while I was in Mandisa's house, we waited for the ANC, *these ANC people* to come. They said they would come and visit me, but the whole weekend they said I must not go to ... (indistinct), they would come to me. But at the end, on Sunday evening, the Clinea brothers came and said, "The ANC people are not coming to see you, they are saying you must go to the refugee offices and if you want Sizwe's belongings, we don't want a woman, a man must come alone." and I think they meant his father. This is the message I got, *I never met the ANC people.*
> (...)

> MRS KONDILE: I don't know, when I asked him (Sizwe's father, sic) he said, he was never there when Sizwe was kidnapped, he feels he, I don't know why he's not here, but he said he's got nothing to witness. *He is a depressed man about all this matter.*

Mrs. Kondile appears to be very disappointed about the attitude of the ANC. She describes her search for Sizwe and how she constantly came up against disbelief and distrust from the side of the ANC people. Her use of the demonstrative pronoun "these" and the indefinite determiner "some" especially convey a negative impression of the terms "ANC people" and "ANC officials". In the second extract, Mrs. Kondile's facial expression shows utter disgust when pronouncing the words "these ANC people", a facial expression that is even more revealing than the actual words. The ANC members are pictured as dishonest people who did not live up to their promises. They did not even show compassion and understanding towards a mother who is desperately looking for her lost son. Mrs. Kondile also indicates that her husband is very depressed about "all this matter", probably meaning the attitude of the ANC.

Later on she stresses that the Kondile family has a history of resistance against apartheid; it is hard for her to hear Sizwe being accused of treason. This tells us that on a more fundamental level Mrs. Kondile is a strong supporter of the liberation movement. Throughout the testimony Mrs. Kondile also identifies people by the term "Comrade" – even her own son is sometimes called "Comrade Sizwe". 'Comrade' was (and is) the typical term by which members of the liberation movement address each other. Apparently, the identification with the ANC is Mrs. Kondile's overall attitude. This attitude is challenged while testifying before the TRC, although it remains dominant. Her negative attitude refers to an identification she does not fully incorporate; it is merely a situational identification, which turns up at this particular moment of testifying before the TRC.

Teddy Williams is another witness whose testimony exhibits a shift in identification with the ANC. Mr. Williams was detained and tortured in an ANC camp in Angola. Similar to Mrs. Kondile's case, Mr. Williams displays a different identity on a macro- and a micro-level. This testifier begins by talking about his growing up in the former Transkei and about his involvement with the liberation movement, which started at a very early age:

> MR WILIAMS: When Mr Mqwalu came and he was introduced to me I freely talked to him and told him that it is not that I am against the PAC, but because I am already – I am already used, or rather I have contacts with the ANC, I would like to go to the ANC because *I already know some policies of the ANC because I knew about the Freedom Charter and some of the books of Mandela – like "His walk to Freedom" I had it at home.*

Mr. Williams was then taken to an ANC camp in Angola for military training. From then onwards we notice a shift: Mr. Williams starts to differentiate between different people within the liberation movement. He identifies with the men who had high moral visions about the future of South Africa. This group is positioned against another group of freedom fighters who merely boosted their morale through abusing girls:

> MR WILLIAMS: (…) so you know there was *this type of situation where these young girls were abused or Officers would help themselves, I don't know maybe it was a question of trying to boost their moral or what, you see some of us we had our morale boosted through the visions that we had about the New South Africa.* So these guys they used to call these girls part of their – mostly they were administrators, to listen to their orders, it is good of course when you are a subordinate to take orders from above, it is good to respect authority even, because tomorrow you will be authority yourself, but then what happened is *that these senior Comrades, some of them they appointed these section Commanders in order to use them, they used to call these girls to the camps* – actually to the Administration as if they needed them for something serious and in that way they do what they had wished to do to them.

Mr. Williams' identification with the ANC is no longer unconditional. He continues by relating how he was appointed as an instructor in those military camps. At that time he and his friends started to challenge the abuses taking place. From then onwards he conveys a negative image of the ANC officials leading the camps:

> MR WILLIAMS: We were innocent, *we were among wolves*, it is a pity that I should say this. Most of the leadership you see, or rather the leaders that used to address us in the camps, *were men who didn't address to our problems.* Those who didn't come to the camps, the man that we needed to come to the camps so that we could speak to – they didn't come to the camps, they didn't come to the camps. When we wanted to speak to … (indistinct) and explain some of these things to him, *we were not given the chance …*

Not only did the officials abuse girls, they were not prepared to listen to the concerns of the soldiers – in this part Mr. Williams paints a bleak picture of some ANC officials. Gradually, his attack on the ANC gets more manifest and he starts to explicitly distance himself from the liberation movement:

> MR WILLIAMS: *I was severally maltreated by the African National Congress.* I want to say by the African National Congress because the people who did these things were the forefront leaders.

At this point, Mr. Williams directly attacks the ANC. He might realise how unusual it is to attack the ANC at this TRC site and that is probably why he emphasises "I want to say the African National Congress" – also note that he uses the full name of the liberation movement instead of the commonly used abbreviation, probably to make a stronger impression with his words. In the rest of the testimony the ANC as a movement is strongly attacked, while Mr. Williams disassociates himself more and more from the organisation. He keeps emphasising that he and his friends were committed freedom fighters, who seemed to stand on their own with their idealistic values. They wanted to liberate South Africa instead of witnessing abuse in a faraway military camp:

> MR WILLIAMS: *We want to go home and fight*. We don't want to fight UNITA. We don't want this corruption that is happening here – people abusing other people's wives,
> (…)
> MR WILLIAMS: (…) Some Comrades were taken to fight UNITA, they refused. When they refused Joe Modise called them half-baked soldiers, cowards and so on and yet the Comrades explained that "Listen, it is not that we are scared to fight, their bosses want to fight the Boers not UNITA. If we fight UNITA we are going to die here in Angola." *We want to go inside South Africa and die in South Africa fighting.*

Finally, after a number of interruptions by the commissioners, Mr. Williams relates the ways in which he personally was maltreated in the camps. He then gets rather emotional when asking for personal protection. He stresses again that although strongly victimised by the liberation movement, he was able to survive. The ANC is no longer the movement he looks up to as a moral guideline, but it is rather pictured as an enemy – apparently an enemy Mr. Williams is afraid of even today:

> MR WILLIAMS: Yes sir. As mutineers, we were rounded up – excuse me, *I would the Commission to try and protect me also* – because you see I am a determined person. When I stand for a principle, I stand for it, I don't think anybody or anyone – that's why I was able to survive up to this point. *And that's why the 16th[10] couldn't break me – including the National African Congress itself.*

---

10. It is not clear what Mr. Williams refers to here, maybe a battalion or the number of a training camp.

When the issue of the requests is raised, Mr. Williams accuses the ANC of being unwilling to face the truth. The ANC is projected as a perpetrator that should "cleanse itself" and address the abuses that took place under its authority:

> MR WILLIAMS: What I would like to request the Commission *to do for the sake of the people of South Africa*, especially for the sake of those fathers and mothers who had their children killed in exile without any reason – *that the African National Congress if it's prepared to face the truth, to cleanse itself;* it should come up at least with all the names who died in exile and along each name an explanation be attached or be given that this one died of malaria at such and such an hour. This one died at the hands of UNITA, at such and such an hour. This one died because he was resisting the ANC security or whatever, or this one died because the Security killed him – for this reason or that reason. Or this one committed suicide.

This testifier again opposes the ANC to his own moral values: for the sake of the well-being of South Africa the ANC has to reveal what has happened in exile. As presented by Mr. Williams it looks as if the movement is no longer concerned about the citizens of South Africa – and especially those citizens who participated in the struggle. According to the testifier, the ANC has abandoned its principles now that it has risen to power. Mr. Williams therefore presents his own moral position as superior to the ones held by the movement.

Throughout this testimony we see how Mr. Williams gradually disassociates himself from the liberation movement. This gradual disassociation coincides with his personal history. Mr. Williams started off as an idealistic supporter of the ANC but these high ideals were destroyed during his training in a military camp. After he was abused he felt isolated with his moral principles, ending up disappointed and embittered towards the ANC. At the end of the testimony the liberation movement is pictured as an enemy, an enemy identification that culminates in loaded terms such as 'personal protection' and 'for the sake of the people of South Africa the ANC has to cleanse itself'.

In none of these examples is there a univocal identification with the ANC. Charity Kondile and Teddy Williams have a tradition of supporting the liberation movement. On a meta-level Mrs. Kondile still supports the ANC, but on the level of her concrete discourse we can detect various layers of association and disassociation. Mr. Williams used to be a staunch supporter of the ANC. In the course of his life he was often disappointed by the movement, which results in the gradual discursive shift from identifying with the movement to opposing and accusing the ANC.

These two testifiers illustrate how different identifications towards the ANC could be expressed at this moment of testifying before the HRVC, again stressing the inclusive nature of the HRV Committee and its reconciliation discourse. A mixed identity was often constructed, consisting of layers that were to a certain extent approved of by the TRC. These testifiers tended to switch between identifications spontaneously, which means that they were involved in the creative self-construction of an identity they saw as appropriate at this present moment of testifying before the Commission.

## 5.5 The ideal testifier

### 5.5.1 Introduction

On the basis of the discursive analysis described in the previous chapters, I noticed that certain utterances, expressions or words by the testifiers appeared to be more highly valued than others by the commissioners. In this chapter I will first go back to the ten distinguished features to explain which utterances were welcomed before the HRV Committee, after which the concept of the *ideal testifier* will be clarified.

Feature One talked about a type of ideological layering – the introduction of the term reconciliation/forgiveness in the testimonies of the HRV victims. A number of illustrations showed us how the commissioners tended to encourage testifiers to speak out in favour of reconciliation or how they specifically wanted to hear the terms 'reconciliation' or 'forgiveness' from the mouth of the testifier. An atmosphere of reconciliation – a reconciliation-oriented frame – was deliberately created, making it sometimes very hard for victims to actually express their personal sentiments.

Feature Two also involved ideological layering, namely emphasising what I have called 'community spirit'. Testifiers were urged to show concern for their fellow South Africans – preferably for fellow South Africans belonging to a different population group. The impression was also given that symbolic or communal requests regarding the well-being of community members were sometimes embraced to a greater extent than personal and material requests. Expressing solidarity with the community and the nation, with fellow victims and with perpetrators was highly valued. In both Feature One and Feature Two the HRV commissioners employed various discursive techniques to inquire about or to remind people of their commitment to reconciliation and peaceful coexistence.

Feature Three, dealing with the level of respect that was paid to the testifiers has also been classified as a kind of ideological layering. On the basis of a number of examples we could conclude that showing respect to the testifiers was one of the key values of the TRC proceedings. Overall, victims were praised and supported, their suffering was acknowledged and the commissioners showed understanding and compassion while listening to their stories. Demonstrating respect for the testifiers happened in different ways, mainly in the opening and closing statements of the testimonies, but also through valuing their experiences, their requests and their communicative competences. Paying respect to the testifiers was unconditional, it was an absolute necessity for the HRV Committee and it can probably be seen as one of the most preferred discursive positions taken by the commissioners.

The last feature dealt with under the heading of ideological layering had to do with the emphasis on emotional discourse – Feature Four. Testifiers were encouraged to describe gruesome details of the way they were tortured. They were also repeatedly asked about their physical and mental conditions since the time the particular gross human rights violation took place. It appeared as if talking about emotionally loaded topics, such as experiencing torture, watching a beloved one being assassinated or suffering from medical problems as a result of the related incident, was more or less appreciated. If these kinds of topics were not forthcoming, the commissioners sometimes explicitly asked about them, pressuring testifiers to manifestly relive traumatic experiences.

Features Five, Six and Seven talked about historical layering. In Feature Five I have distinguished the so-called 'apartheid-talk', referring to discursive elements from the apartheid era that were recontextualised in narratives before the HRV Committee. Quite remarkably, this apartheid-talk was not met with overt disapproval by the commissioners. It might have indicated how deeply traumatised these victims were as a result of their experiences under apartheid. It could also show how parts of their beings were still firmly rooted in the past. The use of apartheid-talk clearly illustrated how crucial the TRC was in the efforts of the country to deal with the apartheid past. This feature could be positive for the image of the Commission, so the HRV commissioners did not seem to be unfavourably disposed towards these utterances.

Testifiers not only shifted back and forth between the past, the present and the future by using apartheid-talk. In the course of their testimonies they also connected, for instance, a traumatic past with a miserable present, or a hopeful present with a bright future. Illustrating which discursive techniques were used to establish this historical layering was the subject of Feature Six. Through the use of direct speech and the present tense testifiers tried to relive or animate the past and link it to their present or future situations. Testifiers also complained about the fact that their lives remained as unsafe, as painful and as miserable as under apartheid. The TRC commissioners did not reject such utterances since they could be highly relevant in post-apartheid South Africa. They could be seen as an indispensable element of the HRV reconciliation discourse because they stressed what South Africa still had to achieve in order to realise this reconciled and unified nation.

Feature Seven analysed the interaction between the testifiers and the TRC audience, an item belonging to the present TRC moment, but with strong repercussions to the future – especially for the testifiers themselves. We have seen how certain victims took advantage of the discursive space provided. The commissioners tolerated this interaction to a certain extent: the public hearings were a core element of the cathartic function of the TRC, so the audience had to be prominently present. However, certain types of interaction with the audience tended to be more preferred than others. In addition, this audience interaction was never allowed to overwhelm the proceedings. The commissioners always had to stay in control and it was their interaction with the testifiers that was to dominate the HRV proceedings.

Finally, I have also distinguished three types of identity layering, meaning that testifiers shifted back and forth between different identifying indexicalities in the course of their testimonies. Three testifiers seemed to struggle with their Afrikaner/white identity, which was the topic of Feature Eight. By appearing before the HRV Committee, people categorised themselves as TRC victims, thus participating in an institution whose aim was to help rectify an era of white oppression and non-white suffering. It looked as if this meta-categorisation was contradictory to the manifest identification as white/Afrikaner South Africans of some of the testifiers. This contradiction turned their identifications as Afrikaners into a highly valued commodity before the TRC. It was crucial for the inclusive-oriented image of the TRC to have white victims relating their sufferings at the hands of the liberation movements. Also the fact that certain testifiers could not come to terms with their Afrikaner identity before the TRC, such as Mrs. Kemp, was an acceptable stance before the Commission. It showed to what extent the apartheid past still burdened people from different levels of South African society – not only black, but also relatively well-off white people.

Before the HRV Committee, testifiers predominantly identified as apartheid victims. In a number of cases, however, perpetrator identities came to the surface in the course of testimonies – an identity layering that was the topic of Feature Nine. This multifaceted identification was appreciated by the TRC: illustrating that the majority of South Africans possessed a victim as well as a perpetrator identity was one of the aims of the Commission. We saw that this mixed identity was sometimes projected by the testifiers themselves; sometimes, it was an identity referred to by the commissioners, whereupon it was either rejected or accepted by the testifier.

Within the course of one and the same testimony certain testifiers also shifted back and forth between supporting and opposing the African National Congress.

It seemed as if this Feature (number Ten) was also appreciated by the TRC. Allowing testifiers to be critical of the ANC suited the Commission's image of impartiality. It also showed how complex identifications could be in post-apartheid South Africa. Testifiers sometimes felt wronged by one group, while still supporting this group on an ideological level. Multivoiced identifications like these showed the world what kinds of challenges the new South Africa was facing. In fact, it was an identity layering that was not only favourable to the image of the Commission, but that was also highly relevant in present-day South Africa.

I should stress that, on the one hand, while discussing these ten features, I have paid a lot of attention to constructionism from the side of the commissioners. On the other hand, it should be clear that the level of discursive participation from the side of the testifiers was substantial. Victims did not always follow the commissioners when it came to the framing of the HRV reconciliation discourse; instead, they often actively participated by giving their own interpretations. The construction of HRV discourse was definitely an interactional enterprise: it was guided by the HRV committee members, but constructively supplemented by the testifying victims.

By juxtaposing these ten features we can now distinguish a number of *ideal testifiers*. In fact, by employing these ten features in a specific manner, certain victims expressed themselves in a way that was more preferred by the HRV commissioners than the ways in which other victims expressed themselves. More specifically, certain testifiers presented themselves as apartheid victims in a discursive manner highly valued by the HRV Committee. It seemed as if these people complied with the image of a HRV testifier the TRC wanted to project into the future. On the basis of their ideological stance, their self-identification and their historical positioning, these testifiers expressed themselves in a way that suited the specificity of the TRC.

In this book, the concept of the ideal testifer is crucial, because it is especially on the basis of the discourse of these ideal testifiers that we will be able to deconstruct the archive of the reconciliation discourse that was created at the HRV hearings. Let me give one example of such an ideal testifier, namely Gregory Beck.

### 5.5.2 Mr. Gregory Beck

Mr. Beck testified in Johannesburg, on the 29th of April 1996. He was a policeman who, while on patrol in Soweto, had been shot by members of the UDF. Mr. Beck belonged to the Coloured community, a population group that had been disadvantaged under apartheid, but that sometimes also feels disadvantaged under the new dispensation (Frost 1998:106–107). It is a mixed group, consisting of people with various identifications vis à vis the other population groups in the country. The Coloured community cannot straightforwardly be categorised: members of this group practice various religions, they speak different languages, they belong to different social classes and also physically there can be considerable variation. In itself, this group could actually function as a symbol for the multiracial, multilingual and multireligious nation of South Africa that the TRC wanted to promote. In addition, it is a group to which great attention should be paid by the new government, especially because of their identity struggle both under apartheid and in post-apartheid South Africa. It is quite likely that testifiers belonging to the Coloured community were highly valued before the TRC.

Mr. Beck testified in English, which was probably his mother tongue. This was a language of wider communication, so definitely welcomed before the TRC. Very interesting is Mr. Beck's professional background. He is a police officer, so belonging to a group generally identified as apartheid perpetrators. While on duty he was attacked by members of the liberation movement. He was not a black victim who had suffered at the hands of white security forces, but a Coloured policeman who was victimised by members of the liberation movement. These kinds of a-typical victims probably took a special position at the HRV hearings: they deviated from the stereotypical TRC image of black victims testifying about atrocities committed by Whites, thus underscoring the inclusive nature of the Commission.

Apart from his socio-political and racial background, which was probably valued by the HRV Committee, Mr. Beck was also discursively identified as an ideal testifier throughout his testimony. Mr. Beck was very committed to national unity in South Africa (Feature Two). He identified himself sharply as a citizen of the new South Africa, referring proudly to "our President", "our people" or "this new South Africa of ours". When asked about his relationship to other people, he claimed to be ready to forgive, especially following the example of Nelson Mandela. He twice emphasised that he did not bear any grudges and he seemed to be very reconciliation-oriented. In terms of a reparation policy with regard to policemen, he stated that a transformation of the new police force is a necessity. In Mr. Beck's words: "every policeman should be community oriented and policemen who are still not prepared to abide with the new South Africa must be kicked out of the police service". He did not say anything about material compensations or personal reimbursements for what he had suffered.

Mr. Beck also displayed a fairly mixed identity with regard to the liberation movement (Feature Ten). At first he was rather critical of the liberation movement, identifying it as the cause of the death of many policemen. Later on, he claimed to understand the motives of the liberation movement, he even identified with Nelson Mandela and he was grateful for the sacrifices made in order to achieve liberation in the country. This shift in identification towards the ANC might well have been valued by the TRC. It not only showed that testifiers were allowed to voice criticism about the ANC at the HRV hearings; it also indicated that people could change their attitudes for the better, in this case from an intolerant police officer to an understanding citizen of a united South Africa. This discursive shift from being against to being pro ANC displayed in the course of his testimony was actually a concrete illustration of the individual transformation Mr. Beck had gone through in the period following apartheid.

Indeed, Mr. Beck clearly testified to a change in mentality and in his attitudes towards the liberation movements. In earlier days he had been a committed policeman, devoting his life to the hunt for liberation activists. Now, after the transformation, and especially through hearing stories at the TRC, he had become more tolerant. He had come to realise the perspectives of the liberation movement and he had understood that living peacefully together was of the utmost importance in the new South Africa:

> MR BECK: (…) and as we are now in the transparent and new South Africa more of these incidents are now revealed. Now it becomes more clear to me what was really going on and the balance between the State at that time and the liberation movements, and I can see the viewpoint of the liberation movement as well, which they hold, or which they held to bring about what we are experiencing in this new South Africa of ours, and that cost us all to be liberated, so therefore *I don't bear any grudges against anybody for what happened, although I was a victim of it, but I understand now. Before I didn't, no. And if these things were not revealed maybe I would have held a different opinion.*
> (…)
> MR BECK: Yes more than likely. If all these things didn't come to the fore of what happened, then maybe I would still bear a grudge. *The reason why my life changed is that I've now learnt from all the stories I've learned from and the example that our State President has brought us for forgiving after he went through all these atrocities as well, and he can forgive,* and I became more tolerant now and more understanding, which before I wasn't. *I can understand now from both sides,* and people's problems daily in my job as well.

Mr. Beck is very explicit about his personal transformation and, even more importantly, he links this transformation not only to the example of Mr. Mandela, but also to the revelation of atrocities before the TRC – it is through the truth revealed at the TRC that he can forgive and that he can now understand the issues from both sides. In fact, Mr. Beck could be regarded as a symbol of the transition the TRC stood for, a transition to democracy, to freedom of speech, to open-mindedness. He has incorporated this transition process as promoted by the TRC and he has applied it to his own consciousness.

Mr. Beck received considerable praise in Archbishop Tutu's closing statement (Feature Three). His commitment to reconciliation and national unity were especially applauded, in that he seemed to personify the transformation process the TRC stood for. Being an a-typical victim who nevertheless supported the ideological values the TRC represented and who identified in a manner highly appreciated before the TRC, turned Mr. Beck into an ideal testifier.

### 5.5.3 Discussion

Let me first elaborate on the fact that, in addition to being regarded as an ideal testifier, Gregory Beck can also be seen as an a-typical testifier. An a-typical testifier, a term I have already used earlier, is a testifier who, on the basis of his or her particular profile did not belong to one of the majority groups appearing before the HRVC. According to the TRC database (TRC Report 1998, 1/6:164–173), the majority of victims who told their stories to the TRC were African (89.9%).[11] The other population groups were represented as follows: Coloured: 1.7%, Asian: 0.2%, White: 1.1%.[12] Most of the non-white victims who came to the TRC had suffered human rights violations committed by apartheid security forces – though the Inkatha Freedom Party too, was found to be responsible for a large number of killings and cases of severe ill-treatment (TRC Report 1998, 3/1:8–10). Most of the white victims had been victimised by the liberation movements. With regard to gender, difference in proportion was marginal: 55.3% of the victims who came to the TRC were female, while 44.7% of them were male. Regarding the type of violation reported, the majority of victims talked about non-fatal gross human rights violations to men, followed by non-fatal gross human rights violations to women and fatal human rights violations to men. The HRV Committee listened to people from all age groups, the majority consisting of those aged thirty-seven and older.

In short, a testifier who belonged to one of these majority groups – for instance by being a middle-aged African lady, talking about her husband who was killed in prison – has been labelled a *typical testifier*. It is a category I have estab-

---

11. 'Victims who told their stories before the TRC' refers to people who gave a written statement to the TRC – as explained in section 2.3.1 there are no statistics or figures available on public HRV testifiers.

12. Apparently, the population group of a number of victims was unknown (see Footnote 27 in the TRC Report 1998, 1/6:167).

lished on the basis of pre-hearing victim characteristics; it took shape depending on the overall composition of the group of HRV testifiers.

Mr. Beck, as a Coloured, English-speaking member of the police force was definitely an a-typical testifier. With regard to either typical or a-typical testifiers, the HRV Committee had probably made sure that a representative selection of both typical and a-typical victims appeared at the public hearings.[13]

It looked as if a-typical victims were usually warmly welcomed by the HRV commissioners. These victims were praised for their courage to come forward and they tended to be highly respected. This was quite understandable, since these a-typical testifiers were crucial for the impartial image of the TRC. By allowing a wide range of different apartheid victims to come forward and tell their stories, the Commission tried to prove that it was unbiased and unprejudiced. All victims were seen as equal and each and every human rights violation should be equally condemned. Everyone had gone through the same misery and apartheid had affected everybody – that was the inclusive message the TRC wanted to spread. It was mainly through hosting a number of these a-typical testifiers that the TRC would be able to make this statement. So, although every testifying victim was shown respect before the HRV Committee, the a-typical victims were even more highly esteemed.

Some of these a-typical testifiers then went on to express themselves in an ideal way in the course of their testimonies – although this was definitely not the case of all of them. These a-typical testifiers who framed their discourse according to the TRC master narrative, like Mr. Beck, were particularly embraced by the TRC. They embodied the values the TRC stood for; they could in fact be seen as personifications of the TRC ideological master narrative. It is these testifiers that should be the point of reference for future generations when recalling the TRC process, and the testimonies of these victims should form an inherent component of the material TRC archive.

Finally, to conclude my discussion of the ideal testifiers, and to clarify this concept further, I will give an example of a testifier who was certainly not a model testifier, a person whose testimony was largely disapproved of by the commissioners. My illustration of a *non-ideal testifier* comes from Nelson Jantjie. Mr. Jantjie testified together with his mother in Karoo, on the 8th of October 1996. His sister was killed by the police and Mr. Jantjie was very angry while testifying. He blamed the police, the Magistrates and the Judges for his miserable situation, both in the

---

13. Again, I deliberately use the qualifier 'probably', since there do not exist any statistics or databases of the victims who were allowed to tell their stories in public. I can thus only suppose that the group who gave most statements to the HRV Committee was also largest represented at the public hearings.

past and in the present day. Leading commissioner Seroke paid little attention to these fierce reactions. She seemed almost to ignore this hatred while she kept talking about the necessity to arrive at peace and forgiveness:

> MR JANTJIE: I am angry, I am not working – I have been tortured by police, I suffer, I am of ill health, I am unemployed, I suffer, my kidneys are not all right.
>
> MS SEROKE: *We understand – we understand.*
>
> MR JANTJIE: These people – the perpetrators they are alive, what are you doing about them – my life is ruined, what are you doing about them? They were not even jailed, I could not even go to my sister's funeral, I was in detention.
>
> (…)
>
> MS SEROKE: *Mr Nelson we understand your situation.*
>
> MR JANTJIE: I am in pain, this police that tortured me, they are working, I am unemployed, these people walk pass me everyday, the others are in De Aar – they still under employment, I cannot work for myself because of them. I don't gain anything from that – my children they all over the streets, they are criminals, they do not go to school.
>
> MS SEROKE: We understand your pain, *but we ask that you try to control yourself.* So that even when we ask our investigation team to find – to find out what happened, *we as the Truth Commission would like to reach a place where there can be peace and forgiveness.*

In the course of Mr. Jantjie's testimony there was a constant shifting between his victim and his perpetrator identity. In contrast with other testifiers, Nelson Jantjie did not introduce his perpetrator identity himself. It was commissioner Potgieter who, quite suddenly, shifted the perspective by inquiring why the victim had been charged and accused – thus focussing on Mr. Jantjie's perpetrator identity. Mr. Jantjie completely rejected this perpetrator identity and it is quite likely that such a self-identification was not appreciated by the commissioners.

Nelson Jantjie also clearly interacted with the audience, especially when uttering the Afrikaans terms and phrases (see Feature Five). His feelings of hatred and anger were intensified by projecting them onto the audience. These Afrikaans terms attracted the attention of the audience, so it was a perfect way of highlighting these personal sentiments. Through this interaction Mr. Jantjie managed to raise empathy for his feelings, even though these feelings were not entirely preferred before the HRV Committee.

Although the non-ideal HRV testifiers expressed their sentiments in a manner that was not always appreciated by the HRV commissioners, even they were respected by the HRV Committee. Also these testifiers were thanked for their willingness to come forward and they were honoured for what they had endured under apartheid. Although these victims deviated from the master narrative established at the HRV hearings, they were still incorporated in the TRC project, illustrating the inclusive character of the TRC – an element I will return to later on.

It is clear that also these non-ideal testifiers had a specific function at the HRV hearings. These testifiers proved that the TRC was necessary – even indispensable with regard to the future of South Africa. These people had not yet brought this internal transformation into practice, but the HRV Commissioners seemed confident that this change towards reconciliation would be realised soon, most likely thanks to the TRC. Hence, it was useful if a couple of these non-ideal testifiers appeared at the public hearings of the TRC.

In this chapter I have distinguished between ideal and non-ideal testifiers before the HRV Committee, ideal testifiers being the embodiment of the ideal discursive position that could be taken before the HRVC. It is now the ideal testifiers' testimonies that give us an overview of the – preferred – rules of formation of this HRV discourse – the Foucaultian archive. Let me briefly, as a reminder, recapitulate which utterances formed the preferred core of the HRV discourse. We can state that utterances that corresponded to reconciliation and forgiveness were preferred, especially utterances in which the actual words 'reconciliation' and 'forgiveness' were explicitly used by the testifying victims. Along the same lines, expressions of solidarity with the community or the nation tended to be highly valued. Emotional discourse, such as descriptions of torture experiences and elaborations on physical or medical conditions, tended to be valued. Apartheid-talk was an aspect of the preferred utterances, similar to expressing continuity between past experiences and the present circumstances. White South Africans were allowed to struggle with their identities before the HRV Committee and identifying the same testifier as both a victim and a perpetrator was highly valued. Within one and the same testimony, victims were allowed to shift back and forth between supporting and opposing the ANC. An inherent and indispensable element of the HRV reconciliation discourse consisted of paying respect to the testifier, and also certain types of interacting with the audience belonged to this preferred discourse.

We can say that the HRV discourse was constructed through the spontaneous utterances of the testifiers as well as through the interaction with the commissioners. In fact, this discourse took shape mainly on the basis of the stimulating input of the HRV committee members. It was these commissioners who guided the testimonies and who dominated the interaction with the testifiers. While paying a lot of attention to the personal desires of the testifiers, they appeared to be framing the testimonies so as to comply with the pre-established structure of the

HRV testimonies and with the aims of the HRV Committee. Although the voice of the commissioners was dominant, the HRV testimonies were definitely co-constructed. This means also that the individual testifiers provided significant input, by accepting or rejecting the framing of the commissioners and by constantly negotiating acceptable indexicalities.

To a large extent, victims were indeed allowed to recount past incidents in their own words. They were allowed to express hatred and demand personal requests. They were allowed to criticise the ANC, to interact with the public or to refuse a perpetrator-identification. However, these kinds of disapproved utterances were restricted by the commissioners, which turned the entire HRV hearings into a strictly contained discursive process – a process whereby the unique expressive space provided to the testifiers was somewhat limited.

## 5.6   Conclusion

In this work, the regimentation of the testifiers' linguistic space has been revealed through a critical discursive analysis. Mostly, this confinement of the discursive freedom of testifiers was not all that obvious. Consequently, it seemed as if the testifiers were not always aware of it at the actual time of testifying. In any case, they basically never reacted explicitly against the fact that certain discursive items or structures were explicitly introduced in their testimonies. One single exception in my selection of thirty testifiers comes from Mr. Bernadine Mwelase. This testifier is the only one I came across who manifestly accused the commissioners of keeping him short while testifying. I merely give this fragment to illustrate how certain testifiers seemed to sense this curtailment of their linguistic freedom. Bearing in mind that this was a rare exception, I will not go deeper into this issue:

> COMMISSIONER: Mr Mwelase, we've heard that, and we are clear that you want the community to know that you were used.
>
> MR MWELASE: *And I haven't disclosed many things here because your questions also are disturbing me as well. There are many and lots of things I would like to disclose in this Commission, but due to time* – and there are people right there who could be saying, "There he is." You know, here there is security, but outside there are no police, there's no security, maybe anything could happen, lo and behold. *Your questions are keeping me short in explaining.*

Although this might have been one of the rare examples where a testifier openly reacted against a perceived lack of freedom of expression, it has become clear in the course of these chapters that victims often implicitly refused to follow the master narrative sought after by the HRV Committee. They often introduced their own interpretations, and in this way they contributed to the conceptualisations put forward by the commissioners. They added their own layers of indexicality, either on an historical, ideological or identity level. There was a constant shifting back and forth between accepting, rejecting or ignoring each other's discourse, both on the side of the testifiers and on the side of the commissioners. Whether manifested superficially or explicitly experienced by the testifiers, it was through this interactional process that a specific kind of so-called *reconciliation discourse* was constructed.

I have labelled this term accordingly because the inclination towards national reconciliation was one of the main and all-embracing elements of this discourse. This discursive drive for reconciliation was actually based on the entire set of ten features, which means that many of the other distinguishing features can be regarded as elements of this focus on reconciliation. In one way or another, all of the above mentioned features emphasised that South Africans had all gone through the same experiences, that many of them were both victim and perpetrator, that the entire nation was to be healed and that everyone needed to work together to transform the nation and to build a united and peaceful society.

Importantly, this reconciliation discourse was based both on the preferred HRV utterances and on the disapproved utterances. For a large part, this discourse was personified by the ideal testifiers, but also the non-ideal testifiers played a significant role in its construction. The combination of these two types of utterances turned the reconciliation discourse into a very complex and inclusive phenomenon. It is to the relation between this multilayered reconciliation discourse, its rules of formation and the social relevance of the term reconciliation that I will turn in the next chapter. We will then see that the inclusive character of the TRC particularly related to the notion of reconciliation, and that both the ideal and the non-ideal testifiers contributed greatly to the polysemic conceptualisation of this reconciliation concept.

# CHAPTER 6

# Reconciliation discourse, truth and society

## 6.1 Reconciliation as a multidimensional term at the HRV hearings

### 6.1.1 Introduction

The analysis in Chapter 5 has led us to conclude that at the Human Rights Violations hearings of the TRC a multilayered reconciliation discourse was constructed. The rules of formation upon which this reconciliation discourse was based were highly complex, depending both on personal motivations and on socio-ideological considerations. In this chapter I will concentrate on the core of this reconciliation discourse, namely the conceptualisation of the term reconciliation. As we will see, this term was open to a broad range of interpretations, which will be illustrated by referring to a number of – ideal – testifiers. In this I will follow an *anti-essentialist* theory of language, namely that meaning or value are not inherent properties of a word or a sentence (Gardiner 1992: 86–87). It will become clear that the contextual situation, the socio-historical circumstances and the dialogic nature of discourse are the crucial items to lend value and meaning to language.

In a second part of this chapter I will suggest a relation between this multivocal HRV reconciliation discourse and South African socio-political and rhetorical reality. Numerous sources have mentioned the prevalence of the term reconciliation in both political and social public discourse, especially in the years immediately following the TRC process. I will give an indication of how reconciliation discourse has 'colonised' various domains in current day South African society, thus indicating the possible impact and repercussions of the TRC reconciliation discourse on the future of the country. Although this research concentrates on the exact TRC moment as a crystallisation point in South African history, the link between HRV discourse and post-TRC society will enable us to formulate assumptions regarding future evolutions. Post-TRC South African society is not the central focus of this volume, but it deserves some attention to investigate how, in the aftermath of the TRC, South Africa has dealt with the reconciliation issue in everyday reality.

### 6.1.2 Constructing truth through discourse

In what follows I would like to define the earlier distinguished HRV reconciliation discourse as an *order of discourse*. Based on Foucault (1969), Fairclough (1992: 43) calls institutional and societal 'orders of discourse' "the totality of discursive practices within an institution or society, and the relationships between them". According to Rojo & Pujol (2002) Foucault's proposal of an order of discourse is mainly focused on the "procedures of regulation of the production, reception, and circulation of discourse". As a result of this regulation, and as has become clear through the analysis in Chapter 5, "it is socially established which discourses can be produced and spread, within which context, which features of the discourse can authorise them, and which features de-authorise them and prevent their circulation".

An order of discourse can be seen as a group of statements that belong to a *discursive formation* (Foucault 2002: 121). A discursive formation is that which in a given ideological formation "[...] determines what can and should be said" (Pêcheux 1982: 111). What I am undertaking in this work is to uncover the discursive formation of the reconciliation discourse, whereby I have labelled this discursive formation with the term *archive*. Indeed, "to describe statements, to describe the enunciative function of which they are the bearers, to analyse the conditions in which this function operates, to cover the different domains that this function presupposes and the way in which those domains are articulated, is to try to uncover [...] the discursive formation" (Foucault 2002: 130). The discursive formation governs a group of verbal performances, and a statement belongs to a discursive formation as a sentence belongs to a text. As Fairclough (1992: 42–43) clarifies, "[...] what happens inside a discursive formation [depends on] the interdiscursive relations between discursive formations and [on] the relations between discursive and non-discursive practices" – hence my emphasis on the extralinguistic socio-political context of the HRV hearings throughout this text.

The concrete discursive practices taking place at the HRV hearings comprise what Foucault has termed a *discursive regime* (see Kellsall in his discussion of courtroom discourse at the Special Court for Sierra Leone, 2004: 7). Such a discursive regime is always linked to a *regime of truth* – or, put differently, discourse always contributes to the creation of new truths (Gqola 2001: 4). According to Foucault (in Gordon 1980: 13):

> 'Truth' is to be understood as a system of ordered procedures for the production, regulation, distribution, circulation and operation of statements. 'Truth' is linked in a circular relation with systems of power which produce and sustain it, and to effects of power which it induces and which extend it. A 'régime of truth'.

And further:

> Each society has its regime of truth, its 'general politics' of truth: that is, the types
> of discourse which it accepts and makes function as true; the mechanisms and
> instances which enable one to distinguish true and false statements, the means
> by which each is sanctioned; the techniques and procedures accorded value in
> the acquisition of truth; the status of those who are charged with saying what
> counts as true.

At the HRV hearings a specific discursive regime was constructed. As the previous chapter has shown, a law of what could and could not be expressed – the production and circulation of discourse – was established at the HRV hearings. Through this selective procedure, this strictly regulated and controlled discourse contributed to the creation of new realities, new truths.

This means that the TRC not only focussed on retrieving the truth about the past (see TRC Report 1998, 1/5:109–113), it also had the authority to capture, to establish and to codify the truth. This dimension of truth recovery was not so much oriented to the past; it was rather directed towards the present and the future – in this case we are talking about political-ideological truth, as will become clear later on. It is this dimension that will be taken into consideration when dealing with the *regime of truth* that was established by the TRC through its discourse. This regime of truth had its foundations in the apartheid past since it was based on the memory that was transferred from the past. By applying specific rules of formation, resulting in the construction of a specific kind of reconciliation discourse, a reconciliation-oriented truth was then projected onto the future.

### 6.1.3  The term 'reconciliation' at the TRC victim hearings

The HRV reconciliation discourse partly took shape on the basis of preferred utterances. In Chapter 5 these preferences have been categorised, based on the analysis of ten features. The so-called *ideal testifiers* could be seen as illustrations/personifications of the most-preferred HRV reconciliation discourse. What all of these ideal testifiers had in common was that they were in favour of reconciliation. Nevertheless, there clearly was individual variation regarding the ways in which reconciliation was conceptualised. Let me give some examples.

In the case of Gregory Beck, reconciliation was mainly framed by referring to national unity. Mr. Beck was the prototypical example of an individual who had undergone a complete transformation, from supporting the apartheid state in earlier days to appreciating the anti-apartheid struggle and the new dispensation in the present. This testifier did voice some critical reflections with regard to the liberation movements, but this was accepted since it functioned as evidence for his transformation process. Mr. Beck strongly identified with the new South Africa and this identification was then the point of departure to emphasise his commitment to reconciliation. Taking "our State President" as an example, he explicitly mentioned that he had been turned into a forgiving, tolerant and under-standing citizen. We clearly get an interpretation of reconciliation that was highly valued by the TRC commissioners, since it was based on an internal transformation process and a strong commitment to national unity.

According to Wilson (2001a: 107), it was this national, more abstract inter-pretation of reconciliation – what he calls the *mandarin-intellectual narrative* – that approached the official TRC view on reconciliation. This official view was formulated in 1996 by Research Unit Director, Charles Villa-Vicencio, who ar-gued that the Commission should promote reconciliation at the level of the South Africa nation, rather than enhancing reconciliation between individuals or social groups; the inclusive dimension of the TRC is clearly at stake when considering this idea. We see, indeed, that a number of TRC victims expressed this point of view, which might have turned their discourse into a highly valued commodity.

A second ideal testifier, Paul Williams, predominantly framed reconciliation religiously. It was mainly as a committed Christian that he wanted to reach out to his perpetrators. He did not feel any bitterness in his heart and he claimed to have completely forgiven them "out of Godly love". It was the bible that had taught him to love his enemies and it was also based on his belief that he supported the TRC amnesty process. This interpretation of reconciliation fitted in the *religious-redemptive narrative* of reconciliation, as distinguished by Wilson (2001a: 109). The religious-redemptive narrative sought not just the reconciliation of 'the na-tion', but also between individuals within the nation. Here we are dealing with an approach to reconciliation in which the personal self plays only a minor role: Mr. Williams was prepared to forgive his attackers, but based solely on his religious conviction. In this testimony reconciliation was conceptualised on a meta-level, since it was believed to find its source not in human encounters, but in supranatu-ral forces. Also such a religiously-oriented interpretation of reconciliation was explicitly appreciated by the HRV commissioners.

The testimony of Metro Bambiso formed the basis for yet another way of framing reconciliation. As a victim of state security violence, Mr. Bambiso want-ed to reconcile with the perpetrators; he was prepared to accept their apologies and to forgive them. Like Mr. Beck, Mr. Bambiso expressed community aware-ness, which gave his individual reconciliation a national dimension. In this case, though, reconciliation was even further developed, since Mr. Bambiso also played the role of a repenting perpetrator. He was the personification of both a forgiving victim and a remorseful perpetrator. Hence, he was a prime example of reconciliation in the new South Africa – where every one, according to Archbishop Tutu for instance, was a victim as well as a perpetrator. Such a highly inclusive notion of reconciliation was obviously welcomed by the commissioners.

When considering the testimony of Phebel Robinson, there are significant resemblances to that of Mr. Beck. Ms. Robinson expressed a strong sense of community spirit, with regard to her late husband as well as with regard to her present-day personal position. As has been explained, this kind of solidarity with members of the community can be seen as an aspect of national awareness – it indicated that one is prepared to live peacefully together with fellow citizens, regardless of their positions under apartheid or their social or ethnic backgrounds. Ms. Robinson explicitly appealed to the audience in order to have this community spirit confirmed – an interaction with the audience that was highly effective, as we have seen in 5.3.4.

Also like Mr. Beck, Ms. Robinson clearly interpreted reconciliation in a more abstract, non-individual sense, approaching it from a national/communal rather than from an individual angle. The fact that both of these victims belonged to the Coloured community, a group of people who sometimes struggled with their national identity in the new South Africa, might be indicative. Therefore, proclaiming their affinity with post-apartheid South Africa and its symbols like Nelson Mandela, and stressing their solidarity with fellow community members was particularly relevant in their case.

In the testimony of Mzothuli Maphumulo reconciliation was lifted to the political level. Although a member of the IFP, and a victim of ANC violence, Mr. Maphumulo presented himself as a mediator between these political factions. Importantly, his tolerance and understanding towards the different political parties not only referred to the past, it also extended to the present and the future. This testifier was open-minded and prepared to cooperate constructively to the building of a reconciled society. In the course of his testimony reconciliation was in the first place given a personal interpretation. Indeed, Mr. Maphumulo had lost three sons as a result of political violence, which turned his reconciliation-oriented attitude into a great sacrifice. The commissioners appreciated this attitude enormously and considered the ability to forgive the perpetrators after such a terrible tragedy as a feature of unsurpassed personal merit. In addition to this personal touch, reconciliation was also given a political dimension, transcending the individual incident, and being made relevant to South African society at large. Reconciling different political factions was indeed crucial immediately after the transition to democracy – and also later on it remained a major political issue.

Finally, there is Stephanie Kemp, a final ideal testifier. Her approach to reconciliation also fitted in the mandarin-intellectual narrative, since she explicitly expressed her support for national reconciliation. However, in this case reconciliation was given an extra dimension that was not so much a political rather than an ethno-cultural one. We have seen that Mrs. Kemp seemed to struggle with her white/Afrikaner identity, since she actually presented a symbiosis between an anti-apartheid activist and a beneficiary of the apartheid system. In her testimony the opposition between white/Afrikaner and victim of the apartheid regime/Communist was transcended. Clearly, it was reconciliation between bearers of the Afrikaner culture and speakers of Afrikaans on the one hand, and ANC activists and apartheid exiles (so people who tended to be opposed to both the Afrikaner culture and Afrikaans) on the other hand, that was at stake. Based on Mrs. Kemp's testimony reconciliation was given a national dimension, whereby reconciliation should take place in the first place between Afrikaners and non-Afrikaners – not, as was the case with Mr. Maphumulo for instance, between members of the IFP and the ANC.

### 6.1.4 Ideal versus non-ideal testifiers

By focussing on these ideal testifiers, we should not forget to pay attention to the other – less ideal, or even non-ideal – testifiers. As stated before, all of the victims who appeared before the HRV Committee contributed to the construction of the HRV reconciliation discourse. It is by surveying the whole range of HRV testifiers (or my representative sample of thirty) that we are able to gain better understanding of the various interpretations of the term reconciliation that were accepted before this Committee.

The above-mentioned ideal testifiers represented one end of the spectrum of ways in which reconciliation could be interpreted before the TRC. Their conceptualisations of reconciliation were very inclusive, broad or abstract; they sometimes even fitted in the 'official' TRC view on reconciliation. We could say that the testimonies of these ideal testifiers approached an imaginary *upper limit* of the way in which reconciliation could be interpreted. This was probably the vision on reconciliation the TRC wanted to present to the nation, the vision they hoped would be followed by South Africans at large. I call this upper limit 'imaginary' because in reality there did not exist an upper limit: the more dimensions were attributed to the notion of reconciliation and the broader it was interpreted, the better. Even in cases where the victim's manifest commitment to reconciliation appeared to be exaggerated, which was slightly the case with Mr. Beck, victims were never asked to temper their enthusiasm. Nor were they ever asked whether their reconciliation-oriented statements were sincere, or whether these attitudes were implemented in their everyday lives.

Let me now turn to the *lower limit* of interpreting the reconciliation concept, the way reconciliation was conceptualised in a less preferred, but usually still acceptable manner. To illustrate the other extreme in which reconciliation could be understood before the HRV Committee, I will discuss a number of non-ideal testifiers.

The first victim who identified in a manner probably less appreciated by the HRV Committee was Johannes van Eck. This victim was highly critical of the TRC and the ANC government. Although prompted by some of the leading commissioners, Mr. van Eck refused to explicitly speak out in favour of reconciliation. The terms 'reconciliation' or 'forgiveness' were never mentioned; Mr. van Eck mainly addressed his personal situation. Nevertheless, Mr. van Eck was not straightforwardly vengeful, nor did he express hatred towards the perpetrators. He seemed aggrieved and sad, rather than angry or resentful. In addition, this victim also referred to God as a source of strength, so in fact he subscribed to the religious narrative that was sometimes put forward by the TRC. Mr. van Eck was very disappointed, disillusioned and distressed, but not explicitly opposed to reconciliation. Moreover, despite the fact that reconciliation was never mentioned in this testimony, the message spread by Mr. van Eck was that reconciliation was possible, but only under the condition that the TRC and the government would be consistent in their attempt to establish an equal and just society.

Interestingly, in the closing statement of the chairperson (Alex Boraine), the testimony was given a reconciliation-oriented twist. Mr. Boraine stressed how this testimony taught us that violence is always terrible and unjust, no matter what the motives are and no matter which ideals are defended. By doing so, Mr. Boraine emphasised that all apartheid victims deserved unconditional respect and that all acts of violence were to be reproached – the bottom-line being that all victims should try to reach out towards one another, in order to have aggression and hate replaced by peace and forgiveness. In this way, Mr. van Eck's testimony was given a reconciliatory dimension, which had probably not been the testifier's intention. Mr. van Eck rather seemed to be determined not to openly commit himself to reconciliation, as can be gathered from his carefully chosen discourse. The HRV Committee put forward its own interpretation of this testimony, adding a coordinating reconciliation-directed dimension.

The willingness to reconcile, but only under certain conditions was a point of view held by a number of testifiers, which contrasted to the position of the ideal testifiers in which the interpretation of reconciliation was largely unconditional. Nhlanhla Buthelezi, for instance, began by claiming that he would only reconcile if he would be given the opportunity to meet the people who called him an informer. At this stage, though, his approach to reconciliation might not have been ideal in the eyes of the commissioners, it was definitely acceptable. However, and perhaps as a result of the way his discourse was framed by the committee members, Mr. Buthelezi's testimony became less reconciliation-oriented towards the end. In this phase of the testimony, the audience participation was clearly restricted: Mr. Buthelezi was not allowed to appeal to the public or to gain acknowledgement with regard to his expressed emotions (see also 5.3.4). The testifier's growing opposition to reconciliation culminated in the explicit sentence "I am not going to, I am not going to reconcile, I am not about to". Utterances like these were probably not acceptable and we see, indeed, that Mr. Buthelezi is cut short by the chairperson:

> MR BUTHELEZI: I suffered a lot, I almost was affected mentally. Even today, I think somehow I am affected mentally. So, I am not going to, *I am not going to reconcile, I am not about to.*
>
> MRS SEROKE: Order please, order.
>
> CHAIRPERSON: Buthelezi, could you, I think you have come to the end, could you please take questions. Thank you.

At the end of the testimony we get a similar situation. Mr. Buthelezi explicitly rejects the reconciliation concept: "No, no, I have no peace whatsoever and I will not forgive", whereupon the chair immediately reacts. In a rather aggressive way Mr. Buthelezi is reprimanded and dismissed:

> MR BUTHELEZI: No, no, no. *No, I have no peace whatsoever and I will not forgive.* I do not even see why the TRC is existing and how it is helping us in a way. If the TRC was conducting its work the right way, it was supposed to let me make mention of the names because I know those names, but if you refuse me to mention those names how I am going to reconcile.
>
> CHAIRPERSON: Mr Buthelezi.
>
> MR BUTHELEZI: I want to mention the names now. Why did they decide to call me a ...
>
> CHAIRPERSON: Could you please ...
>
> MR BUTHELEZI: ... police informer because ...
>
> CHAIRPERSON: Could you please listen. We have never stopped you from mentioning those names. If you did not for the time that you were sitting there, do not blame it on this body. *We are saying thank you, let us give others a chance.*

The message learnt from this testimony is obvious: approaching reconciliation conditionally could still be taken into consideration before the HRV Committee; explicitly rejecting reconciliation could not. These utterances could be situated below the lower limit of possible interpretations of reconciliation. By means of such kinds of expressions the testifier openly contradicted the HRV reconciliation discourse, an attitude that was to be avoided as much as possible. Citizens of the new South Africa were not supposed to openly refuse to forgive or to reconcile.

Next, there is Mr. Morake. This testifier did not openly speak out against reconciliation like Mr. Buthelezi. Nevertheless, he did express clear resentment vis à vis white people:

> COMMISSIONER GCABASHE: How do you feel ever since this has happened?
>
> MR MORAKE: This occurrence changed my life so drastically. *I feel I have this deep hatred for a white person.* When I see a white person, especially at night I have these negative thoughts and even at work when I white person speaks to me I just look at him. *I totally distrust them because during the day they are people and in the evening they are killers.* Even when I'm driving a car and passing through Brandfort these thoughts come back to me so vividly as if it only happened yesterday. I just don't know how to explain this. Each time I think of this occurrence and I think of this attack ... (incomplete)
>
> (...)
>
> COMMISSIONER GCABASHE: Now, when you say, ever since this incident took place and you have this problematic relationship with white people, *did you ever try to get any treatment or some counselling with regard to that?*
>
> MR MORAKE: No, I've never thought of getting any treatment because *I feel that where they are, they are the ones who should be getting the treatment.* I think where they are they are the ones who are supposed to receive the treatment because I think they were the ones who are sick.

In this fragment Mr. Morake argues that he feels this deep hatred for white persons; he distrusts them completely, since "they are people during the day, but killers at night". It is likely that utterances such as these were not appreciated by the HRV commissioners. However, in contrast with the explicit rejection of reconciliation in the testimony of Mr. Buthelezi, these utterances could still be rectified. Indeed, Mr. Morake was not cut short, or prohibited to continue; instead, his resentment was framed as a psychological illness. Proclaiming hatred was an attitude not valued at the HRV hearings, but where they occurred the commissioners set an interpretation on these emotions in order to suit a particular dimension of the reconciliation discourse: this hatred was presented as a curable desease, which means that the possibility was left open for reconciliation in the future.

The last non-ideal testifier I would like to refer to is Nelson Jantjie. The terms reconciliation or forgiveness were not mentioned in this testimony. The testifier was clearly very angry, but he did not openly refuse to reconcile. Also in this case reconciliation seemed to be regarded as a possibility by the HRV commissioners. Although Mr. Jantjie's emotions were largely ignored, his testimony was not curtailed. Commissioner Seroke tried to temper his anger by emphasising the necessity for peaceful coexistence; she even argued that she understood Mr. Jantjie's anger. Let me, for the sake of clarity, repeat this fragment, which I already referred to in section 5.5.3:

> MR JANTJIE: I am angry, I am not working – I have been tortured by police, I suffer, I am of ill health, I am unemployed, I suffer, my kidneys are not all right.
>
> MS SEROKE: *We understand – we understand.*
>
> MR JANTJIE: These people – the perpetrators they are alive, what are you doing about them – my life is ruined, what are you doing about them? They were not even jailed, I could not even go to my sister's funeral, I was in detention.
> (…)
> MS SEROKE: *Mr Nelson we understand your situation.*
>
> MR JANTJIE: I am in pain, this police that tortured me, they are working, I am unemployed, these people walk pass me everyday, the others are in De Aar – they still under employment, I cannot work for myself because of them. I don't gain anything from that – my children they all over the streets, they are criminals, they do not go to school.
>
> MS SEROKE: We understand your pain, *but we ask that you try to control yourself.* So that even when we ask our investigation team to find – to find out what happened, *we as the Truth Commission would like to reach a place where there can be peace and forgiveness.*

The underlying message here appeared to be that resentful testifiers could also be moved towards reconciliation. Mr. Jantjie's expressions of hatred were definitely not appreciated, but according to the reaction of the commissioner all hope should not be abandoned when it comes to reversing these attitudes and promoting reconciliation.

When considering these four non-ideal testifiers, we notice that before the HRV Committee essentially every expression and motivation of reconciliation was accepted. Testifiers were allowed to express hatred and resentment, as long as these sentiments could be rectified, for instance by framing them as an illness, or by ignoring them and stressing peace and forgiveness instead. Sometimes, reconciliation was explicitly *not* mentioned by the testifier, even after instigation by the commissioners. This did not seem to be a problem; in some of these cases reconciliation was then raised by the commissioners themselves – sometimes even in a very subtle way by openly interpreting the testimony in a reconciliation-oriented manner. Although none of these testifiers expressed themselves in a manner preferred by the HRV Committee, these testimonies were framed and interpreted in such a way as to suit the reconciliation-oriented master narrative. These expressions with regard to the reconciliation concept formed the lower limit of what was acceptable. It was only the testimony of Nhlanhla Buthelezi that could be situated below this limit. Openly proclaiming that one was not prepared to reconcile could not be accepted.

### 6.1.5  Accepting various interpretations of reconciliation

Between the upper limit, embodied by the ideal testifiers, and the lower limit, embodied by some of the non-ideal testifiers, there existed a wide range of acceptable interpretations of the term reconciliation. Let me deal with some of these intermediate interpretations.

I have hinted before at some of the testifiers who were only prepared to reconcile under certain conditions. Such a conditional reconciliation was acceptable, but much also depended on the expressed condition. For instance, a number of testifiers claimed that they were willing to reconcile if the perpetrator would tell the truth – this truth could refer to what had happened to disappeared loved ones, to the role played by informers, or to the exact manner in which someone was killed. By framing reconciliation accordingly, testifiers subscribed to the *legal-procedural narrative* on reconciliation, as described by Wilson (2001a: 104–106). This approach to reconciliation came closest to the mandate of the TRC Act. It was a legal positivist, procedural view of reconciliation, which emerged as a result of the application of legal principles contained within the Act. According to the Act, perpetrators were not expected to express guilt, but they were obliged to tell the truth if they wanted to be granted amnesty. Based on this stipulation and extending it to the Human Rights Violations Committee, it was understandable that victims linked their willingness to reconcile in a similar way to the revelation of the truth. Amnesty in exchange for truth or reconciliation and forgiveness in exchange for truth were principles that were clearly inherent to the TRC concept. Therefore, demanding truth as a condition for reconciliation seemed to be embraced by the HRV Committee.

Another condition that was acceptable was the condition that perpetrators should apologise for their deeds before being forgiven. Ms. Lizzy Phike, for instance, agreed to live in peace with her perpetrators, but only if they would come forward to say they were sorry. Although, in contrast with truth, remorse was not required in order to be granted amnesty before the TRC, from a human point of view it was understandable that people expected an apology before being able to forgive or to reconcile. After all, the fact that remorse was not a condition for amnesty had been a highly controversial issue all along the TRC process. Remorse had not been made a requirement because one was afraid of insincere declarations of remorse. Nevertheless, many critics saw this as a shortcoming since an apology from the perpetrators was seen as morally crucial to the victims. In addition, it was commonly claimed that creating a reconciled South African society would never be possible without an apology from the apartheid perpetrators (see Frost 1998; Minow 1998; Ericson 2001; Taylor 2002). On a more general, supranational, level Jacoby (1983: 347) and Schimmel (2002: 141) even argue that both acknowledgement and genuine remorse are essential and necessary conditions in order to forgive. The fact that a victim demanded remorse before he or she would be willing to reconcile was a psychological approach to reconciliation that was probably understood and appreciated by the commissioners.

Sometimes, however, reconciliation was predicated on material redress/compensation. That was the case with Kedu Mahlangu, who argued that he would only be prepared to reconcile if the perpetrators were going to compensate him. I have explained before that material requests were not really welcomed before the Commission. We can speak here about a tension between the quasi-legal TRC frame (based on retributive justice and material compensation), and the quasi-religious TRC frame (based on restorative justice, charity and love of one's neighbour). Before the HRV Committee there was a tendency – definitely in the case of certain commissioners – to openly promote the quasi-religious frame. In general, symbolic or collective reparations, the revelation of truth, or a peaceful solution for a regional conflict were requests the TRC was much more willing to try to fulfil. In the same way, also offering reconciliation and forgiveness solely in exchange for money was an approach to reconciliation the HRV Committee preferred not to address. People were allowed to present such a materialistic interpretation of reconciliation, but it was probably not highly valued.

In section 5.2.4 I have referred to the testimony of Mrs. Lilian Kadi. Initially, when commissioner Meiring quoted from her written statement, this testifier stated that she would be prepared to meet the perpetrators. Later on, though, she talked about the disastrous effects of the incident on the everyday lives of her family and herself, thus indicating that a willingness to reconcile with the perpetrators can go hand in hand with feelings of anger and resentment. Within one and the same testimony we were confronted with a multidimensional interpretation of reconciliation. It appeared as if Mrs. Kadi wanted to forgive the perpetrators, but she was still very bitter about what they had done to her family – one sentiment did not exclude the other. Such a mixture of reconciliatory-oriented feelings might have been common among testifying apartheid victims. However, this testimony of Mrs. Kadi is the only one from my selection where this emotional tension is openly expressed. It is likely that the way Mrs. Kadi approached reconciliation was accepted before the HRV Committee, although the interpretative turn based on anger and grief was probably less appreciated by the commissioners.

Finally, I would like to come back to the redemptive-religious approach to reconciliation, as referred to already in the case of the ideal testifier Paul Williams. Although Mr. Williams was prepared to forgive his attackers primarily on the basis of his Christian belief, he personally did not seem to be averse to reconciliation. He would even like to communicate with the perpetrators in order to find out why they had killed so many innocent people – he portrayed them as, in the first instance, human beings. Mr. Williams also referred to the fact that this attack was not unique. He was aware of a more national suffering, by showing compassion for victims on either side of the apartheid divide. This testifier also displayed a positive attitude towards the South African health system and he was positive about the relief fund that had been established in order to help victims.

It is interesting now to contrast Mr. Williams' testimony to that of Mrs. Bernice Whitfield. Mrs. Whitfield's approach to reconciliation can also be categorised as belonging to the redemptive-religious narrative. She constantly referred to God as the source of reconciliation and forgiveness. She claimed that she held no grudges against anybody because "if God forgives us, we can forgive others". Taking this dimension into consideration, her interpretation of reconciliation resembled the highly valued interpretation of Mr. Williams. However, throughout her testimony Mrs. Whitfield was extremely negative about the new government. She also despised the TRC process, since she stated "As far as I am concerned I'm wasting my time; I'm here for Jesus". Mrs. Whitfield did not show any compassion towards her fellow South Africans; she was primarily concerned with her own misery. In addition, though she was prepared to reconcile as a faithful Christian in the present, she did hope that later on the perpetrators would be judged and punished when coming face to face with Jesus. Apart from her Christian belief, Mrs. Whitfield's attitude was not directed towards reconciliation – rather towards retribution and revenge. Still, I would not define Mrs. Whitfield as a non-ideal testifier. Her approach towards reconciliation was clearly religiously inspired, which was appreciated by the HRV Committee. Her conceptualisation of reconciliation seemed to be accepted, but it probably ranked lower on the 'acceptability-scale' than that of Mr. Williams.

This last example has been given in order to demonstrate the large variety of possible approaches to reconciliation established at the HRV hearings. Sometimes, different interpretations were combined in one and the same testimony, sometimes there was an overlap between various – preferred and less-preferred – strands.

To sum up, reconciliation formed the core component of the HRV reconciliation discourse. The term was not clearly defined by the TRC; in addition, the reconciliation discourse constructed at the hearings was multilayered and highly complex, on an ideological, historical, as well as an identity level. The fact that this discourse was multifaceted, combined with the fact that reconciliation was not unambiguously defined by the Commission, resulted in a very broad conceptualisation of the term at the HRV hearings.

The HRV Committee only tried to determine the limits of acceptable interpretations of reconciliation. In theory, there did not exist an upper limit – the more inclusively reconciliation was approached, the better. In practice, however, we notice that this upper limit could be inferred from the testimonies of some of the ideal testifiers. Their attitudes towards reconciliation could be explicitly religious or they could be oriented towards nation-building and communal solidarity, both of which seemed to be much preferred by the HRV committee members. Reconciliation could also be framed on a more personal level, for instance by incorporating the identity of a forgiving victim as well as the identity of a remorseful perpetrator. Within these different interpretations, considerable variation and layering was possible, such as political or ethno-cultural dimensions, as illustrated above. All of these approaches to reconciliation belonged to the preferred set of interpretations in the repertoire of the HRV Committee.

The lower limit of the way in which reconciliation could be interpreted was outlined more clearly. Victims were allowed to refuse to use the term reconciliation. They were even allowed to express hatred and vengeance. Usually, though, emotions like these were channelled by the leading commissioners, either by completely ignoring them while still stressing the necessity to reconcile, or by projecting them as temporal and superficial. In any case, it is quite likely that expressing anger and a desire for retributive justice ranked very low in the repertoire of acceptable approaches to reconciliation, even when given a reconciliation-oriented turn. Interpretations below the border of acceptability involved explicit refusals to reconcile or to forgive. In my entire corpus of thirty testimonies only one testifying victim seemed to approach reconciliation in an unacceptable manner – and only in the second part of his testimony. Based on the overall reading of the 1819 victim testimonies I can claim that this appeared to be a regular pattern. Only very rarely did victims explicitly refuse to reconcile by actually using the exact words. The majority of victims seemed to be favourably inclined towards reconciliation, giving the term a whole range of different interpretations.

These findings tell us a lot about the way in which reconciliation discourse was constructed at the hearings, through interaction with the commissioners. Despite the fact that this discourse was extremely layered and contained many different dimensions, certain rules had to be respected, certain types of expressions could not be permitted. Already at the onset of the hearings the majority of testifying victims tended towards reconciliation. In the course of the hearing they were then further encouraged to commit themselves to a reconciled and united South Africa. This predominantly happened through the establishment of this multifaceted reconciliation discourse, where reconciliation could be interpreted manifold – but could not be straightforwardly and openly rejected.

The provisional suggestion hinted at here is that the HRV reconciliation discourse was partly constructed intentionally, starting at the level of selecting testifiers (see also the critique of authors such as Jefferey 1999; Brent Harris 2002; and Carin Williams 1999) and then continuing by framing the victim's discourse at the actual HRV site Through this process, the term reconciliation was given a very broad interpretation.

In the next section I will illustrate how the TRC reconciliation discourse influenced post-TRC South African society. Reconciliation became mainstream in South African society, on the level of political rhetoric, education, social regulations and institutional policy. In all of these domains, reconciliation was not only used as merely a discursive category, it was also consciously implemented, leading to a reconciliation-oriented reality. We will bear in mind, though, that this reconciliatory reality was also multidimensional, leading to a broad spectrum of ways in which reconciliation could be employed or implemented.

## 6.2   A multilayered reconciliation discourse in South African reality

### 6.2.1   Introduction

The idea of this section is not to add to the controversy on whether or not the TRC has resulted in or contributed to reconciliation among South Africans. This discussion has been dealt with in numerous articles, books and dissertations, and will not be continued here. What I will illustrate, though, is how reconciliation has become a key term in South African public discourse, finding its way not only into the realm of the arts, but also into the domains of political institutionalisation and policy making. This will tell us how reconciliation has been implemented in South Africa, and how, in the aftermath of the TRC process, a reality based on reconciliation was taking shape in the liberated nation. We will see how the divergent manners in which reconciliation was interpreted before the TRC might have contributed to the coming into existence of a wide variety of reconciliation-related practices in South Africa's reality.

After the transition to democracy in 1994 a new discourse had to be established to talk about South African society. As claimed by Gobodo-Madikizela

(2003b: 56), it is always necessary to forge a vocabulary of peace in the aftermath of mass tragedy. People had to start thinking about one another differently, which also involved talking about and to one another by means of a language adapted to the new dispensation. According to my interpretation, it is in this search for a new socio-political discourse that the TRC acted as a catalyst, and the HRV reconciliation discourse forming the foundation of this wider societal discourse.

### 6.2.2 Reconciliation discourse pre-TRC

Even before the TRC was established various aspects of this reconciliation discourse to be had come to the surface. The implementation of reconciliation did not begin with the Commission, nor did it end when the TRC handed over its Report (Doxtader 2000: 131). The pursuit of national reconciliation has a long history in South Africa, being a key-component of the ideology of Albert Luthuli, South Africa's first Nobel Peace Prize winner in 1961 (de Gruchy 2002: 33). In the '60s, '70s and '80s several members of the Christian community in South Africa were clearly reconciliation-oriented in their resistance to apartheid (de Gruchy, Cochrane & Martin 1999: 4; de Gruchy 2002: 32–38). At the end of the '80s negotiations gradually developed between the ANC and the Afrikaner community (such as the Afrikaner Broederbond and the corporation Anglo American). This first stage was difficult and dangerous, but it is in these initial contacts that the seeds were sown of the later reconciliation process (Villa-Vicencio & Ngesi 2003: 269–271). Apart from a number of tentative initiatives, though, the notion of reconciliation was not embraced by the wider population during the apartheid era.

Everything changed after the liberation of Nelson Mandela in February 1990, which unofficially marked the end of apartheid. From that point on the political transition to democracy was gradually introduced. Analogous to this socio-political transformation the search for a new kind of discourse also came into being. This transition period was characterised by outbursts of extreme violence – according to the TRC Report (1998, 1/6: 171) most violations reported by deponents took place in the period after the unbanning of political parties (so in the period 1990–1994). Although this was a period where reconciliation discourse might have been adopted by the negotiating political parties, the aggressive climate inherited from the apartheid era was still much too intense for this kind of discourse to be incorporated by South African population at large.

The true foundations of the truth and reconciliation process were laid after the democratic elections of 1994. During these years reconciliation gradually came into vogue as a national symbol and reconciliation discourse gradually became accepted as one of the national discourses. However, it was initially still the political elite who were the bearers of this reconciliation-oriented language. According to Norval (1996a: 294), a number of organisations, predominantly the ANC, started to employ a discourse of non-racialism, equality and reconciliation after the transition in 1994. The period from 1994 to 1999 has been labelled the *Mandela era*, and it is commonly suggested that the person of Nelson Mandela has been highly significant in the establishment of a reconciliation process in South Africa (see for instance Frost 1998). And indeed, the search for reconciliation seemed to be largely initiated by the personality of Nelson Mandela – one only has to think about his appearance at the 1995 World Rugby Cup and about the numerous times when he reached out to former apartheid icons, thus turning non-racialism into the new 'civil religion' of South Africa (Waldmeir 1997: 268). It was especially the message of non-racialism and reconciliation as embodied by Mandela that dominated those early days of the transition.

During the presidency of Mandela a new vocabulary emerged to describe the social order, a vocabulary that spoke of nationhood, unity and racial harmony. It seemed as if from 1994 onwards positive attempts were made in order to give South Africans a new language for speaking about – and to – each other (Fullard 2004: 2). At the beginning of the Mandela era it looked as if reconciliation discourse was still largely limited to the domain of politics, since national reconciliation became the mantra of mainly South Africa's political discourse. It was primarily on this political level that reconciliation discourse began to crystallise as the chief mode of reading the 'nation'. A major step by which this political reconciliation discourse was made explicit was in the formulation of the Constitution of the new South Africa. Reconciliation seemed to be firmly enshrined in this 1996 Constitution, as the preamble stated that the Constitution was to:

> Heal the divisions of the past and establish a society based on democratic values, social justice and fundamental human rights; lay the foundations for a democratic and open society in which government is based on the will of the people and every citizen is equally protected by law; improve the quality of life of all citizens and free the potential of each person; and build a united and democratic South Africa able to take its rightful place as a sovereign state in the family of nations.
>
> (Constitution of the Republic of South Africa 1996: preamble)

Gradually, reconciliation discourse spread to popular domains. Terms like *rainbow nation* or *Madiba magic*, which were inherent elements of the reconciliation discourse, took on a talismatic quality and became characteristic of the new South Africa – and they were frequently used among large sections of the population (Jacobs 2000).

### 6.2.3 Reconciliation discourse after 1995

Despite the crucial role of Nelson Mandela and despite the fact that reconciliation discourse had already started to trickle into mainstream discourse before 1995, it was especially the establishment of the Truth and Reconciliation Commission in 1995 which heralded a period marked by the use of *reconciliation discourse* (see also Wilson 2001a: 9–10). We could argue that it was the Commission that was mainly responsible for the permanent introduction and the popularisation of the term reconciliation in South African society. It was especially the individual public hearings, along with extensive media coverage, that caused the notion of reconciliation to filter through to South African society (Goodman 2003: 80).

From the time the TRC was established and even more so from the time the public hearings started to take wide effect in South African society, the discourse of reconciliation could no longer be escaped. Together with the term reconciliation, expressions such as *affirmative action, transformation, transition, healing, democratisation* and *rainbow nation* made up the body of the South African reconciliation discourse. Throughout the process, however, opinions regarding the interpretation of the term reconciliation diverged considerably.

One very interesting and equally debatable term that came into being largely as a result of the TRC reconciliation discourse is *ubuntu*. During and after the TRC proceedings South African reconciliation became conceptualised as something unique, a rather exceptional moral value that was captured under the label of *ubuntu*. This term has been given various interpretations, but it usually includes respect for human dignity, solidarity, restoration and justice. In addition, it is often connected to concepts such as humanity, mutuality, community and compassion. As Tutu (1999b: 34–36) puts it: "A person with *ubuntu* is open and available to others, affirming of others, does not feel threatened that others are able and good; for he or she has a proper self-assurance that comes from knowing that he or she belongs in a greater whole and is diminished when others are humiliated or diminished".

According to Tutu, *ubuntu* is a typical African concept and he argues that the term is very difficult to render in a Western language. Gerloff (1998: 49) even calls *ubuntu* an African philosophical concept, meaning the organic wholeness of humanity. Based on forgiveness in community it is a concept "inconceivable in Western thought". Just like reconciliation, *ubuntu* also is a highly polysemous ideological concept. As Wilson (1996: 13–14) points out, "it connects human rights, reconciliation and nation-building in the populist terms of a relatively benign African nationalism".

As a matter of fact, *ubuntu* had already been employed in South African political discourse slightly before the TRC came into existence. Like reconciliation, *ubuntu* appeared in a number of post-apartheid judicial texts. In the postamble of the 1993 Interim Constitution, for instance, it is stated that "there is a need for understanding but not for vengeance, a need for reparation but not for retaliation, a need for *ubuntu* but not for victimization" (Wilson 1996: 12). Nevertheless, the above-mentioned passage also appeared in the preamble of the 1995 National Unity and Reconciliation Act to establish the TRC, and we could say that it was mainly through the TRC process that the term gained popularity among South African population.

The word *ubuntu* was used quite often at the hearings of the HRV Committee, mainly by chairperson Tutu, but also by other committee members. These are a few examples; only the first one is taken from my selection of thirty testifiers:

> Chairman Mgojo in the closing statement of Patrick Morake's testimony:
>
> "I think the whole thing of the Truth Commission is that the victim must be helped and that the perpetrator must be helped. That's what I just want to say. You need to tell yourself you also need a treatment just as you have rightly said that the perpetrators need the treatment because they need to be healed and retain that *ubuntu* which God had given them."
>
> CHAIRMAN: Ndade Moleke I want again to reiterate what has been said by my colleagues here. In fact the great victims are those who tortured you because they lost all their humanity, humanness, *ubuntu*. It is only the beasts or wild animals, which don't have the image of God, could treat a person like that.
>
> CHAIRPERSON: We can say that here you are a young man who is carrying a heavy load to look after the parents who themselves are traumatised and sick and also to look after your brother's two children. And I want to comment you for the *ubuntu* to know that you are also responsible for the children of your brother if your brother is dead. We commend you for that.

Also in the TRC Report, which can be seen as one of the most influential archives reflecting on the TRC process, *ubuntu* takes a central position. In the chapter 'Ubuntu: promoting restorative justice' the TRC Report reads:

> We are also required to look again at the restorative dimensions of various traditions in South Africa, such as the Judaeo-Christian tradition and African traditional values. Neither is monolithic in its approach; both contain strong sources of communal healing and restoration. As such, they are sources of inspiration to most South Africans. As far as traditional African values are concerned, the fundamental importance of *ubuntu* must be highlighted. *Ubuntu*, generally translated as 'humaneness', expresses itself metaphorically in *umuntu ngumuntu ngabantu* – 'people are people through other people'. In the words of Constitutional

Court Justice Makgoro: "Its spirit emphasises respect for human dignity, marking a shift from confrontation to conciliation."

The Report continues by stressing that "a spontaneous call has arisen among sections of the population for a return to *ubuntu*, a call that has been vividly illustrated by the Commission process" (TRC Report 1998, 1/5: 124–127).

It was partly as a result of the reconciliation discourse constructed at the HRV hearings that the term *ubuntu* became firmly anchored in South African public discourse. *Ubuntu* was perceived as a concept typical for post-apartheid South Africa and it was seen as indispensable in the search for a united and peaceful society. All over the world *ubuntu* became the symbol for the new South Africa, implying that this moral characteristic was typically embodied by post-apartheid South Africans. South Africa also proudly identified with this new label and used it to boost its international image. I will come back to the use of this term as an inherent aspect of reconciliation discourse later on, since this term especially gained popularity in the post-Mandela era.

### 6.2.4 Reconciliation discourse following the Mandela era

Up to now, we have been mainly occupied with the ways in which reconciliation discourse took shape in South African society in the years immediately following the TRC process. We have noted that, in addition to the TRC, the role of Nelson Mandela can be considered as crucial in this respect. After 1999, when President Mandela was replaced by Thabo Mbeki, South Africa's rhetorical and socio-political reconciliation discourse was further developed.

Gradually, President Mbeki also came to recognise the power of reconciliation discourse. At the opening of Parliament in 2001, for instance, he openly praised the "Home for All" initiative and, also in the year 2001, he initiated a conference on a search for common values in South Africa. Although reconciliation was no longer the dominant discourse in society, the quest for reconciliation continued in various forms – also on the level of policy making. As stressed by Mda (2002: 281):

It may not be articulated as much as it was during the Mandela era, but it is in the content of government and civil society programmes that recognize the identities and the rights of minorities while affirming the previously disadvantaged majorities, such as women and black people. Indeed, the current president's (Thabo Mbeki) definition of an African in parliament has been inclusive of the members of all racial and cultural groups that call South Africa their home.

In those years, as part of reconciliation discourse, also the term *ubuntu* appeared continuously in political rhetoric, for instance in speeches by various Ministers. President Mbeki himself seemed to employ the term *ubuntu* abundantly in his political speeches and forms of address (see the website of the South African Government (http://www.gov.za/) for an overview of presidential speeches).

In fact, in the years following the Mandela era a subtle kind of competition was going on between two components of political reconciliation discourse, namely reconciliation itself and *ubuntu*. Under Mandela, especially after 1995, reconciliation seemed to be the most outspoken way to characterise the ideal relationship between South Africans. It appears that under the presidency of Mbeki the concept of *ubuntu* gained in popularity. We could say that under Mbeki political rhetoric became slightly more Africanist-oriented, stressing the fact that South Africans should feel proud to be Africans in the first place. As a result of this ideological move, political discourse felt more comfortable to embrace the term *ubuntu* than reconciliation. Reconciliation was strongly associated with the TRC and with the person of Nelson Mandela. *Ubuntu,* on the other hand, also embodied this reconciliatory dimension, but in addition it had a very strong traditional African connotation. Since it was perceived as typically South African, *ubuntu* also had a strong nationalist relevance, which suited the post-Mandela political rhetoric. Moreover, it seemed as if the term reconciliation necessarily referred to the apartheid past, while *ubuntu* rather had implications for the present and the future.

## 6.2.5 Reconciliation discourse outside politics

In addition to the realm of political rhetoric, reconciliation discourse continued to be explored and developed in other domains in the period after 1995. In the discourse of tourism and culture for instance, South Africa was, and still is, regularly framed as a 'rainbow country' or a 'multicultural' nation, characterised by diversity and peaceful coexistence (Rassool 2000: 1). Phrases such as 'South Africa: the world in one country' and 'South Africans, the rainbow people of God' have become strong identifiers of the new nation. Diversity through reconciliation has become an asset to South Africa, a positive characteristic aimed at, among others, attracting tourists. Clearly, not only internally, but also worldwide, reconciliation has become the identifying label of South Africa.

Moving to the domain of culture, post-apartheid theatre was also preoccupied with the themes of reconciliation. A number of plays dealt explicitly with the TRC and explored the general themes of forgiveness and reconciliation. The best known of these is probably 'Ubu and the Truth Commission', by Jane Taylor.

Apparently, in that post-1994 period, even former practitioners of protest theatre turned to the theatre of reconciliation (Mda 2001:281).

On an academic level the discourse of reconciliation has also definitely left its traces. Numerous courses, debates, conferences and discussion groups have been set up, all concentrating on the issue of reconciliation in South Africa. The number of academic publications on reconciliation has skyrocketed in post-1994: Brian Frost's 'Struggling to Forgive, Nelson Mandela and South Africa's Search for Reconciliation' (1998), Mark Hay's 'Ukubuyisana. Reconciliation in South Africa' (1998) and 'Pieces of the Puzzle. Keywords on Reconciliation and Transitional Justice' (2004), edited by Villa-Vicencio & Doxtader, are but a few examples.

On an institutional level, the TRC formed only part of the institutions of 'redress' developed by the new government. As early as the Mandela era, but mainly afterwards, long-lasting initiatives were developed at this institutional level. Let me just mention some of the initiatives taken in post-1994 or post-TRC South Africa (http://www.csvr.org.za/links.htm#tru): the activities of the Centre for the Study of Violence and Reconciliation (CSVR), which was established in 1989, were extended, by for example launching the Khulumani Support Group in 1995 and by setting up a 'Register of Reconciliation' in 1997; the Institute for the Healing of Memories was established in August 1998; and the Institute for Justice and Reconciliation was launched in May 2000. Small-scale initiatives were taken, such as the Lyndi Fourie Foundation and also universities participated in this drive towards reconciliation – for instance the University of Cape Town with its Transitional Justice Project and its Centre for Conflict Resolution.

All of these initiatives were, in one way or another, aimed at establishing a reconciled nation, by promoting the resolution of conflict and the reduction of violence, by offering workshops and discussion groups where people could talk about past traumas, or by promoting democratic nation building through research and analysis. Most of these institutions continue to be highly dynamic enterprises that are well-resourced. In addition, the reconciliation-oriented message is also spread through museums and monuments, such as the recently established Freedom Park in Pretoria and the Robben Island Museum on Robben Island.

Through the activities of some of the above-mentioned institutions we understand that in South Africa there are concerns about whether or not reconciliation is indeed making progress. The Institute for Justice and Reconciliation, for instance, has developed the Reconciliation Barometer project, which is a longitudinal study that will monitor the reconciliation process among South Africans (see http://www.ijr.org.za/baro.html). Also the CSVR has established its Transition and Reconciliation Programme in order to understand the relationship between historical conflicts, reconciliation, the prevention of violence, and the realisation of justice (see http://www.csvr.org.za/annrep/anntrp.htm).

Initiatives have also been taken to introduce reconciliation at the grassroots level of South African society. In 'Learning to Live Together' (Fanie du Toit 2003), Verwoerd gives a few examples of individuals who came together through the TRC and who continued their journey of personal reconciliation after the TRC had finished. Apartheid victims or their relatives help to promote healing among other traumatised victims, while apartheid perpetrators are committed to help reconstructing the communities in which they had caused suffering. In addition to the personal initiatives, this publication also illustrates practices of social reconciliation. All over South Africa community leaders are trying to enhance reconciliation, for instance by creating a platform for interracial cooperation and dialogue. In organisations and companies, reconciliation can be built through training and participation, and also at schools and among student leaders reconciliation is brought into practice. Boraine (2000c: 363) argues that "there are numerous examples in South Africa where the commitment to reconciliation, religious or secular, has transformed lives and has brought about a change of behaviour and a genuine attempt to right the wrongs within society". "Despite our country's history of conflict and prejudice", he continues, "there are countless examples of black and white finding each other and working together".

These examples clearly suggest that the TRC reconciliation discourse has left its traces in South African society on more than a discursive level. This reconciliation discourse also continues to be implemented on a practical basis, mainly on an institutional level, but also on the local community level.

### 6.2.6 A multilayered reconciliation-oriented reality

Based on the preceding paragraphs we can argue that, in the years immediately following the TRC process, as well as in current day South Africa, reconciliation discourse was and remains firmly anchored in both social and political discourse. It is possible that reconciliation discourse will be further developed in the years to come. However, it is very likely that interpretations of this multilayered term will continue to be debated. Various ways of talking about reconciliation will linger on in South African society, where the word will either be associated with political, social, institutional or cultural issues. Right now, it looks as if South Africa is between definitions of reconciliation. As Doxtader (2003: 132) puts it: "[since] its meaning and value [are] in flux, the question becomes how to (re)invent the term in light of the times".

This overview of the ways in which reconciliation discourse has been adopted in South Africa's socio-political and rhetorical reality cannot tell us whether or not reconciliation has indeed been incorporated by the majority of South Africans. It can tell us, though, that great efforts have been made by a variety of groups in South Africa, not least by the government. Quite clearly it is a reconciliation-centred reality – or a reconciliation-centred truth – that is put forward, not only on an individual, but also on an institutional or public level. Therefore, we could suggest that the HRV reconciliation discourse became highly influential in post-TRC South Africa, leading to a preferred although not univocal reconciliation-oriented reality.

Bearing in mind that the HRV discourse was multilayered and inclusive and that the term reconciliation was conceptualised divergently at the TRC site, it should be pointed out that reconciliation discourse has also comprised different facets in the post-TRC era. At the time of the TRC process reconciliation discourse seemed to be dogmatised by the government. At this government level the political aspects of reconciliation were dominant: reconciliation had to be legalised, for instance by making it understood in the 1996 Constitution. Also the institutional dimension of reconciliation was crucial, hence the establishment of a number of institutions trying to promote the reconciliation process.

For many South Africans, though, reconciliation is an interpersonal matter, which cannot be enforced by laws, regulations or institutions, but which can only be built on an individual basis. It is among this group of people that grass-roots initiatives are particularly meaningful. Many people emphasise the racial dimension of reconciliation, which is probably the interpretation of reconciliation South Africa is most commonly associated with in the world. Others concentrate on reconciliation between political factions, or on reconciliation between bearers of different cultures or speakers of different languages. In recent years, economic reconciliation has also become an issue – it is claimed that apartheid in South Africa still exists, though on a socio-economic rather than a racial basis (Mattes & Thiel 1998; Alexander 1999). In all of these cases, the term reconciliation is adopted by various groups in South African society to characterise the ideal situation post-apartheid South Africa is aiming for, be it with a political, a cultural, a national or an interpersonal connotation. These people usually frame the term reconciliation as a socio-political objective, or as a standard by which to judge the positive achievements of South Africa since 1994.

In contrast with these people, it seems as if some extremist groups, both white Afrikaners and black extremists, have appropriated the term. For most of these groups reconciliation was not part of their vocabulary before the TRC started to popularise the concept – mainly because most of them did not support the idea of a reconciled South Africa in the first place. It was then in the post-TRC era that they managed to incorporate the term in their political rhetoric. They explored various dimensions of the word, dimensions that had not yet been developed by the advocates of reconciliation. They interpreted reconciliation in a particular way; they changed the meaning and the reach of the term, in order for it to suit their views of society and to reach the target audience they had in mind. In contrast with the very wide interpretation of reconciliation before the TRC, these groups often recontextualised this notion according to their own ideological viewpoint. They also entextualised the term in a wide variety of text formats, usually texts that were highly critical about the TRC. For instance, by interpreting reconciliation narrowly they tried to prove that establishing a reconciled South Africa will hardly be possible in the future. In this way, they turned a term that was internationally recognised as the symbol of the TRC into a mechanism to reject the TRC process.

The differential accentuation of the term reconciliation by particular socio-political groups with divergent interests and experiences could result in what Voloshinov has described as the 'struggle over the sign' (Gardiner 1992: 89). This involves a term being appropriated by various groups in society, each trying to fix the meaning of this term and to ascribe to this term its own indexicalities and contextualisations. Often, it is the ruling socio-political group that tries to lend the sign an external and homogeneous character. In the case of South Africa's reconciliation concept, it appears that the term is indeed used by a wide variety of different groups, with a wide variety of different meanings – we could therefore talk about a 'struggle over the sign'. Up to now, however, it has been the multiplicity of significations that has gained the upper hand, rather than one stable, ideologically coloured meaning imposed by one particular group.

To sum up, in post-TRC South Africa there existed a wide variety of different interpretations regarding the notion of reconciliation. With its multivocal conceptualisation the term took a central position in a well-defined reconciliatory reality. Through its reconciliation discourse the TRC had helped to establish this reconciliation-oriented reality, a reality that could not be ignored or rejected in South African society. In fact, because the HRV reconciliation discourse was so multidimensional and inclusive, a wide variety of South Africans could identify with this discourse. In addition, thanks to the polysemy of the term reconciliation, there was no need for any of South Africa's socio-political groups to openly reject the concept. Even groups that were strongly opposed to the idea of a reconciled nation incorporated the term, sometimes even to express their criticism with regard to the TRC.

It is the existence of multiple versions of the reconciliation-concept, embedded in a multilayered and highly inclusive reconciliation discourse that created the potential for power in many different contexts. What I would like to suggest here is that, through its reconciliation discourse the Truth Commission exerted a great deal of *power* on South Africa's post-TRC society, extending its influence to a large number of different domains. In the next chapter I will contextualise this powerful influence of the TRC by dealing with the broader issue of discourse and power. I will conclude by defining the TRC as a *centring institution,* an institution that might have had a political agenda and which, through its all-embracing impact, has been crucial in the construction of post-apartheid realities.

# CHAPTER 7

# Exercising power through discourse

## 7.1    Introduction

Up to now we have analysed the reconciliation discourse as constructed at the HRV hearings. We have seen that it was a multilayered discourse, on an ideological, a historical and an identity level. By applying this layeredness differently, testifiers expressed themselves in ways that were, to a greater or lesser extent, either appreciated or ignored by the HRV commissioners. We have tried to construct the *archive* of the HRV hearings, the rules that define what in a given situation could or could not be expressed. The most-preferred utterances were embodied by what I have called the *ideal testifiers*. It was the discourse of these testifiers that the TRC wanted to capture, to spread to the nation and to preserve for future generations. Central to this preferred discourse was the notion of reconciliation, although we have seen that the HRV Committee was extremely flexible in allowing different interpretations of this term.

In Chapter 6 we saw how the discursive practices of the TRC were connected to a specific reality. We could claim that, through its reconciliation discourse the TRC not only contributed to the introduction of the term reconciliation in South African socio-political discourse, it also participated in confronting South Africans with a reconciliation-oriented reality. Because of the omnipresent influence of the HRV reconciliation discourse in South African society, this discourse could be seen as very influential and powerful. Its powerful impact was enhanced by the fact that the HRV reconciliation discourse was extremely multidimensional and inclusive and appealed to a wide variety of South Africans. It is with the power of this reconciliation discourse and subsequently with the power of the TRC that I will deal in this chapter. I will first elaborate on the relation between power and discourse; I will then set out how the TRC exercised power. I will recapitulate how the TRC exerted power in the context of the HRV hearings by situating this display of power in a theoretical framework. I will then finish by explaining how the TRC exercised power in South African society.

## 7.2 Power and discourse, the context

As stressed before, the TRC was in charge of establishing an official memory of the apartheid past. The TRC was invested with the authority to create an archive of what had happened in this traumatic period in South African history. The preservation of memory is always selective and implicated in power, hence my reference to the TRC's *archontic power*.

The crucial role discourse plays in the production of knowledge and in the exercise of power has been generally acknowledged among post-structural scholars working in the domain of language, power and ideology. I will not attempt to contribute to this debate; I will only refer to a couple of theories upon which some of my premises will be based. According to Bocock (1986: 16), in his discussion on hegemony, both Althusser's and Foucault's conceptions of power fail to conceptualise the role of human agents. Althusser claims that power is located in the state – and in its two components, the 'Repressive State Apparatus' and the 'Ideological State Apparatus'. Foucault, on the other hand, argues that power and knowledge are predominantly exercised through discourse. For Foucault, wherever there is a discourse in place power is to be seen exercised – especially referring here to discursive practices, such as exposés and writings belonging to institutions. According to Foucault, though, it is not only powerful entities, powerful institutions or powerful personalities that succeed in establishing a discursively constructed truth. Power is also generated because the entire system (also the 'powerless' people) discursively reproduces regimes of truth. This is Foucault's understanding of *positive power*, an item I will come back to with regard to the TRC later on. In the words of Foucault: "[...] truth isn't outside power, or lacking in power [... ]. Truth is a thing of the world: it is produced only by virtue of multiple forms of constraint. And it induces regular effects of power" (Gordon 1980: 131; Sanford 2003: 78). In this work I mainly follow the basic assumptions of Foucault, although also the concept of the Ideological State Apparatus can be applied to the Truth and Reconciliation Commission.

Foucault looked at the institutional causes of power. He identified a historical shift from sovereign power (state power) to disciplinary power (targeted at individuals) and biopower (oriented to the subjugation of bodies and the control of population in general, such as disciplining citizens by means of statistics and demographies) (Clegg 1989: 155; Crais 2002: 10). According to Foucault, power and discourse are closely related, for:

> Discourse can be both an instrument and an effect of power, but also a hindrance, a stumbling block, a point of resistance and a starting point for an opposing strat-

> egy. Discourse transmits and produces power, it also undermines and exposes it, renders it fragile and makes it possible to thwart it.　　(Foucault 1984a: 110)

Through discourse, Foucault argues, truths are 'normalised' and it is through these normalised truths that power is exercised very effectively. Or, as he puts it (in White & Epston 1990: 22):

> There can be no possible exercise of power without a certain economy of discourses of truth which operates through and on the basis of this association. We are subjected to the production of truth through power and we cannot exercise power except through the production of truth.　　(Foucault 1980: 93)

Bourdieu is another key scholar on the relation between power and discourse. He claims that cultural and symbolic elements such as arts and language can be situated on the level of symbolic capital, since they contain symbolic power. These elements are very efficient with regard to exercising power, since they are usually misrecognised as carriers of power (LiPuma 1993: 21–26). In this way, power is exerted in a hidden manner, through *symbolic violence* – hence being more fundamental than overt power relations (Robbins 1991: 66; Thompson 1994: 43–46).

Although Cicourel (1993: 99–107) follows Bourdieu in the view that discourse is indispensable to preserve power relations, he stresses, in contrast to Bourdieu, that discourse can also be used by people to exercise power consciously. A combination of conscious discourse framing and the subconscious introduction of discursive concepts was at stake before the HRV Committee. Importantly, as Bourdieu indicates, discourse is only powerful to the extent that this discourse and its users are perceived as legitimate and powerful. Power is not inherent in discourse (Robbins 1991: 141). The TRC was a highly authoritative and legitimate institution, indeed, hence the power associated with the discourse constructed at its hearings. We will see later that this institutional aspect probably had great implications for the acceptance of reconciliation discourse in South African society.

## 7.3　The TRC exercised power at the HRV hearings

In this section I will recapitulate how the HRV Committee exerted power at the actual site of the victim hearings. I will do this by applying the theoretical framework of Foucault's *procedures of restriction*, as explained in his 'L'ordre du discours' (1971 – the English translation I used dates from 1984). These procedures refer to mechanisms that determine why certain utterances could or could not be expressed. By doing so, I will largely summarise what has been explained in Chapter 5. This summary will be highly relevant, though, since, together with the findings on reconciliation discourse in society, as discussed in Chapter 6, Foucault's theoretical framework will serve as a point of departure for my discussion on TRC discourse and power in society later in this section.[14]

It has become abundantly clear in Chapter 5 that testifiers at the site of the HRV hearings did not have outright freedom in terms of what they said and how they said it. As a first set of mechanisms of restriction Foucault refers to *procedures of exclusion*. According to Foucault, the most obvious and also the most familiar procedure of exclusion is the *prohibition*. It is mainly through this concept of the prohibition that the link between discourse on the one hand and power and desire on the other is revealed. Foucault talks about three kinds of prohibition, which intersect, reinforce each other, compensate for each other and form a complex and ever-changing network. These three types are: 'taboo on the object of speech', 'the ritual of the circumstances of speech' and 'the privileged right of the speaking subject'.

At the HRV hearings the application of these varieties of prohibition is apparent. We have seen that in the discourse of the testifying victims certain topics were taboo. Narratives revolving around hatred, vengeance and intolerance were not appreciated, nor were statements involving individualism or racism. The hearings could not be used as a platform to spread political messages either. At a hearing in East London (on the 22nd of July 1996), for instance, a lady asked permission to "give a message to the Africans as we are gathering here", after she had finished giving her testimony. This lady was known as a militant member of Poqo, the military wing of the Pan-Africanist Congress. The leading commissioner seemed to be afraid that she would start sloganising and the testifier was cut short abruptly. The hearings could not be turned into a political rally and the commissioners had to keep control at all times.

The second kind of prohibition has to do with the ritual of the circumstances of speech. Although, as interpreted by Foucault, the word ritual should probably not be taken literally, it is a fact that the TRC proceedings have often been characterised as a ritual (Ross 1997; Bozzoli 1998; Krog 1998b; Buur 2003; Goodman 2003). In this ritual setting the atmosphere of religious reconciliation was overwhelming. Also on the level of the props (banners, slogans, candles, the cardinal dress of Desmond Tutu), the HRV hearings radiated a message of reconciliation

---

14. I use 'power' here as a shorthand, to refer both to *authority* and to actual *power*, and this in contrast with f.e. Arendt (1970). In an authoritative way the TRC could obviously influence events taking place at the HRV site. It could also determine events, so exercise power, for it was the TRC who determined according to which frame future generations would interpret the apartheid past, how they would cope with the present and how they would envisage the future.

and forgiveness. This setting – the circumstances of speech – imposed a reconciliation-oriented grid onto the testifying victims. The ritual setting was supposed to be cathartic and to contribute to the building of a reconciled South Africa. However, the pressure to comply with this ideal was so overwhelming that it probably limited certain expressions.

The third kind of prohibition distinguished by Foucault is the privileged or the exclusive right of the speaking subject. The victims who told their stories at the HRV hearings were given a special social status. As a result of the TRC proceedings a new category of South Africans emerged: victims of gross human rights violations. This referred to South Africans who had a lot of prestige in South African society, since they had testified before the TRC. Not only did TRC victims have a special status, it was also a status that granted them specific privileges – the right to get reparations for instance (only South Africans that were labelled 'TRC victims' could apply for reparations).

The importance of these testifying victims was not only based on the status attributed to them by the TRC itself, it could also be connected to the esteem given to them by their communities. We may not forget that these victims were purposely selected to represent a typical human rights violation and a larger group of victims of this human rights violation. They had a huge responsibility in that they were also supposed to represent the suffering of fellow community members. These testifiers were privileged in post-apartheid South Africa; they had the exclusive right to speak in the name of others.

This privilege granted them a great deal of discursive freedom, but it also imposed restrictions. Since they talked before the eyes of the world, it was to a large extent impossible to be untruthful. After the TRC hearings these victims would go back to their community members and families, who were sometimes familiar with the particular gross human rights violations or with the context in which these atrocities had taken place. As a result, telling lies was often highly improper.

Another principle of exclusion, according to Foucault, is not another prohibition, but *a division and a rejection*. We have seen in section 5.2.6 that all of the victims who appeared before the TRC were respected. Their discourse was never considered worthless; on the contrary, it was esteemed and valued. Because this appreciation was not unqualified and because it was not attributed to each testifier to the same extent, the issues of division and rejection also play a role here. First, on an overt level, division resulting in rejection could be detected at the stage preceding the actual hearings. On this meta-level testifying victims had to comply with a number of well-defined criteria. This led to a division and a rejection of a certain group of victims, first at the level of the statement taking and then on the level of selection to appear in public. Victims who were rejected at this stage did not get the favourable label of TRC victim, nor could they apply for reparations.

At the actual HRV hearings this division and rejection took place in a much more subtle way, since it was embedded in the constructed reconciliation discourse. In Chapter 5 I elaborated on the manners in which the testifier's discourse was pushed in a certain direction, resulting in the – sometimes explicit – rejection of certain discursive practices. I have argued that this rejection led to a division on the level of the concrete HRV testifiers: one group could be defined as *ideal testifiers,* while another group was less or non-ideal. The ideal testifiers would be the preferred victims to make up the TRC archive. The non-ideal testifiers were not excluded at the actual TRC site, but their voices were generally less frequently heard, mentioned or remembered in post-TRC discourse. For instance, when taking renowned reflections on the TRC process, such as 'No Future Without Forgiveness', by Desmond Tutu (1999b), or 'A country unmasked', by Alex Boraine (2000c), we notice that the examples taken are often illustrations of the incredible willingness to forgive expressed by a number of HRV victims. Archbishop Tutu (1999b: 82, 120) describes the victims who testified to the Commission as "remarkable, extraordinary and special"; he even calls them "VSPs, or Very Special People". No doubt that when using these favourable definitions, Archbishop Tutu has mainly those victims in mind who openly claimed to support reconciliation and forgiveness. Also other publications predominantly point at the victims whose discourse was reconciliation-oriented, while testifiers who were less cooperative are hardly mentioned.

Foucault considers the *opposition between true and false* as a third system of exclusion. This opposition was crucial before the Truth Commission. Foucault (1984a: 111–113) talks about the will to truth as a historical construction and as an institutionally constraining system, leading to a desire to classify, measure and observe. At the TRC the 'will to truth' was given a special dimension. One of the TRC's objectives was to reveal the truth as had happened under apartheid. At the HRV hearings this truth was to be derived from the victim testimonies, whereby especially narrative and personal truth were seen as crucial (these truths being two of the four truths distinguished by the TRC, see TRC Report 1998, 1/5: 109–113). We have seen that at the HRV hearings there was a preference for a specific kind of truth. As an institution aimed at breaking away from a terrifying past, the TRC was interested, amongst others, in emotionally loaded apartheid truths, in truths that portrayed South Africans as both victims and perpetrators, or in truths that originated in the past, but seemed to be continued in the present. I am talking here about a kind of *meta-truth,* which was different from the truth related to the actual content of the narrative.

As explained before, the TRC not only revealed past truths, it also tried to establish new realities and to introduce them into South African society. Therefore, the will to truth was both applied to the past, and projected onto future South Africa. However, not just any kind of truth was acceptable. The truth that was desired, constructed and subsequently made available to the public was clearly a truth that centred around the concept of reconciliation. The desire to understand and grasp the apartheid truth was in fact transformed into a desire to possess and control the present and the future truths.

Of the three great systems of exclusion that forge discourse – the forbidden discourse, the division leading to rejection, and the will to truth, Foucault sees the third one as the most dominant. He claims "the first two [systems of exclusion] are constantly becoming more and more fragile and more uncertain, to the extent that they are now invaded by the will to truth, which for its part constantly grows stronger, deeper and more implacable" (Foucault 1984a: 113–114). What is at stake in this will to truth, according to Foucault, is nothing more than desire and power – or a *desire for power*. We could already argue, indeed, that it was mainly through the desire to establish truthful discourse that the Commission managed to exercise power in post-TRC South Africa.

Foucault also distinguishes internal procedures of restricting discourse, namely *the genre, the author* and *the discipline.* At the HRV Committee the discursive genre could be described as oral narratives of trauma, largely situated in the past, combined with techniques taken from the genres of interrogation and the media. These narratives had an externally determined structure: victims first had to give some general information about their families, they then had to talk about the gross human rights violation suffered and they finally had to answer questions posed by the commissioners. This was a format that clearly involved discursive limitations. The structures of the oral traumatic narrative, the interrogation and the media discourse also contained internal restrictions inherent to the genre – for instance, testifiers had to speak comprehensibly in order to be understood by the commissioners and the interpreters, extralinguistic parameters of emotion were allowed and the interrogation had to be conform to the question-answer format.

With 'the author' Foucault does not necessarily mean the speaking individual who pronounces a word or writes a text. Rather, it is a principle that establishes the coherence and unity of discourse; it lies at the origin of the discourse's meaning and it acts as the focus of its coherence. In the case of the TRC, this author principle was fulfilled by what I have called *the archons* in Chapter 3. It was the archons who had the power to organise discourse, to unify it and to make it available for future archiving efforts. These archons imposed specific restrictions to the HRV narratives: the TRC structure, so also the discourse allowed at its hearings, was determined by a parliamentary act; next, the TRC commissioners and the testifying victims tried to bring coherence and unity in the HRV narratives at the actual site of the hearings; and finally, all of the actors involved in the continuous entextualisation process of the TRC narratives transformed these pieces of discourse, added extra layers of meaning, and then tried to unify all of the fragments of TRC discourse to create a coherent whole.

The final internal procedure to delineate discourse is related to the discipline. The reconciliation discourse constructed at the HRV hearings derived its forms from various disciplines, including legal discourse, a therapeutic consultation by a psychologist and a religious confession, all of which was cloaked in a strictly contextualised narrative of nation building and reconciliation. This network of complementary disciplines determined what could be accepted as truthful, as coherent and as systematic. It was this network that imposed the rules of the production of discourse. The testifiers had to express themselves in a manner that conformed to the rules of these disciplines that were operative in this specific historical TRC context. It was this disciplinary network that determined how testifiers had to frame their discourse on a historical, ideological and identity level, and that also determined how the commissioners were to react to these statements.

Foucault concludes his exposé on the discursive procedures of restriction by stressing that it is very abstract to separate some of these systems. Most of the time, he maintains, "they are linked to each other and constitute kinds of great edifices which ensure the distribution of speaking subjects into the different types of discourse and the appropriation of discourses to certain categories of subject" (Foucault 1984a: 123).

By implementing Foucault's framework on the reconciliation discourse established at the HRV hearings, I did try to deconstruct this framework. We have noticed, though, that the recurring pattern is always the same. In many different ways the discourse of the testifying victims was limited, controlled and managed. The final result was always a particular kind of reconciliation discourse, whereby the concept (and the term) of reconciliation formed a multidimensional central truth.

## 7.4    Power exertion yes, but …

Let me emphasise here that the exertion of power at the HRV hearings should be put in perspective. A number of authors are quite critical about the freedom of expression granted to testifying HRV victims (Bock et al. 2000; Harper 2000: 69; Grunebaum-Ralph 2001: 201) and indeed, as illustrated in Chapter 5, discursive constructionism was definitely an issue at the HRV hearings. Nevertheless, one should be aware of the fact that discursive power is a multifaceted concept and that the terms linguistic regimentation/manipulation cannot be used lightly.

We have seen that at the HRV Committee we could speak about inequality among the various discourse participants. To a greater or lesser extent, testifiers were indeed urged to direct their language in a certain direction. The HRV commissioners did set the boundaries to the types of statements that were permissible or sayable. It is important to stress, though, that at the actual hearings this execution of power should not be generalised. The discussion of Foucault's framework has told us that power was indeed at stake at various levels of the HRV process. However, at the same time, testifiers were respected, acknowledged and listened to, which was a new experience to many of them. In addition, although the commissioners sometimes tried to constrain the discourse of the testifiers, these victims also reacted against this discursive pressure. This resulted in complex *discursive struggles* (Hardy & Phillips 1999: 5) between members of this institutional field, as each tried to influence the way it was defined. This intricate network of different dimensions of power exertion, revealed through the interaction between speech participants, helped to co-construct the institutional context of the Commission.

As with any institution with asymmetric power relations between its participants, power was an issue at the TRC. We have clearly seen, though, that the HRV testifiers reacted against this division of power. Some of them manipulated the situation and participated actively in the construction of reconciliation discourse. In fact, all of the discourse participants possessed a certain amount of discursive power. They employed this power differently, but through the reconciliation discourse they all helped to establish the TRC setting.

In what follows I will continue to elaborate on the way the TRC exercised power, not only in the context of the hearings itself, but also on a wider societal level. Nevertheless, it did seem important to me to stress that this execution of power should not be conceptualised one-sidedly. Later on, we will see that also the TRC's socio-political execution of power should not necessarily be framed negatively, hence being reminiscent of Foucault's conviction that power is not always a negative force.

## 7.5    The TRC and power in society

Chapter 6 told us that the HRV reconciliation discourse had a considerable impact on post-TRC South Africa, leading to a reconciliation-oriented socio-political reality. The HRV Committee not only exercised power in the course of its process, it also left a powerful imprint on South African society. I have therefore suggested that the adoption of HRV reconciliation discourse corresponds to the fact that the TRC could be seen as a powerful institute in post-apartheid South Africa.

Because this reconciliation discourse was multilayered it appealed to many South Africans; people from different backgrounds felt appreciated and respected by the Commission. This multivocal discourse turned the TRC into a very inclusive institution, an institution that aroused a sense of belonging and that left a great impression on citizens in South Africa and beyond. The fact that reconciliation itself, as a multidimensional concept, also tended to be accepted by a wide variety of different groups, added to this powerful aspect of the Commission. In the following paragraphs I will attempt to deal with the wider implications of the power exerted by this HRV reconciliation discourse, implications going beyond the mere fact that this discourse became a favourite type of discourse in South Africa. Rather, I would like to offer some suggestions with regard to the impact the TRC might have had on the relative peace, stability and reconciliation in current day South African society.

## 7.6    The historical setting of the TRC process

We can argue that particular discourses only become visible at certain moments in time; time has to be ripe for certain discursive regimes to appear. For a number of decades the victim narratives that emerged at the TRC had been circulating among people oppressed by the apartheid regime or belonging to the liberation movements. It had often been prohibited to talk about apartheid atrocities outside of this group of subjugated people. If people were allowed to relate their experiences, these narratives were dismissed and the narrators were ridiculed.

After the fall of apartheid it became less risky to relate apartheid atrocities. The TRC was then regarded as a *safe space*, where experiences from the past could be relived in a reassuringly secure space (Ericson 2001; Gready 2003:23). More importantly, it was only after the fall of apartheid that these HRV stories were accepted and believed. It is commonly perceived, indeed, that the acknowledgement of the past was one of the main achievements of the TRC (Bizos 1998:132; Christy 2000:57). It was only after 1994 that narratives of apartheid atrocities could be related and accepted as a truthful past; it was only after 1994 that these narratives could start to exercise power on a wider socio-political scale.

I have suggested that the truth as established at the HRV hearings revolved around the concept of reconciliation. Also the fact that such a reconciliation discourse was deemed acceptable in post-TRC South Africa was connected to the historical setting. The majority of South Africans seemed to be convinced that a reconciliation-oriented transition process was the only alternative when trying to establish a peaceful society. They realised that after the TRC process had come to a conclusion, reconciliation had to be embraced – only then could civil war or extreme violence be avoided; only then could attempts be made to build a united nation.


## 7.7    The TRC as a powerful state institution

Clearly, the historical time frame was right in order for reconciliation discourse to be introduced in South Africa and for a reconciliation-oriented reality to be established. Therefore, the power of the TRC had a macro-dimension. This macro-dimension was not only based on the right historical period, but also on the fact that the TRC was established through a parliamentary act, which turned it into a widely recognised and authoritative state institution. As has been discussed by a number of scholars, it is mainly institutions that, in any society, exercise power through their discourse.

Foucault's work offers many theoretical suggestions to conceptualise discourse and to analyse it in relation to the historical rise of institutions. He stresses that actually occurring discourse is firmly and inextricably embedded in dimensions of social being and social organisation, and he compels us to see occurrences of discourse as intrinsically historical (Blommaert 2005: 100). According to Foucault, an institution necessarily has two poles: 'apparatus' and 'rules'. It is on the basis of these two elements that an institution exercises power (Deleuze 1988: 76–77). Especially state power is executed by institutional apparatus; in fact, the most general characteristic of an institution, whether or not this is a state institution, consists of organising the relations between power and government. The TRC, being established by a parliamentary act, was definitely a state institution. This means, following Foucault, that the power it exercised was not local, or limited to privileged places; instead, it was diffuse and all-embracing (Deleuze 1988: 26).

Since the TRC was clearly a powerful and authoritative institution, it is most likely that this institutional force promoted the introduction of reconciliation discourse in South Africa. I would therefore like to define the TRC as a *centring institution*, an institution which produces meaning and which creates indexicalities that gradually become mainstream in societal discourse. According to Blommaert (2005: 79) these centring institutions occur at all levels of social life. Blommaert (2005: 170–171) connects these centring institutions to *orders of indexicality*, which he defines as "stratified patterns of social meanings often called 'norms' or 'rules' and defining what kind of meanings and values the semiotic action or process would have in specific contexts". People have to orient their discourse to these orders of indexicality in order to have a voice and be acceptably understood in a given context.

It is the reconciliation discourse as an order of indexicality that is linked to the TRC as a centring institution. At every discursive moment people are subject to the pressure of these centring institutions. Together with the educational system, the church and political movements, the TRC as a state institution can be considered as a centring institution with a very wide scope – predominantly exerting influence within South Africa, but also beyond. Finally, Blommaert (2005:218) describes the state as the determining centring institution, since it is the state that controls access to language, that interprets and evaluates discourse and that determines the significance of terms. Other, non-state, centring institutions can be dominant as well, but they always occur in relation to the state.

The power the HRV Committee exerted through its discourse was thus grounded in the fact that the TRC can be considered as an authoritative state institution and in the fact that the historical time frame made this kind of discourse acceptable to the wider South African population. It is commonly claimed that the TRC was first and foremost a political instrument. In this context, the power exercised by the TRC is often perceived as politicised (i.e. a negative connotation). I will first give some qualifications with regard to this interpretation of the TRC. In the following section I will then elaborate on what I understand the implications of this TRC power to be.


## 7.8    The TRC as a political instrument?

A number of critics have claimed that the TRC, in its function as a centring institution, was purely an instrument of the ANC. In the elections of April 1994, indeed, the African National Congress won the elections with 62.6% of the votes (http://electionresources.org/za/provinces.php?election=1994). A Government of National Unity was established, which was a constitutionally defined multi-party government consisting of the seven political parties that were voted to power in these first democratic elections. In her discussion of the HRV hearings at Alexandra Township, Bozzoli (1998:173) clearly states that the choice of witnesses was heavily influenced by the ANC. As a result, it was the ANC that was openly identified with the public telling of the story of Alexandra's past. Also other authors claim that the impact of the ANC on the TRC process was a recurring feature. According to Roodt (2000), for instance, the TRC was definitely biased, since it underestimated and ignored black violence, NP-committed atrocities were exaggerated, while ANC crimes tended to be neglected. As stated by Jefferey (2001:85), the TRC treated the ANC delegation with friendliness and respect, while subjecting the NP delegation to persistent cross-questioning. Another critique, voiced by the IFP, said that in the selection of TRC commissioners and the appointment of TRC senior staff "loyalty to the ANC appeared to be a prerequisite" (Jefferey 2001: 86).

It was mainly the NP and the IFP who were convinced that the TRC was prejudiced in its dealing with apartheid and anti-apartheid violence (Christie 2000: 131). A large majority of the 17 TRC commissioners was 'pro-struggle', as also noted by Laurence (1998). Not a single one could be categorised as a representative of either the NP or the IFP. Only commissioner Chris de Jager had links to Afrikaner nationalism, but he resigned, accusing the Commission of bias. At the grassroots level people with ANC affiliations appeared to be less fearful of the Commission, while people with different ideological convictions lacked the same kind of trust (Laurence 1998). Norval (2001: 183) tells us that the critique that the TRC was an instrument of the ANC was not only voiced in 'conservative' quarters. The IFP and the PAC (Pan-Africanist Congress), but also some NGOs, were suspicious of the TRC's political agenda. Norval continues that this accusation might contain a grain of truth, not on the basis of straightforward partiality, however. Rather, it was with regard to the non-racial, homogeneous conception of nationhood in which the TRC resembled the vision of the ANC. On a more general, long-term level, Kjeldgard & Nexo (1999: 45) state that the ANC needed a Commission like the TRC "to consolidate the new state and to help the ANC in the ongoing struggle for hegemony". It is clear that according to quite a number of people, a political agenda was at stake when establishing the TRC.

Notwithstanding the numerous accusations of partiality, the Commission itself manifestly upheld its reputation of impartiality. People like Alex Boraine and Desmond Tutu pointed out that the TRC was objective and even-handed, for instance by maintaining that the liberation movements had also committed gross human rights violations in their 'just war against an unjust regime' (Buur 2000a: Chapter 10). In fact, the Commission was quite severe in its findings on the ANC, which resulted in a major disagreement between the ANC and the TRC. The ANC was dissatisfied about the way they had been portrayed by the Commission, nor did the TRC and the ANC-led government reach an agreement on the issue of Urgent Interim Reparations to apartheid victims, after the closing down of the HRV Committee (Buur 2000a: 72). In essence, the fact that all major political parties were dissatisfied with the conclusions of the TRC, proved that the Commission had been largely even-handed (Boraine 2000c: 231; Cherry 2000: 6).

Based on my discursive analysis, we can conclude that the HRV Committee tried its best to lend a voice to victims from all sides of the apartheid conflict. All political groups, social classes and ethnic groups were represented at the HRV hearings; since white victims formed such a small minority, these white apartheid victims even tended to be overrepresented at the HRV hearings, which completely overrules the critique of the National Party. The HRV committee members themselves belonged to various population groups, religions and professional backgrounds. It is true that commissioner de Jager, as a member of the Afrikaner community, resigned after some time. The other white, Afrikaans-speaking commissioner, Mr. Wynand Malan, submitted some minority positions prior to the publication of the TRC Report (see TRC Report 1998, Volume 5, Chapter 9). This might indicate that the TRC's method of working was rather in line with the non-Afrikaans commissioners. It should be recognised, however, that the Afrikaner community was in no way excluded from the Commission. All this confirms the inclusive character of the TRC, a centring institution that addressed the entire nation in an attempt to forge a common understanding of the necessity to live together peacefully.

At the level of the actual discursive practices we can note that the HRV commissioners tended to be largely unbiased when addressing the testifiers. Sometimes, ANC policy was explicitly defended, but in the same way, the ANC was also criticised. In particular, when victims of anti-apartheid crimes were allowed to speak, the commissioners often openly stated that violence could never be justified, no matter what the ideological motivations are. On the basis of this concrete discourse analysis, together with the arguments from people such as commissioners Boraine and Tutu, it becomes rather difficult to classify the TRC as an instrument of the African National Congress. Moreover, the first proposals and discussions regarding the TRC already took place during the negotiation period between 1990–1994. At that time, the National Party was still in charge, although the ANC was its main fellow negotiator. So, the TRC concept was also approved by the NP – some ANC negotiators were even convinced that the ANC had been pressurised to great concessions, since the amnesty process was an explicit condition from the side of the NP. When, in December 1995, the TRC Act came into effect, South Africa was ruled by the Government of National Unity. This meant that it was not only the ANC that was to decide how the country should be governed, and that the TRC came into existence as a result of a political compromise.

Rather than an instrument of the ANC, we could call the TRC an instrument of the ruling/decision-making parties between 1990-1998 (being the year in which the first part of the TRC Report was published). Indeed, it is clear that the TRC did have a political agenda: its objective was to start a process of national reconciliation, whereby inclusive nation building was definitely a political exercise. Therefore, it is also clear that the power exercised by the TRC in South African society can be seen as politicised. This politicised power did not seem to be dominated by one political ideology, though, which already tempers the negative connotations sometimes associated with TRC power.

## 7.9   TRC power and its impact on South African society

Let me now elaborate on the fact that, although part of a political agenda, the TRC's exertion of power should not necessarily be conceived as a negative force. According to Foucault, power does not only contain an oppressing or suppressing character, it can also be productive (in Devos 2004: 65). Indeed, we have noted in the previous chapters that the power exercised by the TRC, through its discourse, was first and foremost a reconciliation-oriented force, leading to a reconciliatory reality. What I would like to explain here is how TRC power might have had a favourable impact on South African society.

It is quite likely that the HRV Committee's reconciliation discourse and consequently also the reconciliation discourse in South African society, have shaped the way South Africans think, feel and act. As Gerwel (2000: 123) puts it, the initial idea of the TRC was to deal with the past as quickly and efficiently as possible, so that South Africans could put the past behind them. However, the TRC became so dominant in everyday life that it began to take a life on its own. The TRC became a kind of monument in and of itself to the past.

First of all, we can argue that the vagueness of the term reconciliation was a deliberate choice from the side of the TRC. It was an inevitable choice: defining reconciliation unambiguously and restricting reconciliation discourse in such a way that it would only allow for a number of limited interpretations, would never have had the same impact on South African society. If this had been the case, the debate on reconciliation would not have become so dominant in South Africa and never would so many people – both nationally and internationally – have started to reflect on the value of restorative justice and peaceful conflict resolution.

The power exercised by the TRC on a socio-political level can also be conceived as positive since it was a mechanism to *decentralise* power. All people who had participated in the TRC process – victims, perpetrators, TRC staff, but also the media, politicians, researchers and artists who used TRC material – felt as if they had contributed to 'the building of a unified and reconciled nation'. All of these people felt powerful to a certain extent and they felt proud to be part of the new nation. Because they were given a *voice* before the TRC they understood that they were now esteemed citizens of the new South Africa; they had gone from *subjected* people to *subjects* of the new state. It is even possible that the entire nation and the entire socio-political scene gained power as a result of the TRC proceedings, since not only TRC participants, but most South Africans might have felt committed to the TRC. They realised that their country was setting an example to the world and they might have felt part of this unique undertaking. This also means that powerless South Africans (uneducated, poor, marginal) might have felt a certain amount of power because of their emotional attachment to the TRC – here we clearly see the productive power of the TRC discourse at work. Everybody talked, discussed and read about the Commission, so it was this discursively produced regime of truth of the entire state system that generated power. This is what Foucault means when he talks about *positive power* – power that is rooted in society as a whole, power that belongs to everybody and power everybody can contribute to.

All this can be connected to the inclusive character of the TRC, a notion I have used throughout this text. I would consider inclusiveness as the superstructure of the entire TRC concept. First of all, this inclusive dimension was highlighted when discussing the diversity of the HRV testifiers. Through this diversity the TRC emphasised that apartheid had affected everybody, that the entire nation was a victim and that everybody should be healed. It was also as a result of this inclusiveness that testifiers – victim and perpetrator – could possess a double identity before the TRC. The respect that was attributed to each and every testifier before the HRV Committee also formed an important element of the inclusive nature of the Commission. Chapter 5 told us that the HRV reconciliation discourse was highly layered on an ideological, historical and identity level, which also stressed the inclusive nature of the Commission. A storytelling template was provided to the testifying victims, but within that format a lot of discursive freedom was accepted – thus appealing to a majority of South Africans. In section 6.1 we have seen that at the HRV Committee the reconciliation-oriented master narrative and the term reconciliation itself were constructed in a very vague and multidimensional manner. Most South Africans could relate to the polysemic concept of reconciliation, so also here the inclusive dimension is at stake.

Reconciliation not only became a national symbol, but also an internationally recognised identifier of the new South Africa. Clearly, by including all South Africans into the TRC process, by constructing a common narrative of the past and by stressing that all South Africans now had to work together to live in peace and stability, the TRC had inclusive national unity as its main objective. The inclusiveness of the TRC is like a Leitmotiv running through this work. It appears in different segments of this text and it is part and parcel of some of my main findings. Through the reconciliation discourse a majority of South Africans recognised themselves in one central concept. They all related to the term reconciliation and in many divergent ways they all identified with this concept. As a result of this reconciliation discourse, a majority of South Africans also felt connected to the TRC. Consequently, they all felt united, which could have formed a solid basis for the construction of new, democratic South Africa.

To sum up, the suggestion offered here is that as a result of the reconciliation discourse constructed at the HRV hearings, a reconciliation-oriented reality was established in South Africa. This reality was multifaceted, since the concept of reconciliation could be interpreted in manifold ways and because the reconciliation discourse in itself was inclusive and multidimensional. Ultimately the TRC's institutional power was extremely influential in South Africa. This power should not be seen as detrimental, but rather as a constructive and advantageous force in terms of South Africa's future.

# CHAPTER 8

# Towards a conclusion

## 8.1 In short: The main findings of this study

In this book I started from a socio-political phenomenon, located in one particular historical and geographical context, but with an influence on various other transitional processes, namely the South African Truth and Reconciliation Commission. The main objective was to try to gain insight into the ways in which the TRC contributed to a reconciled post-apartheid society in South Africa.

On the basis of a discursive analysis of the TRC Human Rights Violations hearings and a deconstruction of the Foucaultian archive of these hearings, we concluded that both at the actual HRV hearings and in South African society the TRC exerted a reconciliation-oriented power. In both of these contexts power should be interpreted as a complex and multidimensional concept. At the hearings we noted a fascinating combination of the granting and constraining of discursive freedom. The TRC also exercised power in South African reality, partly based on political motivations, but also inspired by a reconciliation-driven social consensus. In all this, TRC power should be regarded as a constructive and stimulating force, and not as a confining and adverse one.

## 8.2 The researcher's perspective

### 8.2.1 Methodology

Right from the start I explained that for this study I mainly borrowed from methods used in the domain of Critical Discourse Analysis. I did, however, also try to avoid some of the problems sometimes associated with CDA. Blommaert (2005: 38–41) mentions three negative features in relation with CDA: linguistic bias, closure to particular societies and closure to a particular time frame. CDA is said to be too restricted to solely a linguistic-textual analysis, without paying attention to the social context. It is crucial, as also Wodak (2006: 604) states, to investigate "what is not said, what happens after something was said, who has access to speak [..] and so forth". A variety of empirical data, as well as sufficient background information are inherent aspects of CDA (Wodak 2001: 65). Although we should not generalize, as rightly claimed by Wodak, it is true that few CDA researchers have paid attention to these contextual features. It has become clear that in this study South Africa's socio-political reality was the issue of special interest, although the construction of discourse formed the point of departure. It is also claimed that CDA mainly concentrates on discourse patterns in Western societies – this was clearly not the case in this work. Furthermore, in this book I also expressed a clear sense of history, another indispensable prerequisite of CDA research (Wodak 2006: 605). Power and linguistic repertoires have long histories, also in South Africa. Therefore, I elaborated on the differences regarding linguistic inequality under apartheid and in post-apartheid South Africa, and I devoted a great deal of attention to aspects of historical layering. In addition, I also concentrated on where reconciliation discourse comes from and where it goes to. I explained how this discourse came into existence and how it still reverberates in South African society at large. Finally, and in addition to Blommaert's critique on CDA, Critical Discourse Analysis essentially has to be diverse and multidisciplinary, since it should integrate "the best work of many people, from different disciplines, countries, cultures and directions of research" (Van Dijk 2001: 95–96). This study combined theories from Blommaert, Foucault and other poststructuralists, integrating insights taken from domains such as pragmatics, sociology and political sciences – thus creating an original framework.

In fact, I would stress that the domain of CDA contained most potential for this study, although I added my own interpretation to this academic field by applying it to an exceptional kind of data.

### 8.2.2   Evaluating the TRC?

In Chapter 2 I indicated that in the field of TRC studies an abundance of both positive and negative evaluations of the South African Commission can be found. Already during the time of its existence the TRC was highly controversial in South Africa. Especially in the aftermath of the process, though, the domains of reconciliation studies and conflict resolution flourished and worldwide the TRC was either praised or condemned. From all of these   often contradictory – opinions we can only draw two tentative conclusions: the TRC process cannot straightforwardly be classified as either positive or negative, and the results of this process will only be revealed in due time.

My intention has never been to evaluate the Commission. Nevertheless, in accordance with Critical Discourse Analysis, where the impossibility of impartiality is acknowledged – CDA offers a *critical awareness* in the first place (Blommaert 2005: 33), I did take a particular position vis-à-vis the TRC. By dealing with the aspects of power in and through discourse and by regularly using terms such as 'controlling', 'guiding' and 'directing', the impression might have been conveyed that I consider the TRC as an institution that was not able to live up to its grand ideals. I also claimed that the freedom of expression of testifying victims was regimented to a certain extent at the HRV Committee. Therefore, at the end of Chapter 5, the reader might have concluded that I merely regarded the entire HRV discourse as being solely constructed on the basis of underlying ideological motivations – hence not really serving the interests of the apartheid victims.

In the remainder of this text it became obvious that a certain amount of power exertion and discursive constructionism was indeed at stake. However, I also explicitly stated that exercising power and constraining discourse should not necessarily be conceived negatively in the case of the TRC. It has to be clear that I see the TRC first and foremost as a positive initiative. Not only was the Commission the only possible and indispensable option in post-apartheid South Africa; also in its concrete proceedings the TRC attempted to successfully fulfil its ambitious mandate. It is therefore quite understandable that conflict-resolving mechanisms in other countries have openly taken the South African TRC as a model. This means that the influence of the TRC reaches far beyond its local context. Not only did the Commission facilitate a national discussion on gross human rights violations and on issues of justice, reconciliation and democracy. It is also quite likely that the TRC instigated the worldwide debate on the value of restorative versus retributive conflict resolution.

In any case, it seems to me that the negative features of the TRC sink into insignificance when compared to the long-term implications this initiative might have had on South African society. One of the suggested conclusions of this study was that the TRC probably contributed to the continuation of an atmosphere of reconciliation among South Africans after 1994. This is also put forward by Gibson (2004) after having carried out his research on current day attitudes towards reconciliation in South Africa. He maintains that "[those South Africans] who are more accepting of the TRC's version of the truth are more likely to be reconciled" and "accepting the TRC's truth certainly did not contribute to 'irreconciliation'" (Gibson 2004: 334–335). Also du Toit (2006: 204) argues that "The TRC's most important legacy was to promote reconciliation that applied to national, community and individual needs". Recognising the discursive contribution of the TRC, he continues that "Reconciliation includes modest and open-ended efforts to draw all sides of the conflict into a society-wide debate [...]".

To me, the impact of the TRC might not have been manifest; it is not a tangible result we can clearly pinpoint. Instead, it can be described as an underlying current, a *tendency to reconciliation* many South Africans might not be openly aware of. This corresponds to the ideas expressed by Antjie Krog in the epilogue to the 1999-edition of her book 'Country of My Skull'. In this postscript she wonders whether the TRC process has indeed achieved reconciliation in South Africa. What is *not* visible, she claims, is "reconciliation as a mysterious Judaeo-Christian process". Instead, what we see daily is "reconciliation as one of the most basic skills applied in order to survive conflict". Following this line of thoughts she argues that survival is the essence of reconciliation. Therefore, Krog also seems to be convinced that it is first and foremost in the daily lives of South Africans that we find this intangible spirit of reconciliation. Krog also maintains that the word 'reconciliation' still resounds in the land. Indeed, in this work I have tried to demonstrate that it is partly as a result of the HRV reconciliation discourse that reconciliation became a point of discussion in South Africa. The concept became firmly rooted in South African public life, which might have influenced people's perspective on society.

### 8.2.3 Suggesting vs. concluding

What I suggest here is that the TRC *might* have been *one of the factors* leading to a reconciled South Africa. As many scholars have pointed out, the TRC was only part of a *reconciliation process* (see amongst others Bizos 1998: 238; Connor 1998: 8; Christie 2000: 178; Villa-Vicencio & Ngesi 2003). A direct causality between the TRC and reconciliation in South African can never be proven. Actors such as churches, civil organisations, community networks and government agencies have also contributed – and are still contributing – to the preservation of reconciliation in the country. It is sometimes also claimed that the traditional African concept of *ubuntu* might have been one of the factors underlying the willingness among South Africans to try and build a peaceful future together. I have argued before that charismatic figures such as Mandela and Tutu played a significant role in getting the notion of reconciliation accepted by a larger public. Finally, it is also possible that the rise in the standard of living of some South Africans, or the material provisions supplied by the government could have enhanced reconciliatory feelings.

In the course of this book I have not devoted too much attention to these alternative factors, as it is my assumption that it was mainly the TRC that instigated, stimulated and promoted this process.

This final suggestion has to be formulated very carefully, not only because of the largely unprovable nature of my findings, but also because I have been discussing and analysing South African society from an outsider's perspective. This means that, although I have tried to formulate my conclusions cautiously, it is quite possible that certain points of view will be controversial for people more familiar with South African society. However, it must not be forgotten that from the outset it was my deliberate intention to approach the Commission from an outsider's perspective. I have studied the TRC as it showed itself to the outer world through its publications on the internet and through the media. Just as looking at the TRC from the outside could be advantageous, approaching South Africa's socio-political reality as an outsider might also be interesting. It has given me the opportunity to investigate a crystallisation point in South African society without being too influenced by recent developments in the country. Since I looked at South Africa from a distance, my research was not affected by the country's terrifying history, nor by present-day sensitivities. Nevertheless, I would like to emphasise that I am very much aware of the difficulties connected to this outsider's perspective. I would never pretend that I have actually gained insight into South African society. I have merely offered some suggestions with regard to one single aspect of this complex nation.

This book might have opened up the debate on TRC reconciliation discourse and its relation with peace, stability and tolerance in South Africa. We may never forget that each reading and interpretation of records becomes a new reading. Each reading provides new insights into what actually happened, to the context and to the quest for understanding the past. In different ways this study has tried to add to these insights and by doing so it has tried to contribute to the TRC archive. Quite evidently, a huge domain of investigation in South Africa is still reserved for many more generations of researchers to come. The Commission and especially its implications on South African society need to be further investigated – the final aim being to add to the global debate on restorative justice and conflict resolution.

## 8.3    The South African TRC and beyond

To conclude this book I would like to discuss the uniqueness and/or the universal relevance of the South African TRC process. There is no doubt that the TRC was a unique kind of conflict-resolving mechanism. To begin with, the South African context in itself was rather unique. In South Africa the transition to democracy had not taken place as the result of a coup d'état or a civil war, but as a result of negotiations. Consequently, all of the parties previously in a state of war had to sit together to work out the democratic dispensation, which was an exceptional situation. South Africa also possessed a very good infrastructure, a democratic media institute and a highly developed legal system. All of this greatly enhanced the functioning and the decision-making of the TRC.

In addition, there were the unique elements of the TRC itself. Although the South African Truth Commission was the sixteenth commission of its kind, starting with the Ugandan Commission of Inquiry in 1974 (Hayner 2001:291), at the time of being established it did have a number of particular characteristics. One such unique aspect was that the TRC provided for individual amnesty while no blanket amnesty was granted, this in contrast with the Commission on the Truth for El Salvador, for instance. Another element was that the TRC had impressive powers of subpoena, search and seizure. Although these powers were not always used, the TRC did have the power to subpoena high-level politicians, or it could issue search orders against key individuals or institutions (for instance the head-quarters of the South African Defence Force or the ANC). In comparison, the well-known National Commission on Truth and Reconciliation in Chile had no power of subpoena and received very little cooperation from the armed forces (Hayner 2001:36). Furthermore, the TRC was also unique in its transparency, for example in the selection of the commissioners, the openness to the media and the holding of public hearings. This contrasted with similar initiatives, like the National Commission on the Disappeared in Argentina, which did not hold pub-lic hearings at all. This Commission heard testimony in private and information only emerged with the release of the final report. Finally, the South African TRC was also the first to create a witness protection programme, which strengthened its investigative powers and allowed witnesses to come forward with information that might put them at risk (TRC Report 1998, 1/4:54–55).

In the final years of the 20th and in the beginning of the 21st century there was a worldwide tendency to approach conflict resolution from a restorative rath-er than from a retributive perspective. The International Centre for Transitional Justice (ICTJ) is currently working in close to thirty countries, either to help set-ting up truth commissions, such as in Kenya, Burundi, Indonesia or Northern Ireland, or to follow up on truth and reconciliation processes that have taken place already, such as in Morocco, South Africa, Guatemala, Ghana, Liberia and Peru (for more information see http://www.ictj.org). The activities of this Inter-national Centre prove that establishing reconciliation in a divided country is a burning issue all over the globe.

South African TRC experts have been involved in the establishment of many of these processes of transitional justice, in for example Burundi, Lebanon, Mo-rocco, Kosovo and Peru and indeed, many of the features that turned the South African TRC into a success, especially the unique characteristics mentioned above, could be adapted and then used in other situations. One example can be given from the Truth and Reconciliation Commission in Sierra Leone. The estab-lishment of this Commission was also guided by staff members from the South African TRC and this Commission completed its work in October 2004. One striking aspect of the Sierra Leone Commission is that it has a very informative and transparent website (http://www.trcsierraleone.org/drwebsite/publish/index.

shtml). This website contains the entire final report and many very useful links and is comparable to the South African TRC website. It is characteristics like these that can easily be taken over in other transitional justice processes.

Importantly, as a result of the very special local context, the South African model should always critically be examined while trying to find out which elements can be copied. The ICTJ has always provided a critical voice in countries where the South African model has been adopted as a one-size-fits-all approach to transitional justice, with little or no attempt made to customise it to the particular context. Countries such as Ghana and Algeria were planning to simply adopt the South African amnesty legislation, although this would have been pernicious to their own peace process (http://www.ictj.org/en/where/region1/625.html).

However, based on my discursive research in particular, I would like to highlight three fundamental elements of the South African TRC that could be taken over by other countries trying to address a violent past. First of all, the Human Rights Violations Committee provided a forum for thousands of victims to talk about their sufferings under apartheid. These victims came from South African towns, villages or remote areas and the majority of them did not have a high political, social or religious profile. These victims can be considered as ordinary South Africans, testifying in their own mother tongue and surrounded by family and friends to support them. One of the great merits of the TRC is that it gave a voice to these ordinary citizens. By testifying before the TRC they participated in the story of nation-building; in this way they might have felt more committed to the new South African nation and they might have been more willing to work together in the construction of a peaceful future. Giving a voice to citizens and especially to victims of past atrocities is one of the main characteristics of the South African TRC that could be repeated in other contexts. In transitional processes or truth commissions all over the world, particular attention should be paid to listening to and respecting ordinary citizens. This is not only beneficial to the TRC process itself, but also to the future of previously divided nations.

Secondly, by means of the testimonies of apartheid victims and perpetrators, the TRC composed a collective memory, an official archive of the apartheid past. This archive was reflected in the TRC Report and, even more importantly, in the recordings and the transcriptions of the testimonies. This officially authorised and undeniable archive will for ever be cherished by future generations. There does exist a record of the apartheid past now and this record will always be there to be consulted and analysed. Creating an officially recognised archive that is open to the public and to national and international researchers is also an aspect of the TRC that could be copied by other countries.

Thirdly, the Human Rights Violations hearings formed a template for talking about a traumatic past. Previously, people did not know how to talk about atrocities, how to express emotions of grief and anger – definitely not in public. As a result of this testimonial format smaller truth commissions were set up in schools, in companies and in local neighbourhoods in South Africa (see section 2.7). People now knew how to listen to victims, how to pay respect and how to deal with their emotions and memories. Similarly, in other countries where truth commissions have been established, the reconciliation discourse created at the hearings could be taken as an example for initiatives of the same kind but on a smaller scale. We must not forget that in many countries a truth commission is only a first step on the way to unity and reconciliation. In view of this, it is often important that there is a follow-up to the TRC process, for instance in the form of micro-commissions in various contexts all over the country.

The three above-mentioned characteristics also played a role in the fact that the TRC reconciliation discourse greatly impacted on South African society, as described in this book. We could therefore wonder whether it would be possible for other truth commissions to have a same reconciliation-oriented impact on society, through its reconciliation discourse. Based on the analyses in this work, we can claim that reconciliation discourse might definitely be constructed in other countries as well and that the impact on society might indeed be similar as in South Africa. We have also seen, though, that the South African transitional process contains a number of specific elements, which makes it impossible to merely duplicate this process.

During my research I have only concentrated on the South African TRC; I do not have specialised knowledge with regard to other reconciliation processes. However, nation-building and reconciliation are often – if not always – at stake in transitional processes. Besides, in all countries where a truth commission has been established since the year 2000, public hearings were organised and the media was involved. Taking all these elements together, it is conceivable that a same kind of reconciliation discourse was created – with the same features of encouraging reconciliation, steering away from anger and revenge, and offering freedom of expression to previously silent population groups.

Nevertheless, everything always depends on the TRC legislation, on the local context, on the individual histories of the testifiers, on the profiles and attitudes of the TRC commissioners, on the reaction of the audience and on the national security situation. Based on the South African situation I can only say that a similar link between reconciliation discourse, power and society *might be possible* in other countries.

Finding out whether these findings for South Africa can in any way be expanded to other countries dealing with a traumatic past is a challenge to be taken up by future researchers.

# References

Abu-Lughod, L. & Lutz C. A. 1990. "Introduction: Emotion, discourse, and the politics of everyday life." In *Language and the politics of emotion*, C. A. Lutz & L. Abu-Lughod (eds.), 1–23. Cambridge: Cambridge University Press.

Ackermann, D. 1996. "On Hearing and Lamenting, Faith and Truth Telling." In *To Remember and to Heal. Theological and Psychological Reflections on Truth and Reconciliation*, R. H. Botman & R. Petersen (eds.), 44–59. Cape Town: Human & Rousseau.

Adam, H. 1997. "Contradictions of Liberation: Truth, Justice and Reconciliation in South Africa." *Paper presented at the Vancouver Institute Lecture*. November 29, 1997, University of British Columbia, Vancouver.

Adam, H. & Adam, K. 2000. "The politics of memory in divided societies." In *After the TRC, Reflections on truth and reconciliation in South Africa*, W. James & L. Van de Vijver (eds.), 46–52. Cape Town: David Philips Publishers.

Adebayo, A. 1996. "Towards a New African Order with a New South Africa." In *South Africa & Africa. Within or Apart?*, A. Adebayo (ed.), 217–236. Cape Town: Sadri Books.

Africa, N. 1999. "Les politiques publiques en faveur du bien-être. Les ressources de l'institionnalisation." In *La République d'afrique du Sud. Nouvel Etat, Nouvelle Société*, G. Conac, F. Dreyfus & N. Maziau (eds.), 127–142. Paris: Economica.

African History Online. 2005. http://africanhistory.about.com/library/glossary/bldef-inDuna.htm.

Afrikaans-English Online Dictionary. 2000. http://dictionaries.travlang.com/AfrikaansEnglish/.

Ailola, D. A. & Montsi, F. L. 1999. "Language, Law and Power in South Africa: The Alienation of the Majority from the Legal System." In *Knowledge in Black and White*, Kwesi Kwaa Prah (ed.), 133–142. Cape Town: Centre for Advanced Studies of African Society.

Alexander, N. 1999. "Prospects for a non-racial future in South Africa." *Unpublished Paper*. University of Cape Town.

Alexander, N. 2002. *An Ordinary Country*. Pietermaritzburg: University of Natal Press.

Allan, A. 2000. "Truth and reconciliation: A psycholegal perspective." *Ethnicity & Health* 5 (3): 191–219.

Allan, S. 1998. "News from NowHere: Televisual News Discourse and the Construction of Hegemony." In *Approaches to Media Discourse*, A. Bell & P. Garrett (eds.), 105–141. Oxford: Blackwell Publishers Limited.

Allen, J. 1999. "Balancing justice and social unity: Political theory and the idea of a truth and reconciliation commission." *49 University of Toronto Law Journal*: 315–353.

Allen, J. 2001. "Between retribution and restoration: Justice and the TRC." *South African Journal of Philosophy* 20 (1): 22–41.

Ally, R. 1999. *The Truth and Reconciliation Commission: Legislation, Process and Evaluation of Impact, Occasional Paper No 12 June 1999*. Pretoria: Centre for Human Rights.

Althusser, L. 1971. *Lenin, philosophy and other essays*. London: Verso.

Alvarez-Caccamo, C. 1996. "The power of reflexive language(s): Code displacement in reported speech." *Journal of Pragmatics* 25 (1): 33–59.

Alvarez-Caccamo, C. 1998. "From 'switching code' to 'code-switching': Towards a reconceptualization of communicative codes." In *Code-Switching in Conversation. Language, interaction and identity*, P. Auer (ed.), 29–50. London: Routledge.

Amadiume, I. & An-Na'im, A. 2000. "Introduction: Facing Truth, Voicing Justice." In *The Politics of Memory. Truth, Healing and Social Justice*, I. Amadiume & A. An-Na'im (eds.), 1–20. London: Zed Books.

ANC Manifesto Online. 1999. www.anc.org.za/elections/manifesto/manifestotext.txt.

Anderson, B. 1983. *Imagined Communities*. London: Verso.

Anderson, C. 2002. "Off the Hook: Winnie Mandela, White Guilt and the TRC." *African Studies Association 45th Annual Meeting*. Washington DC, December 2002.

Andrews, P. E. 1999. "Affirmative action in South Africa: Transformation or tokenism?" *Law in Context* 15 (2): 80–109.

Anthonissen, Ch. 2007. "Critical discourse analysis as an analytic tool in considering selected, prominent features of TRC testimonies." In *Discourse and Human Rights Violations,* Ch. Anthonissen & J. Blommaert (eds.), 65–88. Amsterdam: John Benjamins Publishing Co.

Arendt, H. 1970. *Geweld, Macht en Onmacht*. Utrecht: Spectrum.

Asad, T. 1993. "The Concept of Cultural Translation in British Social Anthropology." In *Genealogies of Religion. Discipline and Reason of Power in Christianity and Islam*, T. Asad (ed.), 171–199. Baltimore: The John Hopkins University Press.

Ash, T. G. 1997. "True confessions." *New York review of books*, 49: 17 (7): 33–38.

Ashforth, A. 1990. *The Politics of Official Discourse in twentieth-century South Africa*. Oxford: Clarendon Press.

Asmal, K. 1996. "South Africa in Africa: A South African perspective." In *South Africa & Africa. Within or Apart?*, A. Adebayo (ed.), 29–36. Cape Town: Sadri Books.

Asmal, K., Asmal, L. & Roberts, R. S. 1997. *Reconciliation Through Truth, a Reckoning of Apartheid's Criminal Governance*. Cape Town: David Philip Publishers.

Asmal, K., Asmal, L. & Roberts, R. S. 2000. "When the assassin cries foul: The modern Just War doctrine." In *Looking Back, Reaching Forward, Reflections on the Truth and Reconciliation Commission of South Africa*, Ch. Villa-Vicencio & W. Verwoerd (eds.), 86–98. Cape Town: University of Cape Town Press.

Auer, P. 1984. *Bilingual Conversation*. Amsterdam: John Benjamins Publishing Company.

Auer, P. 1998. "Introduction: *Bilingual Conversation* revisited." In *Code-Switching in Conversation. Language, interaction and identity*, P. Auer (ed.), 1–24. London: Routledge.

AWEPA & the African European Institute. 1998. *Truth and Reconciliation in Democratic Transition: The South African example*. Amsterdam: AWEPA.

Bakhtin, M. M. 1981. *The Dialogic Imagination*. Austin: University of Texas Press.

Bakhtin, M. M. 1984. *Problems of Dostoevsky's poetics*. Manchester: Manchester University Press.

Barnard, R. 2001. "Speaking Places: Prison, Poetry, and the South African Nation." *Research in African Literatures* 32 (3): 155–162.

Barnett, C. 2000. "Language Equity and the Politics of Representation in South African Media Reform." *Social Identities* 6 (1): 64–90.

Barrell, H. 1990. *MK, the ANC's armed struggle*. Harmondsworth: Penguin Books Ltd.

Battersby, J. 1997. "It is time for acknowledgement." In *Rhodes Journalism Review, Online Edition 14*, A. Garman & G. Berger (eds.). School of Journalism and Media Studies, Rhodes University, South Africa.

Bauman, R. 2000. "Language, Identity, Performance." *Pragmatics* 10 (1): 1–5.

Bauman, R. & Briggs, Ch. L. 2000. "Language Philosophy as Language Ideology: John Locke and Johann Gottfried Herder." In *Regimes of Language. Ideologies, Polities, and Identities*, P. V. Kroskrity (ed.) 139–204. Santa Fe: School of American Research Press.

Beaman, K. 1984. "Coordination and Subordination Revisited: Syntactic Complexity in Spoken and Written Narrative Discourse." In *Coherence in Spoken and Written Discourse*, D. Tannen (ed.), 45–80. Norwood: Ablex Publishing Corporation.

Becker, C. 1999. "Memory/Monstrosity/Representation." *The TRC: Commissioning the Past Conference*. Johannesburg: University of the Witwatersrand, 11–14 June 1999.

Bell, A. 1998. "The Discourse Structures of News Stories." In *Approaches to Media Discourse*, A. Bell & P. Garrett (eds.), 64–104. Oxford: Blackwell Publishers Limited.

Bell, T. & Ntsebeza, D. B. 2001. *Unfinished Business. South Africa, Apartheid & Truth*. Observatory: RedWorks.

Bellamy, R. 1994. "The Social and Political Though of Antonio Gramsci." In *The Polity Reader in Social Theory*: 32–38. Cambridge: Polity Press.

Benezer, G. 1999. "Trauma signals in life stories." In *Trauma and Life Stories. International Perspectives*, K. L. Rogers & S. Leydesdorff with G. Dawson (eds.), 29–44. London: Routledge.

Benke, G. & Wodak, R. 2003. "Remembering and forgetting: The discursive construction of generational memories." In *At War with Words*, M. N. Dedaic & D. N. Nelson (eds.), 215–244. Berlin: Mouton de Gruyter.

Bennett, J. F. 1997. "Credibility, plausibility and autobiographical oral narrative: Some suggestions from the analysis of a rape survivor's testimony." In *Culture, Power & Difference, Discourse Analysis in South Africa*, A. Levett, A. Kottlet, E. Burman & I. Parker (eds.), 96–108. Cape Town: University of Cape Town Press.

Bernstein, B. 1971. *Class, Codes and Control. Volume 1. Theoretical Studies towards a Sociology of Language*. London: Routledge & Kegan Paul.

Bester, R. 2000. At the edges of apartheid memory. *Paper Online:* http://www.museums.org.za/sam/conf/enc/bester.htm.

Bester, R. 2002. "Trauma and Truth." In *Experiments with Truth. Documenta 11_Platform2*, O. Enwezor et al. (eds.), 155–174. Ostfildern-Ruit: Hatje Cantz Publishers.

Bethke E. J. 1997. "True Confessions." *New Republic* 217 (19): 12–14.

Bhabha, H. K. 1990a. "Introduction: Narrating the nation." In *Nation and Narration*, H. K. Bhabha (ed.), 1–7. London: Routledge.

Bhabha, H. K. 1990b. "DessemiNation: Time, narrative, and the margins of the modern nation." In *Nation and Narration*, H. K. Bhabha (ed.), 291–322. London: Routledge.

Bhargava, R. 2000. "The moral justification of truth commissions." In *Looking Back, Reaching Forward, Reflections on the Truth and Reconciliation Commission of South Africa*, Ch. Villa-Vicencio & W. Verwoerd (eds.), 60–67. Cape Town: University of Cape Town Press.

Bharucha, R. 2002. "Between Truth and Reconciliation: Experiments in Theater and Public Culture." In *Experiments with Truth. Documenta 11_Platform2*, O. Enwezor et al. (eds.), 361–388. Ostfildern-Ruit: Hatje Cantz Publishers.

Biber, D. & Finegan, E. 1989. "Styles of stance in English: Lexical and grammatical marking of evidentiality and affect." *Text* 9 (1): 93–124.

Biko, N. 2000. "Amnesty and denial." In *Looking Back, Reaching Forward, Reflections on the Truth and Reconciliation Commission of South Africa,* Ch. Villa-Vicencio & W. Verwoerd (eds.), 193–198. Cape Town: University of Cape Town Press.

Binns, T. & Nel, E. 1999. "Beyond the development impasse: The role of local economic development and community self-reliance in rural South Africa." *The Journal of Modern African Studies* 37 (3): 389–408.

Bird, E. & Garda, Z. 1998. "Reporting the Truth Commission. Analysis of Media Coverage of the Truth and Reconciliation Commission of South Africa." *Gazette* 59 (4–5): 331–343.

Bizos, G. 1998. *No One to Blame? In Pursuit of Justice in South Africa.* Claremont: David Philip Publishers Ltd.

Black, D. R. & Swatuk, L. A. 1997. "The 'New' South Africa in Africa: Some Tentative Conclusions and Prognostications." In *Bridging the Rift: The New South Africa in Africa,* L. A. Swatuk & D. R. Black (eds.), 221–246. Boulder: Westview Press.

Blom, J-P. & Gumperz, J. J. 1972. "Social Meaning in Linguistic Structure: Code-Switching in Norway." In *Directions in Sociolinguistics. The Ethnography of Communication,* J. J. Gumperz & D. Hymes (eds.), 407–434. New York: Holt, Rinehart and Winston, Inc.

Blommaert, J. 1997. "Introduction: Language and politics, language politics and political linguistics." In *Political Linguistics,* J. Blommaert & C. Bulcaen (eds.), 1–10. Amsterdam: John Benjamins Publishing Company.

Blommaert, J. 1999a. "The debate is open." In *Language Ideological Debates,* J. Blommaert (ed.), 1–38. Berlin: Mouton de Gruyter.

Blommaert, J. 1999b. "The debate is closed." In *Language Ideological Debates,* J. Blommaert (ed.), 425–438. Berlin: Mouton de Gruyter.

Blommaert, J. 1999c. "Analyzing African asylum seekers' stories: Scratching the surface." *Discourse & Society* 12: 413–449.

Blommaert, J. 2001. "Context is/as Critique." In *Critique of Anthropology 21/1,* J. Gledhill & S. Nugent (eds.), 13–32. London: SAGE Publications.

Blommaert, J. 2003. "Orthopraxy, writing and identity. Shaping lives through borrowed genres in Congo." In *Re/reading the past. Critical and functional perspectives on time and value,* J. R. Martin & R. Wodak (eds.), 177–194. Amsterdam: John Benjamins Publishing Co.

Blommaert, J. 2004a. "In and out of class, codes and control: Globalisation, discourse and mobility." In *Dislocations/Relocations: Narratives of displacement,* M. Baynham & A. De Fina (eds.), Manchester: St.Jerome.

Blommaert, J. 2004b. *Workshopping. Professional vision, practices and critique in discourse analysis.* Gent: Academia Press.

Blommaert, J. 2005. *Discourse. A Critical Introduction.* Cambridge: Cambridge University Press.

Blommaert, J. & Bulcaen, C. 2000. "Critical Discourse Analysis." *Annual Review of Anthropology* 29: 447–466.

Blommaert, J. & Slembrouck, S. 1995. "La construction politico-rhétorique d'une nation flamande." In *Les grands myths de l'jistoire de Belgique, de Flandre et de Wallonie,* Anne Morelli (ed.), 263–280. Bruxelles: Editions Vie Ouvrière.

Blommaert, J. & Slembrouck, S. 2000. "Data formulation as text and context: The (aesth)etics of analysing asylum seekers' narratives." *LPI Working Paper n°2.* Gent (http://bank.rug.ac.be/lpi/LPI2.doc).

Blommaert, J. & Verschueren, J. 1992. "The Role of Language in European Nationalist Ideologies." *Pragmatics* 2 (3): 355–375.

Blommaert, J. & Verschueren, J. 1996. "European Concepts of Nation-Building." In *The Politics of Difference. Ethnic premises in a world of power*, E. N. Wilmsen & P. McAllister (eds.), 104–123. Chicago: The University of Chicago Press.

Blommaert, J. & Verschueren, J. 1998. "The Role of Language in European Nationalist Ideologies." In *Language Ideologies. Practice and Theory*, B. B. Schieffelin, K. A. Woolard & P. V. Kroskrity (eds.), 189–210. New York: Oxford University Press.

Blommaert, J., Bock M. & McCormick, K. 2001. "Narrative inequality and the problem of hearability in the TRC hearings." *Unpublished Paper.*

Blommaert, J. et al. 2001. "Discourse and Critique: Part One Introduction." In *Critique of Anthropology* 21/1, J. Gledhill & S. Nugent (eds.), 5–12. London: SAGE Publications.

Bloom, L. 2000. "After the war is over, truth and reconciliation? Impressions and reflections." *Psychology in Society* 26: 43–52.

Bloomfield, D. et al. 2003. *Reconciliation After Violent Conflict. A Handbook*. Stockholm: International Institute for Democracy and Electoral Assistance.

Bock, M., McCormick, K. & Raffray, C. 2000. "Fractured truths: Multiple discourses in South Africa's Truth and Reconciliation Commission." *Paper presented at Centre for African Studies Seminar*, University of Cape Town, August 2000.

Bocock, R. 1986. *Hegemony*. Chichester: Ellis Horwood Limited.

Boraine, A. 1995. "Truth and Reconciliation". *South African Outlook* 55: 55–56.

Boraine, A. 1998. "Reigning in impunity for international crimes and serious violations of fundamental human rights." In *Essays on the Truth and Reconciliation Commission*, Embassy of South Africa (ed.), 21–25. Den Haag: Embassy of South Africa.

Boraine, A. 2000a. "The Language of Potential." In *After the TRC, Reflections on truth and reconciliation in South Africa*, W. James & L. Van de Vijver (eds.), 74–81. Cape Town: David Philips Publishers.

Boraine, A. 2000b. "Truth and Reconciliation in South Africa: The Third Way." In *Truth versus justice: The morality of truth commissions*, R. I. Rotberg & D. Thompson (eds.), 141–157. Princeton: Princeton University Press.

Boraine, A. 2000c. *A Country Unmasked. Inside South Africa's Truth and Reconciliation Commission*. Cape Town: Oxford University Press.

Boraine, A. 2003. "South Africa's Amnesty Revisited." In *The Provocations of Amnesty: Memory, Justice and Impunity*, Ch. Villa-Vicencio & E. Doxtader (eds.), 165–180. Claremont: David Philip Publishers.

Boraine, A. & Levy, J. (eds.). 1995. *The Healing of a Nation?* Cape Town: Justice in Transition.

Boraine A., Levy, J. & Scheffer, R. (eds.). 1997. *Dealing with the Past, Truth and Reconciliation in South Africa*. Cape Town: Institute for Democracy in South Africa.

Borer, T. A. 2001. "Reconciliation in South Africa. Defining Success." *Kroc Institute* Occasional Paper, March 2001.

Boroughs, D. 1997. "Will the Truth set them free?" *US News and World Report* 122 (16): 42–45.

Botman, R. H. 1996. "Narrative Challenges in a Situation of Transition." In *To Remember and to Heal. Theological and Psychological Reflections on Truth and Reconciliation*, R. H. Botman & R. Petersen (eds.), 32–43. Cape Town: Human & Rousseau.

Botman, R. H. 1997. "Justice that Restores. How Reparation Must be Made." *Track Two* 6 (3&4).

Bourdieu, P. 1991. *Language & Symbolic Power*. Cambridge: Polity Press.

Bourdieu, P. 1994. "Social Space and Symbolic Power." In *The Polity Reader in Social Theory*: 111–120. Cambridge: Polity Press.

Bourdieu, P. & Passeron, J.-C. 1977. *La Réproduction: Eléments pour une Théorie du Système d'Enseignement*. Paris: Minuit.

Bozzoli, B. 1998. "Public Ritual and Private Transition: The Truth Commission in Alexandra Township, South Africa 1996." *African Studies* 57 (2): 167–195.

Braid, M. 1997. "South Africa's Bid to Pacify It's Ghosts. Can the Victims Live with Amnesty?" *World Press Review, February 1997*: 11–12.

Braude, C. 1997. "Media should get the truth out." *Mail & Guardian South Africa*. 13th February 1997: 7.

Braudel, F. 1969. "Histoire et sciences sociales: la longue durée." *Ecrits sur l'Histoire*: 41–83. Paris: Flammarion.

Brenneis, D. 1996. "Telling Troubles: Narrative, Conflict and Experience." In *Disorderly Discourse. Narrative, Conflict, and Inequality*, Ch. L. Briggs (ed.), 41–52. New York: Oxford University Press.

Briggs, Ch. L. 1992. "Linguistic Ideologies and the Naturalization of Power in Warao Discourse." *Pragmatics* 2 (3): 387–404.

Briggs, Ch. L. 1996. "Introduction." In *Disorderly Discourse. Narrative, Conflict, and Inequality*, Ch. L. Briggs (ed.), 3–40. New York: Oxford University Press.

Brockmeier, J. & Carbaugh, D. 2001. "Introduction." In *Narrative and Identity. Studies in Autobiography, Self and Culture*, J. Brockmeier & D. Carbaugh (eds.), 1–24. Amsterdam: John Benjamins Publishing Co.

Bronkhorst, D. 1995. *Truth and Reconciliation: Obstacles and Opportunities fur Human Rights*. Amsterdam: Amnesty International Dutch Selection.

Brown, P. & Fraser, C. 1979. "Speech as a marker of situation." In *Social Markers in Speech*, K. R. Scherer & H. Giles (eds.), 33–62. Cambridge: Cambridge University Press.

Brown, P. & Levinson, S. 1979. "Social structure, groups and interaction." In *Social Markers in Speech*, K. R. Scherer & H. Giles (eds.), 291–342. Cambridge: Cambridge University Press.

Bruner, J. 2001. "Self-making and world-making." In *Narrative and Identity. Studies in Autobiography, Self and Culture*, J. Brockmeier & D. Carbaugh (eds.), 25–38. Amsterdam: John Benjamins Publishing Co.

Bucholtz, M. 2000. "The politics of transcription." *Journal of Pragmatics* 32: 1439–1465.

Bundy, C. 1994. "At War with the Future? Black South African Youth in the 1990s." In *South Africa. The Political Economy of Transformation*, S. J. Stedman (ed.), 47–64. Boulder & London: Lynne Rienner Publishers.

Bundy, C. 2000. "The Beast of the Past, History and the TRC." In *After the TRC, Reflections on truth and reconciliation in South Africa*, W. James & L. Van de Vijver (eds.), 1–13. Cape Town: David Philips Publishers.

Bunsee, B. 1996. "Blinded by the light: Debate about reconciliation is superficial." *The Sunday Independent, 3rd November 1996*: 11.

Burton, M. 1999. *The South African Truth and Reconciliation Commission: Looking back, moving forward – revisiting conflicts, striving for peace*. Johannesburg: Centre for the Study of Violence and Reconciliation.

Burton, M. 2000a. "Reparation, Amnesty and a National Archive." In *After the TRC, Reflections on truth and reconciliation in South Africa*, W. James & L. Van de Vijver (eds.), 109–116. Cape Town: David Philips Publishers.

Burton, M. 2000b. "Making moral judgements." In *Looking Back, Reaching Forward, Reflections on the Truth and Reconciliation Commission of South Africa,* Ch. Villa-Vicencio & W. Verwoerd (eds.), 77–85. Cape Town: University of Cape Town Press.

Buur, L. 1999. "Monumental History: Visibility and Invisibility in the Work of the South African Truth and Reconciliation Commission." *The TRC: Commissioning the Past Conference.* The University of the Witwatersrand, Johannesburg, 11–14 June 1999.

Buur, L. 2000a. *Institutionalising truth. Victims, perpetrators and professionals in the everyday work of the South African Truth and Reconciliation Commission.* Ph.D. Dissertation, Aarhus University, Denmark.

Buur, L. 2000b. "Negotiating Ambivalence." *Perspectives. Studies in Translatology* 8 (3): 169–186.

Buur, L. 2001a. "The South African Truth and Reconciliation Commission. A Technique of Nation–State Formation." In *States of Imagination: Ethnographic Explorations of the Postcolonial State,* Th. B. Hansen & F. Stepputat (eds.), 149–181. Durham & London: Duke University Press.

Buur, L. 2001b. "Making findings for the future: Representational order and redemption in the work of the TRC." *South African Journal of Philosophy* 20 (1): 42–68.

Buur, L. 2003. "'In the name of the victims': The politics of compensation in the work of the South African Truth and Reconciliation Commission." In *Political Transition: Politics and Cultures,* P. Gready (ed.), 148–164. London, Sterling, Virginia: Pluto Press.

Calhoun, C. 1993. "Habitus, Field, and Capital: The Question of Historical Specificity." In *Bourdieu. Critical Perspectives,* C. Calhoun, E. LiPuma & M. Postone (eds.), 61–88. Cambridge: Polity Press.

Calland, R. 1999. "Democratic government, South African style 1994–1999." In *Election '99 South Africa. From Mandela to Mbeki,* A. Reynolds (ed.), 1–15. Claremont: David Philip Publishers Ltd.

Cameron, D. 2001. *Working With Spoken Discourse.* London: SAGE Publications.

Carnegie Council on Ethics and International Affairs. 1999. *Perspectives on Ethics and International Affairs* Fall 1999/1.

Carroll, J. B. 1956. *Language, Thought, and Reality. Selected Writings of Benjamin Lee Whorf.* Cambridge: The Massachusetts Institute of Technology Press.

Caruth, C. 1995. "Trauma and experience. Introduction." In *Trauma. Explorations in Memory,* C. Caruth (ed.), 3–12. Baltimore: The John Hopkins University Press.

Centre for the Study of Violence and Reconciliation. 1998. *Survivors' perceptions of the Truth and Reconciliation Commission and Suggestions for the Final Report.* Johannesburg: CSVR.

Centre for the Study of Violence and Reconciliation. 2000. *Workshop Report: The Implementation of the TRC's Recommendations.* Parktonian Hotel, Braamfontein, Johannesburg.

Centre for the Study of Violence and Reconciliation Website. 2005. http://www.csvr.org.za.

Centre for the Study of Violence and Reconciliation & the Khulumani Support Group. 1998. *Survivors' Perceptions of the TRC and Suggestions for the Final report.* Johannesburg: Centre for the Study of Violence and Reconciliation.

Chafe, W. 1998. "Things we can Learn from Repeated Tellings of the Same Experience." *Narrative Inquiry* 8 (2): 269–285.

Chapman, A. R. 1999. "Coming to Terms with the Past: Truth Justice and/or Reconciliation." *The TRC: Commissioning the Past Conference.* University of the Witwatersrand, Johannesburg, 11–14 June 1999.

Chapman, A. R. 2003a. "The TRC's Approach to Promoting Reconciliation in the Human Rights Violations Hearings." *Unpublished Paper.* Johannesburg: Centre for the Study of Violence and Reconciliation.

Chapman, A. R. 2003b. Perspectives on Forgiveness in the Human Rights Violations Hearings. *Unpublished Paper.* Johannesburg: Centre for the Study of Violence and Reconciliation.

Cherry, J. 2000. "Historical truth: Something to fight for." In *Looking Back, Reaching Forward, Reflections on the Truth and Reconciliation Commission of South Africa,* Ch. Villa-Vicencio & W. Verwoerd (eds.), 134–143. Cape Town: University of Cape Town Press.

Cherry, J., Daniel J. & Fullard, M. 2002. "Researching the 'Truth': A View from Inside the Truth and Reconciliation Commission." In *Commissioning the Past: Understanding South Africa's Truth and Reconciliation Commission,* D. Posel & G. Simpson (eds.), 17–36. Johannesburg: Witwatersrand University Press.

Chimombo, M. P. F. & Roseberry, R. L. 1998. *The Power of Discourse, An Introduction to Discourse Analysis.* Mahwah, New Jersey: Lawrence Erlbaum Associates, Publishers.

Chisholm, P. 1996. "Apartheid: Can the truth set a nation free?" *Maclean's* 109 (15): 28–31.

Christie, K. 2000. *The South African Truth Commission.* London: MacMillan Press Ltd.

Chubb, K. & Van Dijk, L. 2001. *Between Anger and Hope, South Africa's Youth and the Truth and Reconciliation Commission.* Johannesburg: Witwatersrand University Press.

CIA World Factbook South Africa Online. 2007. http://www.cia.gov/cia/publications/factbook/geos/sf.html#People.

Cicourel, A. V. 1993. "Aspects of Structural and Processual Theories of Knowledge." In *Bourdieu. Critical Perspectives,* C. Calhoun, E. LiPuma & M. Postone (eds.), 89–115. Cambridge: Polity Press.

Clark, K. & Holquist, M. 1984. *Mikhail Bakhtin.* Cambridge: Harvard University Press.

Clegg, S. R. 1989. *Frameworks of Power.* London: SAGE Publications Ltd.

Clegg, S. R. 1993. "Narrative, Power, and Social Theory." In *Narrative and Social Control: Critical Perspectives,* D. K. Mumby (ed.), 15–48. Newbury Park: SAGE Publications, Inc.

Cleveland, T. 2002. ""We Still Want the Truth….". The Effects of the Experience of the ANC's Angolan Detention Camps upon Post-Apartheid South African Memory." *Unpublished Paper.*

Coetzee, M. 2003. "An Overview of the TRC Amnesty Process." In *The Provocations of Amnesty: Memory, Justice and Impunity,* Ch.Villa-Vicencio & E. Doxtader (eds.), 181–194. Claremont: David Philip Publishers.

Coetzer, J. P. J. 2000. *Gister se dade, vandag se oordeel.* Pretoria: J. P. Van der Walt.

Collins, J. 1996. "Socialization to text: Structure and contradiction in schooled literacy." In *The Natural Histories of Discourse,* M. Silverstein & G. Urban (eds.), 203–228. Chicago: University of Chicago Press.

Collins, J. 1998. "Our Ideologies and Theirs." In *Language Ideologies. Practice and Theory,* B. B. Schieffelin, K. A. Woolard & P. V. Kroskrity (eds.), 256–270. New York: Oxford University Press.

Colvin, C. J. 2003. "Limiting Memory: The Roots of Storytelling in Post-Apartheid, Post-TRC South Africa." In *Telling Wounds. Narrative, Trauma & Memory. Working through the SA armed conflicts of the 20th century. Proceedings of the conference,* C. van der Merwe & R. Wolfswinkel (eds.), 234–244. Stellenbosch: Van Schaik Content Solutions.

Colvin, C. J. 2004. "Ambivalent Narrations: Pursuing the Political Through Traumatic Storytelling." *Paper Online:* http://academic.sun.ac.za/sociology/NSF_2004_03_19_Colvin.doc.

Combrink, N. L. 1998. "History and the Commission on Truth and Reconciliation: The Problem of Collective Guilt." *Journal of Contemporary History* 23 (2): 101–119.

Connor, B. 1998. *The Difficult Traverse. From Amnesty to Reconciliation.* Pietermaritzburg: Cluster Publications.

Conrad, B. 1998. "After the truth, it's time to pay up." *Electronic Mail & Guardian,* November 3rd.

Constitution of the Republic of South Africa Online. 1996. www.polity.org.za/html/govdocs/constitution/saconst02.html?rebookmark=1#30.

Corry, W. & Terre Blanche, M. 2000. "Where does the blood come from?: True stories and real selves at the TRC hearings." *Psychology in Society* 26: 6–17.

Cose, E. 1998. "The limitations of the Truth." *Newsweek* 132 (18): 41–43.

Coulthard, M. 1992. "Forensic discourse analysis." In *Advances in Spoken Discourse Analysis,* M. Coulthard (ed.), 242–258. London: Routledge.

Crais, C. 2002. *The Politics of Evil. Magic, State Power, and the Political Imagination in South Africa.* Cambridge: Cambridge University Press.

Crocker, D. A. 2000. "Truth Commission, Transitional Justice, and Civil Society." In *Truth versus justice: The morality of truth commissions,* R. I. Rotberg & D. Thompson (eds.), 99–121. Princeton: Princeton University Press.

Cronin, J. 2001. "Sorry can help, but on its own is not enough." *Weekly Mail & Guardian,* January 12th 2001.

Crush, J. & McDonald, D. A. (eds.). 2002. *Transnationalism and New African Immigration to South Africa.* Southern African Migration Project & the Canadian Association of African Studies.

Cutting, J. 2002. *Pragmatics and Discourse. A resource book for students.* London & New York: Routledge.

Daley, S. 1997. "Agony Relived in Apartheid Inquiry." *New York Times* 17-7-1997: 10.

Darbon, D. 1999a. "La fermeture du circuit identitaire en Afrique du Sud." In *L'après-Mandela. Enjeux sud-africaines er régionaux,* D. Darbon (ed.), 41–64. Paris: Editions Karthala.

Darbon, D. 1999b. "Une sociéte en travail: réinventer le passé en Afrique du Sud." In *L'après-Mandela. Enjeux sud-africaines er régionaux,* D. Darbon (ed.), 87–102. Paris: Editions Karthala.

Das, V. & Kleinman, A. 1999. "Introduction." In *Remaking a World. Violence, Social Suffering and Recovery,* V. Das, A. Kleinman, M. Lock, M. Ramphele & P. Reynolds (eds.), 1–30. Berkeley: University of California Press.

Davenport, T. R. H. & Saunders, C. 2000. *South Africa: A Modern History.* Houndmills: Palgrave MacMillan.

Dawson, G. 1999. "Trauma, memory, politics: The Irish Troubles." In *Trauma and Life Stories. International Perspectives,* K. L. Rogers & S. Leydesdorff with G. Dawson (eds.), 180–204. London: Routledge.

Deacon, H. 1998. "Remembering tragedy, constructing modernity: Robben Island as a national monument." In *Negotiating the Past: The making of memory in South Africa,* S. Nuttall & C. Coetzee (eds.), 161–179. Cape Town: Oxford University Press.

Deegan, H. 2001. *The Politics of the New South Africa. Apartheid and After.* Harlow: Pearson Education Ltd.

De Fina, A. 2003. *Identity in Narrative. A Study of Immigrant Discourse.* Amsterdam: John Benjamins Publishing Company.

Degenaar, J. 1993. "No Sizwe. The Myth of the Nation." *Indicator SA* 10 (3): 11–16.

Deleuze, G. 1988. *Foucault*. Minneapolis: University of Minnesota Press.

Derrida, J. 1996. *Archive fever. A Freudian impression*. Chicago: The University of Chicago Press.

Derrida, J. 1999. *Sur parole. Instantanés philosophiques*. Saint-Etienne: Editions de l'Aube.

Derrida, J. 2002. "Archive Fever in South Africa." In *Refiguring the Archive*, C. Hamilton et al. (eds.), 38–80. Cape Town: David Philip Publishers.

Devos, R. 2004. *Macht en verzet. Het subject in het denken van Michel Foucault*. Kapellen: Uitgeverij Pelckmans.

Dijk Van, T. A. 1997a. "Discourse as Interaction in Society." In *Discourse as Social Interaction*, T. A. Van Dijk (ed.), 1–37. London: SAGE Publications Ltd.

Dijk Van, T. A. 1997b. "What is Political Discourse Analysis?" In *Political Linguistics*, J. Blommaert & C. Bulcaen (eds.), 11–52. Amsterdam: John Benjamins Publishing Company.

Dijk Van, T. A. 1998a. "Opinions and Ideologies in the Press." In *Approaches to Media Discourse*, A. Bell & P. Garrett (eds.), 21–63. Oxford: Blackwell Publishers Limited.

Dijk Van, T. A. 1998b. *Ideology, a multidisciplinary approach*. London: Sage Publications.

Dijk Van, T. A. 2001. "Multidisciplinary CDA: A plea for diversity." In *Methods of Critical Discourse Analysis*, R. Wodak & M. Meyer (eds.), 95–120. London: SAGE Publications Ltd.

Dixon, J. A. 1997. "Discourse and racial partition in the 'New' South Africa." In *Culture, Power & Difference, Discourse Analysis in South Africa*, A. Levett, A. Kottlet, E. Burman & I. Parker (eds.), 17–30. Cape Town: University of Cape Town Press.

Doxtader, E. 2003. "Easy to Forget or Never (Again) Hard to remember? History, Memory and the 'Publicity' of Amnesty." In *The Provocations of Amnesty: Memory, Justice and Impunity*, Ch. Villa-Vicencio and E. Doxtader (eds.), 121–155. Claremont: David Philip Publishers.

Doxtader E. & Villa-Vicencio, Ch. 2003a. "Introduction: Profiling Violence and the Potential for Reconciliation." In *Through Fire with Water. The roots of division and the potential for reconciliation in Africa*, E. Doxtader & Ch. Villa-Vicencio (eds.), XIII–XXII. Claremont: David Philip Publishers.

Doxtader E. & Villa-Vicencio, Ch. 2003b. "Introduction: Provocations at the End of Amnesty." In *The Provocations of Amnesty: Memory, Justice and Impunity*, Ch. Villa-Vicencio & E. Doxtader (eds.), x–xx. Claremont: David Philip Publishers.

Drew, P. & Sorjonen, M.-L. 1997. "Institutional Dialogue." In *Discourse as Social Interaction*, T. A. Van Dijk (ed.), 92–118. London: SAGE Publications Ltd.

Dube, P. S. 2002. "The Story of Thandi Shezi." In *Commissioning the Past: Understanding South Africa's Truth and Reconciliation Commission*, D. Posel & G. Simpson (eds.), 117–130. Johannesburg: Witwatersrand University Press.

Du Bois, J. W. 1991. "Transcription Design Principles for Spoken Discourse Research." *Pragmatics* 1: 71–106.

Dugard, J. 1998. "Does South Africa's Truth and Reconciliation Process Comply with International Norms?" *Transnational Law & Contemporary Problems* 8: 277–311.

Dunn, K. 1997. "The Painful Truth." *Maclean's* 110 (48): 32.

Dunn, K. 1998. "Power of Forgiveness in South Africa." *Christian Science Monitor* 90 (153): 1–4.

Dupin B. 1999. "Dans une arc-en-ciel de symboles: le spectre de la nouvelle nation sud-africaine." In *L'après-Mandela. Enjeux sud-africaines et régionaux*, D. Darbon (ed.), 103–136. Paris: Editions Karthala.

Durant, S. 1999. "Bearing witness to apartheid: J. M. Coetzee's inconsolable works of mourning." *Contemporary Literature* 40 (3): 430–454.

Duranti, A. 1997. *Linguistics Anthropology.* Cambridge: Cambridge University Press.

Durrheim, K. 1997. "Peace talk and violence: An analysis of the power of 'peace.'" In *Culture, Power & Difference, Discourse Analysis in South Africa,* A. Levett, A. Kottlet, E. Burman & I. Parker (eds.), 31–43. Cape Town: University of Cape Town Press.

Duvenage, P. 1999. "The Politics of Memory and Forgetting after Auschwitz and Apartheid. *The TRC: Commissioning the Past Conference.* Johannesburg: University of the Witwatersrand, 11–14 June 1999.

Dyzenhaus, D. 1998. *Truth, Reconciliation and the Apartheid Legal Order.* Cape Town: Juta & Co. Ltd.

Eades, L. M. 1999. *The End of Apartheid in South Africa.* Westport, Connecticut: Greenwood Press.

Eagleton, T. 1991. *Ideology. An Introduction.* London: Verso.

Eddings, J. 1997. "The shield of truth." *US News & World Report* 122 (5): 13–15.

Edley, N. 2001. "Analysing Masculinity: Interpretative Repertoires, Ideological Dilemmas and Subject Positions." In *Discourse as Data. A guide for analysis,* M. Wetherell, S. Taylor & S.J. Yates (eds.), 189–228. London: SAGE publications Ltd.

Edmondson, W. 1981. *Spoken Discourse. A model for analysis.* London: Longman.

Edwards, J. A. 2001. "The Transcription of Discourse." In *The Handbook of Discourse Analysis,* D. Schiffrin, D. Tannen & H. E. Hamilton (eds.), 321–348. Malden: Blackwell Publishers.

Elder, J. W. 1998. "Expanding Our Options: The Challenge of Forgiveness." In *Exploring Forgiveness,* R. D. Enright & J. North (eds.), 150–164. Madison: The University of Wisconsin Press.

Election Resources on the Internet. 2004. http://www.electionresources.org/za/.

Ellis, S. 2000. "Review Essay. Truth and Reconciliation Commission of South Africa Report, Volumes 1–5. Pretoria: Government Printer, October 1998." *Transformation* 42: 57–72.

ELSAM. 2002. *Truth and Reconciliation Commission.* Online. www.elsam.or.id/kkr/english/index-eng.htm.

Embassy of South Africa. 1998. *Final report: The Truth and Reconciliation Commission. Summary and Guide.* Den Haag: Embassy of South Africa.

Engel, S. 1999. *Context is everything: The nature of memory.* New York: W. H. Freeman and Company.

Enright, R. D. & North, J. 1998. "Introducing Forgiveness." In *Exploring Forgiveness,* R. D. Enright & J. North (eds.), 3–8. Madison: The University of Wisconsin Press.

Ericson, M. 2001. *Reconciliation and the Search for a Shared Moral Landscape.* Frankfurt am Main: Peter Lang.

Erikson, K. 1995. "Notes on Trauma and Community." In *Trauma. Explorations in Memory,* C. Caruth (ed.), 183–199. Baltimore: The John Hopkins University Press.

Eyskens, L. 2001. *Controverses over de Zuid-Afrikaanse Waarheids- en Verzoeningscommissie.* Ma Thesis. Ghent: Ghent University.

Fairclough, N. 1992. *Discourse and Social Change.* Cambridge: Polity Press.

Fairclough, N. 1995a. *Critical Discourse Analysis. The Critical Study of Language.* London: Longman Group Limited.

Fairclough, N. 1995b. *Media Discourse.* London: Edward Arnold.

Fairclough, N. 1996a. "Globalisation of discursive practices." *Paper Online:* http://bank.rug.ac.be/global/programme.html.

Fairclough, N. 1996b. "Technologisation of discourse." In *Texts and Practices. Readings in Critical Discourse Analysis*, C. R. Caldas-Coulthard & M. Coulthard (eds.), 71–83. London: Routledge.

Fairclough, N. 1998. "Political Discourse in the Media: An Analytical Framework." In *Approaches to Media Discourse*, A. Bell & P. Garrett (eds.), 142–162. Oxford: Blackwell Publishers Limited.

Fairclough, N. 2001a. *Language and Power.* Harlow: Longman.

Fairclough, N. 2001b. "Critical discourse analysis as a method in social scientific research." In *Methods of Critical Discourse Analysis*, R. Wodak & M. Meyer (eds.), 121–138. London: SAGE Publications Ltd.

Fairclough, N. 2003. *Analysing Discourse. Textual analysis for social research.* London: Routledge.

Fernandez, L. D. 1996. "Possibilities and limitations of reparations for the victims of human rights violations in South Africa." In *Confronting Past Injustices, Approaches to amnesty, punishment, reparation and restitution in South Africa and Germany,* M. Rwelamira & G. Werle (eds.), 65–78. Durban: Butterworths.

Ferrara, A. 1985. "Pragmatics." In *Handbook of Discourse Analysis, Volume 2. Dimensions of Discourse,* T. A. Van Dijk (ed.), 137–158. London: Academic Press.

Field, S. 1999. "Memory, the TRC and the Significance of Oral History in Post-Apartheid South Africa." *The TRC: Commissioning the Past Conference.* Johannesburg: University of the Witwatersrand, 11–14 June 1999.

Foster, D. 2000. "What makes a perpetrator? An attempt to understand." In *Looking Back, Reaching Forward, Reflections on the Truth and Reconciliation Commission of South Africa,* Ch. Villa-Vicencio & W. Verwoerd (eds.), 219–229. Cape Town: University of Cape Town Press.

Foucault, M. 1969. *L'archéologie du savoir.* Paris: Bibliothèque des Sciences Humaines.

Foucault, M. 1971. *L'ordre du discours.* Paris: Gallimard.

Foucault, M. 1975. *Surveiller et Punir: Naissance de la Prison.* Paris: Gallimard.

Foucault, M. 1984a. "The Order of Discourse." In *Language and politics. Readings in social and political theory,* M. Shapiro (ed.), 108–138. Oxford: Basil Blackwell publisher Ltd.

Foucault, M. 1984b. *De Wil tot Weten. Geschiedenis van de seksualiteit I.* Nijmegen: SUN.

Foucault, M. 1984c. *Het Gebruik van de Lust. Geschiedenis van de seksualiteit II.* Nijmegen: SUN.

Foucault, M. 1984d. *De Zorg voor Zichzelf. Geschiedenis van de seksualiteit III.* Nijmegen: SUN.

Foucault, M. 1988. *De orde van het spreken.* Meppel: Uitgeverij Boom.

Foucault, M. 2001. *Discipline, Toezicht en Straf. De geboorte van de gevangenis.* Groningen: Historische Uitgeverij.

Foucault, M. 2002. *The Archaeology of Knowledge.* London & New York: Routledge.

Fourie, G. 1999. "The psychology of perpetrators of "political" violence in South Africa – A personal experience." *Unpublished Paper.* University of Cape Town: South Africa.

Fowler, R. 1985. "Power." In *Handbook of Discourse Analysis, Volume 4: Discourse Analysis in Society,* T. A. Van Dijk (ed.), 43–60. London: Academic Press.

Fowler, R. 1996. "On critical linguistics." In *Texts and Practices. Readings in Critical Discourse Analysis,* C. R. Caldas-Coulthard & M. Coulthard (eds.), 3–14. London: Routledge.

Fowler, R. & Kress, G. 1979. "Critical linguistics." In *Language and control,* R. Fowler, B. Hodge, G. Kress & T. Trew (eds.), 185–213. London: Routledge & Kegan Paul.

Franz, C. 1997. *South Africa's Truth and Reconciliation Commission: An enquiry into the nature of the 'truth' produced at hearings of the Committee of Human Rights Violations.* Honours Dissertation, University of Cape Town.

Freedom of Expression Institute of South Africa. 1995. "The Truth Commission Bill. Transparency in Government: another Urban Legend?" *FXI Update* January 1995: 1–12.

Freeman, M. 2001. "From substance to story: Narrative, identity, and the reconstruction of the self." In *Narrative and Identity. Studies in Autobiography, Self and Culture,* J. Brockmeier & D. Carbaugh (eds.), 283–298. Amsterdam: John Benjamins Publishing Co.

Freeman, M. & Brockmeier, J. 2001. "Narrative integrity: Autobiographical identity and the meaning of the "good life"". In *Narrative and Identity. Studies in Autobiography, Self and Culture,* J. Brockmeier & D. Carbaugh (eds.), 75–102. Amsterdam: John Benjamins Publishing Co.

Frost, B. 1998. *Struggling to Forgive, Nelson Mandela and South Africa's Search for Reconciliation.* London: Harper Collins Publishers.

Fullard, M. 2004. "Dis-Placing Race: The South African Truth and Reconciliation Commission (TRC) and Interpretations of Violence." *Race and Citizenship in Transition Series.*

Fullard, M. & Rousseau, N. 2003. "Truth, Evidence, and History: A Critical Review of Aspects of the Amnesty Process."In *The Provocations of Amnesty: Memory, Justice and Impunity,* Ch. Villa-Vicencio & E. Doxtader (eds.), 195–216. Claremont: David Philip Publishers.

Gal, S. 1979. *Language shift: Social determinants of linguistic change in bilingual Austria.* New York: Academia Press.

Gardiner, M. 1992. *The Dialogics of Critique. M. M. Bakhtin & the Theory of Ideology.* London & New York: Routledge.

Garman, A. 1997. "Media Creation. How the TRC and the media have impacted on each other." *Track Two* 6 (3&4).

Garrett, P. & Bell, A. 1998. "Media and Discourse: A Critical Overview." In *Approaches to Media Discourse,* A. Bell & P. Garrett (eds.), 1–20. Oxford: Blackwell Publishers Limited.

Gee, J. P. 1996. *Social Linguistics and Literacies. Ideology in Discourses.* London: The Falmer Press.

Gee, J. P. 1999. *An Introduction to Discourse Analysis. Theory and Method.* London: Routledge.

Gerloff, R. 1998. "Truth, a New Society and Reconciliation: The Truth and Reconciliation Commission in South Africa from a German Perspective." *Missionalia* 26 (1): 17–53.

Gerwel, J. 2000. "National reconciliation: Holy grail or secular pact?" In *Looking Back, Reaching Forward, Reflections on the Truth and Reconciliation Commission of South Africa,* Ch. Villa-Vicencio & W. Verwoerd (eds.), 277–286. Cape Town: University of Cape Town Press.

Geslin, N. 2001. "Using Past Events to Construct a Present: Voices at the Truth and Reconciliation Commission hearings." *Poetics and Linguistics Association Conference Papers 1999.* Potchefstroom University.

Gibbons, J. A. 1998. "Contemporary relations of the OAU and South Africa." *Tenth Annual Conference of the African Society of International and Comparative Law, 3–5 August 1998.*

Gibson, J. L. 2003. "The Legacy of Apartheid: Racial Differences in the Legitimacy of Democratic Institutions and Processes in the New South Africa." *Comparative Political Studies* 36: 772–800.

Gibson, J. L. 2004. *Overcoming Apartheid. Can Truth Reconcile a Divided Nation?* New York: Russell Sage Foundation.

Gibson, J. L. & Gouws, A. 1998. "Political Intolerance and Ethnicity. Investigating Social Identity." *Indicator South Africa* 15 (3): 15–20.

Gibson, J. L. & Gouws, A. 1999. "Truth and Reconciliation in South Africa: Attributions of Blame and the Struggle over Apartheid." *American Political Science Review* 93 (3): 501–516.

Gibson, J. L. & Gouws, A. 2003. *Overcoming Intolerance in South Africa: Experiments in Democratic Persuasion.* New York: Cambridge University Press.

Gibson, J. L. and MacDonald, H. 2001. "Truth – Yes, Reconciliation – Maybe: South Africans Judge the Truth and Reconciliation Process." *Research paper for the Institute For Justice and Reconciliation, 11th June 2001.*

Gilbert, G. & Makhudu, D. 1984. *The creole continuum in Afrikaans: A non-Eurocentric view.* Unpublished manuscript, Department of Linguistics, Southern Ill. Univ at Carbondale.

Giliomee, H. 1992. "Broedertwis: Intra-Afrikaner conflicts in the transition from apartheid 1969–1991." In *Peace, Politics and Violence in the New South Africa*, N. Etherington (ed.), 147–161. London: Hans Zell Publishers.

Gilmore, L. 2001. *The Limits of Autobiography. Trauma and Testimony.* Ithaca: Cornell University Press.

Gobodo-Madikizela, P. 1997. "Healing and the racial divide? Personal reflections on the Truth and Reconciliation Commission." *South African Journal of Psychology* 27 (4): 271–276.

Gobodo-Madikizela, P. 2003a. *A Human Being Died That Night. A Story of Forgiveness.* Claremont: David Philip Publishers.

Gobodo-Madikizela, P. 2003b. "Alternatives to Revenge: Building a Vocabulary of Reconciliation Through Political Pardon." In *The Provocations of Amnesty: Memory, Justice and Impunity,* Ch. Villa-Vicencio & E. Doxtader (eds.), 51–60. Claremont: David Philip Publishers.

Goffman, E. 1974. *Frame Analysis.* Harmondsworth: Penguin Books Ltd.

Goldblatt, B. & Meintjes, S. 1997. "Dealing with the aftermath: Sexual violence and the Truth and Reconciliation Commission." *Agenda* 36: 7–18.

Goniwe, N. 2000. "Dealing with the Past: A Memorial for the Cradock Four." *New South African Outlook* Winter 2000, 2 (3): 3–5.

Goodman, D. 1999. *Fault Lines: Journeys into the New South Africa.* Berkeley: University of California Press.

Goodman, T. 2003. "Setting the Stage. A Cultural Approach to the South African Truth and Reconciliation Commission." *Yale Journal of Sociology* 3: 77–92.

Goodman, T. & Price, M. 1999. "Continuing the TRC Project: The Use of Internal Reconciliation Commissions to Facilitate Organisational Transformation – The Case of the Wits Health Sciences Faculty." *The TRC: Commissioning the Past Conference.* Johannesburg: University of the Witwatersrand, 11–14 June 1999.

Goodwin, Ch. 1981. *Conversational Organization: Interaction between Speakers and Hearers.* New York: Academic Press.

Goodwin, Ch. & Duranti, A. 1992. "Rethinking context: An introduction." In *Rethinking context. Language as an interactive phenomenon*, A. Duranti & Ch. Goodwin (eds.), 1–42. New York: Cambridge University Press.

Goodwin Ch. & Goodwin, M. H. 1992. "Assessments and the construction of context." In *Rethinking context. Language as an interactive phenomenon*, A. Duranti & Ch. Goodwin (eds.), 147–190. New York: Cambridge University Press.

Gordon, C. 1980. *Power/Knowledge: Selected Interviews and Other Writings 1972–1977, by Michel Foucault.* New York: Pantheon Books.

Goris, G. 1999. "Geen paradijservaring, Zuid–Afrika's poging tot verzoening." *Wereldwijd* februari 1999: 42–43.

Gouws, A. 1999. "The gender dimension of the 1999 elections." In *Election '99 South Africa. From Mandela to Mbeki*, A. Reynolds (ed.), 159–172. Claremont: David Philip Publishers Ltd.

Govender, R. 1998. *Psychotherapy for Sequelae of Trauma Based on Testimonies of Victims at the Truth and Reconciliation Commission*. Thesis for the Department of Psychology, University of the Western Cape, Bellville.

Govier, T. & Verwoerd, W. 2002. "Forgiveness: The Victim's Prerogative." *South African Journal of Philosophy* 21 (2): 97–112.

Gqola, P. D. 2001. "Defining People: Power and the Metaphors of the New South Africa." *The Burden of Race? 'Whiteness' and 'Blackness' in Modern South Africa Workshop*, University of the Witwatersrand, Johannesburg, 5–8 July 2001.

Graybill, L. S. 1998a. "Pursuit of Truth and Reconciliation in South Africa." *Africa Today* 45 (1): 103–134.

Graybill, L. S. 1998b. "Impact of Christianity on Struggle Against Apartheid." In *Africa's Second Wave of Freedom. Development, Democracy, and Rights*, L. Graybill & K. W. Thompson (eds.), 189–208. Lanham: University Press of America Inc.

Graybill, L. S. 2002. *Truth and Reconciliation in South Africa. Miracle or Model?* Boulder: Lynne Rienner Publishers, Inc.

Gready, P. 2003. "Introduction." In *Political Transition: Politics and Cultures*, P. Gready (ed.), 1–26. London, Sterling, Virginia: Pluto Press.

Gready, P. & Kgalema, L. 2000. "Magistrates under Apartheid: A case study of professional ethics and the politicisation of justice." *Occasional Paper*. Johannesburg: Centre for the Study of Violence and Reconciliation.

Gruchy de, J. 2002. *Reconciliation. Restoring Justice*. Claremont: David Philips Publishers.

Gruchy de, J., Cochrane, J. & Martin, S. 1999. "Faith, Struggle and Reconciliation." In *Facing the Truth. South African faith communities and the Truth and Reconciliation Commission*, J. Cochrane, J. de Gruchy & S. Martin (eds.), 1–17. Cape Town: David Philip Publishers.

Grunebaum-Ralph, H. 2001. "Re-Placing Pasts, Forgetting Presents: Narrative, Place, and Memory in the Time of the Truth and Reconciliation Commission." *Research in African Literatures* 32 (3): 198–212.

Grunebaum-Ralph, H. and Stier, O. 1999. "The Question (of) Remains: Remembering Shoah, Forgetting Reconciliation." In *Facing the Truth. South African faith communities and the Truth and Reconciliation Commission*, J. Cochrane, J. de Gruchy & S. Martin (eds.), 142–152. Cape Town: David Philip Publishers.

Gumperz, J. J. 1972. "Introduction." In *Directions in sociolinguistics: The ethnography of communication*, J. J. Gumperz & D.Hymes (eds.), 1–25. New York: Holt, Rinehart and Winston, Inc.

Gumperz, J. J. 1982. *Discourse strategies*. New York: Cambridge University Press.

Gumperz, J. J. 1984. "Communicative competence revisited." In *Meaning, Form, and Use in Context: Linguistic Applications*, D. Schiffrin (ed.), 278–289. Washington D.C.: Georgetown University Press.

Gumperz, J. J. 1992. "Contextualization and understanding." In *Rethinking context. Language as an interactive phenomenon*, A. Duranti & Ch. Goodwin (eds.), 229–252. New York: Cambridge University Press.

Gumperz, J. J., Kaltman, H. & Catherine, M. 1984. "Cohesion in Spoken and Written Discourse: Ethnic Style and the Transition to Literacy." In *Coherence in Spoken and Written Discourse*, D. Tannen (ed.), 3–20. Norwood: Ablex Publishing Corporation.

Habib, A. 1996. "Myth of the Rainbow Nation: Prospects for the Consolidation of Democracy in South Africa." *African Security Review* 5 (6).

Hall, M. 1998. "Earth and stone: archaeology as memory." In *Negotiating the Past: The making of memory in South Africa*, S. Nuttall & C. Coetzee (eds.), 180–200. Cape Town: Oxford University Press.

Halliday, M. A. K. & Hasan, R. 1985. *Language, context, and text: Aspects of language in a socio-semiotic perspective*. Oxford: Oxford University Press.

Hamber, B. 1996. "The need for a survivor-centered approach to the Truth and Reconciliation Commission." *Community Mediation Update* No 9.

Hamber, B. 1997. "Who Should Apologise to Whom?" *Urgent Public Statement: Endorsed by 17 Organisations, 4th September 1997.*

Hamber, B. 1998. "Reflecting on the Relationship between Transformation, Reconciliation and Socio-economic Change in South Africa." *Medico International Interview, 16th June 1998.*

Hamber, B. 2000. "Righting the Wrongs: Dealing with the difficulties of granting reparations in South Africa." In *From Rhetoric to Responsibility. Making Reparations to the Survivors of Past Political Violence in South Africa*, B. Hamber & T.Mofokeng (eds.), Chapter 8. Johannesburg: Centre for the Study of Violence and Reconciliation.

Hamber, B. & Kibble, S. 1999. *From Truth to Transformation, the Truth and Reconciliation Commission in South Africa*. London: Catholic Institute for International Relations.

Hamber, B. & Van der Merwe, H. 1998. "What is this thing called Reconciliation?" *Goedgedacht Forum After the Truth and Reconciliation Commission*. Goedgedacht Farm, Cape Town, 28th March 1998.

Hamber, B. & Wilson, R. 1999. "Symbolic Closure through Memory, Reparation and Revenge in Post-conflict Societies." *Traumatic Stress in South Africa Conference*. Parktonian Hotel, Johannesburg, South Africa, 27–29 January 1999.

Hamber B., Mofokeng, T. & Simpson, S. 1997. "Evaluating the Role and Function of Civil Society in a Changing South Africa." *The Role of Southern Civil Organisations in the Promotion of Peace Seminar*. DHR Seminar, London, 10th November 1997.

Hamilton, C. 2002. "'Living by Fluidity': Oral Histories, Material Custodies and the Politics of Archiving." In *Refiguring the Archive*, C. Hamilton et al. (eds.), 209–228. Cape Town: David Philip Publishers.

Hamilton, C., Harris, V. & Reid, G. 2002. "Introduction." In *Refiguring the Archive*, C. Hamilton et al. (eds.), 7–18. Cape Town: David Philip Publishers.

Hardy, C. & Phillips, N. 1999. "No Joking Matter: Discursive Struggle in the Canadian Refugee System." *Organization Studies* 20 (1): 1–24.

Harper, E. 2000. "Playing rugby with the truth." *Psychology in Society* 26: 53–72.

Harris, B. 1998. "'Unearthing' the 'Essential' Past: The TRC and the Making of a National Public Memory." *South African and Contemporary History Seminar*. 28th April, 1998, University of the Western Cape, Bellville.

Harris, B. 1999. "Confessing the Truth: Shaping Silences Through the Amnesty Process." *The TRC: Commissioning the Past Conference*. University of the Witwatersrand, Johannesburg, 11–14 June 1999.

Harris, B. 2000. *The Past, the TRC and the Archive as Depository of Memory*. Online publication: http://www.oslo2000.uio.no/program/papers/m3c/m3c–harris.pdf.

Harris, B. 2002. "The Archive, Public History and the Essential Truth: The TRC Reading the Past." In *Refiguring the Archive*, C. Hamilton et al. (eds.), 161–178. Cape Town: David Philip Publishers.

Harris, V. 1999. "'They should have destroyed more': The Destruction of Public Records by the South African State in the Final Years of Apartheid, 1990–1994." *The TRC: Commissioning the Past Conference*. University of the Witwatersrand, Johannesburg, 11–14 June 1999.

Harris, V. 2001. "Seeing (in) Blindness: South Africa, Archives and Passion for Justice." *Silver Jubilee Annual Conference of the Archives and Records Association of New Zealand*, Wellington, New Zealand, August 2001.

Harris, V. 2002a. "A Shaft of Darkness: Derrida and the Archive." In *Refiguring the Archive*, C. Hamilton et al. (eds.), 61–82. Cape Town: David Philip Publishers.

Harris, V. 2002b. "The Archival Sliver: A Perspective on the Construction of Social Memory in the Archives and the Transition from Apartheid to Democracy." In *Refiguring the Archive*, C. Hamilton et al. (eds.), 135–160. Cape Town: David Philip Publishers.

Harris, V. 2002c. "The Truth and Reconciliation Commission: An Exercise In Forgetting?" *South African History Archive*. Paper Online: http://www.zmag.org/content/showarticle.cfm?SectionID=2&ItemID=2576.

Harris, V. 2002d. "Telling Truths about the TRC Archive." *South African History Archive*. Paper Online: http://www.wits.ac.za/saha/publications/FOIP_5_2_Harris.pdf.

Hawkins, B. 2001. "Ideology, metaphor and iconographic reference." In *Language and Ideology. Volume II: Descriptive cognitive approaches*, R. Dirven, R. Frank & C. Ilie (eds.), 27–50. Amsterdam: John Benjamins Publishing Company.

Hay, M. 1998. *Ukubuyisana. Reconciliation in South Africa*. Pietermaritzburg: Cluster Publications.

Hay, M. 1999. "Grappling with the Past: The Truth and Reconciliation Commission of South Africa." *Africa Journal on Conflict Resolution* 1: 29–51.

Hayes, G. 1998. "We suffer Our Memories: Thinking About the Past, Healing, and Reconciliation." *American Imago* 55 (1): 29–50.

Hayner, P. B. 1996. "Commissioning the truth: Further research questions." *Third World Quarterly* 17 (1): 19–29.

Hayner, P. B. 2000. "Same species, different animal: How South Africa compares to truth commissions worldwide." In *Looking Back, Reaching Forward, Reflections on the Truth and Reconciliation Commission of South Africa*, Ch. Villa-Vicencio & W. Verwoerd (eds.), 32–41. Cape Town: University of Cape Town Press.

Hayner, P. B. 2001. *Unspeakable Truths. Confronting State Terror and Atrocity*. London: Routledge.

Henderson, W. 2000. "Metaphors, narrative and 'truth': South Africa's TRC." *African Affairs* 99 (396): 457–465.

Heuvel van den, A. 1998. "The Truth and Reconciliation Commission: A beacon in the ocean. In Embassy of South Africa" *Essays on the Truth and Reconciliation Commission*: 40–43. Den Haag: Embassy of South Africa.

Heyns, M. 2000. "The whole country's truth: Confession and narrative in recent white South African writing." *Modern Fiction Studies* 46 (1): 42–66.

History of the Afrikaans language in South Africa Online. 2002. http://nc.essortment.com/historyafrikaan_rqrs.htm.

Hodge, R. & Kress, G. 1993. *Language as Ideology*. London/ New York: Routledge.

Hodge, B., Kress, G. & Jones, G. 1979. "The ideology of middle management." In *Language and control*, R. Fowler, B. Hodge, G. Kress & T. Trew (eds.), 81–93. London: Routledge & Kegan Paul.

Holiday, A. 1998. "Forgiving and forgetting: The Truth and Reconciliation Commission." In *Negotiating the Past: The making of memory in South Africa*, S. Nuttall & C. Coetzee (eds.), 43–56. Cape Town: Oxford University Press.

Holquist, M. 1986. "Answering as Authoring: Mikhail Bakhtin's Trans-Linguistics." In *Bakhtin. Essays and Dialogues on His Work*, G. S. Morson (ed.), 59–72. Chicago: The University of Chicago Press.

Howe, D. 1998. "In South Africa, the truth can only take you so far." *New Statesman* 127 (4410): 13–15.

Howe, H. M. 1994. "The SADF Revisited." In *South Africa, Twelve Perspectives on the Transition*, H. Kitchen & J. Coleman Kitchen (eds.), 78–92. Westport, Connecticut: Praeger.

Hudson, P. 2000. "Liberalism, democracy and transformation in South Africa." *Politikon* 27 (1): 93–102.

Humphrey, M. 2000. "From Terror to Trauma: Commissioning Truth for National Reconciliation." *Social Identities* 6 (1): 7–28.

Hutchby, I. & Wooffitt, R. 1998. *Conversation Analysis. Principles, Practices and Applications.* Cambridge: Polity Press.

Hymes, D. 1981. *'In vain I tried to tell you' Essays in Native American Ethnopoetics*. Philadelphia: University of Pennsylvania Press.

Hyslop, J. 1999. "Shopping during a revolution: Entrepreneurs, retailers and 'white' identity in South Africa's democratic transition." *The TRC: Commissioning the Past Conference*. University of the Witwatersrand, Johannesburg, 11–14 June 1999.

Ignatieff, M. 1997. "Articles of Faith." In *Echoes of Violence. Niza Cahier no 1, April 1997*, De Balie & the Netherlands Institute for Southern Africa (eds.), 7–12. Amsterdam: NiZa.

Ignatieff, M. 1998. *The Warrior's Honor, Ethnic War and the Modern Conscience*. London: Chatto & Windus.

Institute for Democracy in South Africa. 1994. *Justice in Transition*. Cape Town: IDASA.

Institute for Democracy in South Africa. 2000. *Trends and comparisons in views of democracy*. Rondebosch: Institute for Justice and Reconciliation.

Institute for Justice and Reconciliation. 1998. *Time to Act, the Recommendations of the Truth and Reconciliation Commission*. Rondebosch: IJR.

Institute for Justice and Reconciliation Website. 2004. http://www.ijr.org.za.

International Center for Transitional Justice Website. 2007. http://www.ictj.org/.

Jacobs, S. 2000. "The politics of traditional leadership." *The Institute for Democracy in South Africa* 11.

Jacoby, S. 1983, *Wild Justice. The Evolution of Revenge*. New York: Harper & Row Publishers.

Jaffe, A. 2000. "Comic Performance and the Articulation of Hybrid Identity." *Pragmatics* 10 (1): 39–59.

James, W. 1998. "And now it's up to you and me." *Siyaya* 3: 60–63.

James, W. & Lever, J. 2000. "South Africa – The Second Republic: Race, Inequality, and Democracy in South Africa." In *Three Nations at the Crossroad. Beyond Racism: Embracing an Interdependent Future Series*. Atlanta: Southern Education Foundation.

Jaworski, A. & Coupland, N. 1999. "Introduction: Perspectives on Discourse Analysis." In *The Discourse Reader*, A. Jaworski & N. Coupland (eds.), 1–44. London: Routledge.

Jefferey, A. 2000. "Truth Commission repudiated by its own amnesty committee." Paper On-line: http://www.sairr.org.za/wsc/pstory.htx?storyID=195.

Jefferey, A. 2001. *The Truth about the Truth Commission*. Johannesburg: South African Institute for Race Relations.

Jenkins, C. 2000. "After the dry white season: The dilemmas of reparation and reconstruction in South Africa." *South African Journal on Human Rights* 16 (3): 415–485.

Johnstone, A. 2000. "The Nation, Reconciliation and the Postcolonial Imagination: Narratives of Transition in Australia and South Africa." *Ph.D. Research Proposal, Politics Department, University of Adelaine.*

Johnstone, B. 1990. *Stories, community, and place. Narratives from Middle America*. Blooming-ton: Indiana University Press.

Johnstone, B. 2001. "Discourse Analysis and Narrative." In *The Handbook of Discourse Analysis*, D. Schiffrin, D. Tannen & H. E. Hamilton (eds.), 635–649. Malden: Blackwell Publishers.

Jolly, R. & Attridge, D. 1998. "Introduction." In *Writing South Africa. Literature, apartheid, and democracy, 1970–1995*, D. Attridge & R. Jolly (eds.), 1–13. Cambridge: Cambridge University Press.

Jones, J. & Wareing, S. 1999. "Language and politics." In *Language, Society and Power. An introduction*, L. Thomas & S. Wareing (eds.), 31–48. London: Routledge.

Joseph, J. E. 2004. *Language and Identity. National, Ethnic, Religious*. Houndmills: Palgrave MacMillan.

Joseph, J. E. & Taylor, T. J. 1990. "Introduction: Ideology, science and language." In *Ideologies of Language*, J. E. Joseph & T. J. Taylor (eds.), 1–8. London: Routledge.

Jubilee 2000 South Africa. 2000. *Reparations. A draft position paper*. Cape Town: Alternative Information & Development Centre.

Kelsall, T. 2004. Politics, anti-politics, international justice: notes on the special court for Sierra Leone. *Settling Accounts: Truth, Justice and Redress in Post–Conflict Societies Conference*. Weatherhead Centre for International Affairs: Harvard University, 1–4 November 2004.

Kelsall, T. 2005. "Truth, Lies, Ritual: Preliminary Reflections on the Truth and Reconciliation Commission in Sierra Leone." *Human Rights Quarterly* May 2005.

Kerby, A. P. 1991. *Narrative and the SELF*. Bloomington: Indiana University Press.

Kgalema, L. 1999. "Symbols of Hope: Monuments as symbols of remembrance and peace in the process of reconciliation." *Research paper*. Johannesburg: Centre for the Study of Violence and Reconciliation.

Kgalema, L. & Gready, P. 2000. "Transformation of the Magistracy: Balancing Independence and Accountability in the New Democratic Order." *Research paper*. Johannesburg: Centre for the Study of Violence and Reconciliation.

Kgalema, L. & Van der Merwe, H. 2003. "What is Truth? Victim and Commission Perspectives." *Unpublished Paper*. Johannesburg: Centre for the Study of Violence and Reconciliation.

Khoisan, Z. 2001. *Jakaranda Time, An Investigator's View of South Africa's Truth and Reconciliation Commission*. Observatory: Garib Communications.

Khulumani Support Group Website. 2005. http://www.khulumani.net/about/background.htm.

Kirby, R. 2000. "The TRC's Helderberg tragedy." *Daily Mail & Guardian*, September 5th, 2000.

Kiss, E. 2000. "Moral Ambition Within and Beyond Political Constraints: Reflections on Restorative Justice." In *Truth versus justice: the morality of truth commissions*, R. I. Rotberg & D. Thompson (eds.), 68–98. Princeton: Princeton University Press.

Kjeldgard, P. & Nexo, E. A. 1999. *The South African Truth and Reconciliation Commission – A Tragedy of True Lies and Video-tapes*. Roskilde University, Denmark.

Kleinman, A. & Kleinman, J. 1996. "The Appeal of Experience; The Dismay of Images: Cultural Appropriations of Suffering in Our Times." *Daedalus. Journal of the American Academy of Arts and Sciences* 125 (1): 1–24.

Klerk de, V. 2003a. "The language of truth and reconciliation: Was it fair to all concerned?" *Southern African Linguistic and Applied Language Studies* 21 (1&2): 1–14.

Klerk de, V. 2003b. "Language and the law. Who has the upper hand?" *AILA Review* 16: 89–103.

Kock de, E. 1998. *A long night's Damage. Working for the Apartheid State*. Saxonwold: Contra Press.

Kok de, I. 1998. "Cracked heirlooms: memory on exhibition." In *Negotiating the Past: The making of memory in South Africa*, S. Nuttall & C. Coetzee (eds.), 57–74. Cape Town: Oxford University Press.

Kress, G. 1985. "Ideological Structures in Discourse." In *Handbook of Discourse Analysis, Volume 4: Discourse Analysis in Society*, T. A. Van Dijk (ed.), 27–42. London: Academic Press.

Kress, G. & Fowler, R. 1979. "Interviews." In *Language and control*, R. Fowler, B. Hodge, G. Kress & T. Trew (eds.), 63–80. London: Routledge & Kegan Paul.

Kress, G. & Hodge, R. 1979. *Language as Ideology*. London: Routledge & Kegan Paul.

Krog, A. 1998a. *Country of My Skull: Guilt, Sorrow, and the Limits of Forgiveness in the New South Africa*. Parklands: Random House South Africa.

Krog, A. 1998b. "The Truth and Reconciliation Commission – A National Ritual?" *Missionalia* 26 (1): 5–16.

Krog, A. 1999. "The TRC and National Unity." In *Truth and Reconciliation in South Africa and the Netherlands*, R. Dorsman, H. Hartman & L. Noteboom-Kronemeijer (eds.), 14–31. Utrecht: Netherlands Institute of Human Rights.

Krog, A. 2003. "The Choice of Amnesty: Did political necessity Trump Moral Duty?" In *The Provocations of Amnesty: Memory, Justice and Impunity*, Ch. Villa-Vicencio & E. Doxtader (eds.), 115–120. Claremont: David Philip Publishers.

Kroskrity, P. V. 2000. "Regimenting Languages: Language Ideological Perspectives." In *Regimes of Language. Ideologies, Polities, and Identities*, P. V. Kroskrity (ed.), 1–34. Santa Fe: School of American Research Press.

Kroskrity, P. V. 2004. "Language Ideologies." In *A Companion to Linguistic Anthropology*, A. Duranti (ed.), 496–514. Oxford: Blackwell Publishing Ltd.

Labov, W. 1972. *Language in the Inner City: Studies in the Black English Vernacular*. Philadelphia: University of Philadelphia Press.

Lakoff, R. T. 1990. *Talking Power. The Politics of Language in Our Lives*. New York: BasicBooks.

Lalu, P. & Harris, B. 1996. "Journeys From the Horizons of History: Text, Trial and Tales in the Construction of Narratives of pain." *Current Writing* 8 (2): 24–38.

Langa, M. 1997. "The writing was always on the wall, but where were the reporters?" In *Rhodes Journalism Review, Online Edition 14*, A. Garman & G. Berger (eds.). School of Journalism and Media Studies, Rhodes University, South Africa.

Langellier, K. M. 2001. "'You're marked': Breast cancer, tattoo, and the narrative performance of identity." In *Narrative and Identity. Studies in Autobiography, Self and Culture*, J. Brockmeier & D. Carbaugh (eds.), 145–185. Amsterdam: John Benjamins Publishing Co.

Lapsley, M. 1998. "Confronting the past and creating the future: The redemptive value of truth telling." *Social Research* 65 (4): 741–752.

Laub, D. 1995. "Truth and Testimony: The Process and the Struggle." In *Trauma. Explorations in Memory*, C. Caruth (ed.), 61–75. Baltimore: The John Hopkins University Press.

Laufer, S. 1998. "Truth and apartheid." *Nation* 266 (2): 5–6.

Laurence, P. 1998. "What the TRC won't tell you." *Focus 11.*

Lee, D. 1992. *Competing Discourses. Perspective and Ideology in Language.* London: Longman.

Legassick, M. & Minkley, G. 1997. *Current Trends in the Production of South African History.* Bellville: University of the Western Cape.

Leseka, M. 2000. "The TRC's Recommendations on Rehabilitation and Reparation." In *From Rhetoric to Responsibility. Making Reparations to the Survivors of Past Political Violence in South Africa,* B. Hamber & T. Mofokeng (eds.), Chapter 2. Johannesburg: Centre for the Study of Violence and Reconciliation.

Lever, J. & Wilmot, J. 2000. "The Second Republic." In *After the TRC, Reflections on truth and reconciliation in South Africa,* W. James & L. Van de Vijver (eds.), 191–200. Cape Town: David Philips Publishers.

Levett A., Kottler, A., Burman, E. & Parker, I. 1997. "Power and discourse: Culture and change in South Africa." In *Culture, Power & Difference, Discourse Analysis in South Africa,* A. Levett, A. Kottlet, E. Burman & I. Parker (eds.), 1–14. Cape Town: University of Cape Town Press.

Levinson, S. C. 1983. *Pragmatics.* Cambridge: Cambridge University Press.

Lewin, H. 1997. "Official Voices." In *Rhodes Journalism Review, Online Edition 14,* A. Garman & G. Berger (eds.).

Lewin, H. 1998. "The never-ending story." *Track Two,* December 1998: 40–43.

Leydesdorff, S. et al. 1999. "Introduction: Trauma and life stories." In *Trauma and Life Stories. International Perspectives,* K. L. Rogers & S. Leydesdorff with G. Dawson (eds.), 1–26. London: Routledge.

Liebenberg, I. 1996. "The Truth and Reconciliation Commission in South Africa: Context, future and some imponderables." *South African Public Law* 11: 123–159.

Liebenberg, I. & Zegeye, A. 1998. "Pathway to Democracy? The case of the South African Truth and Reconciliation Process." *Social Identities* 4 (3): 541–559.

Linde, C. 1993. *Life Stories. The Creation of Coherence.* New York: Oxford University Press.

Linde, C. 1999. "The Transformation of Narrative Syntax into Institutional Memory." *Narrative Inquiry* 9 (1): 139–174.

Linde, C. 2001. "Narrative in Institutions." In *The Handbook of Discourse Analysis,* D. Schiffrin, D. Tannen & H. E. Hamilton (eds.), 518–536. Malden: Blackwell Publishers.

LiPuma, E. 1993. "Culture and the Concept of Culture in a Theory of Practice." In *Bourdieu. Critical Perspectives,* C. Calhoun, E. LiPuma & M. Postone (eds.), 14–34. Cambridge: Polity Press.

Llewellyn, J. J. & Howe, R. 1999. "Institutions for Restorative Justice: The South African Truth and Reconciliation Commission." *University of Toronto Law Journal* 49 (3).

Long Night's Journey into Day website. 2000. http://www.irisfilms.org/longnight/index.htm.

Lucius-Hoene, G. & Deppermann, A. 2000. "Narrative Identity Empiricized: A Dialogical and Positioning Approach to Autobiographical Research Interviews." *Narrative Inquiry* 10 (1): 199–222.

Lucy, J. A. 1996. "The scope of linguistic relativity: An analysis and review of empirical research." In *Rethinking linguistic relativity,* J. J. Gumperz & S. C. Levinson (eds.), 37–69. Cambridge: Cambridge University Press.

Lukes, S. 1974. *Power: A Radical View.* London: MacMillan Press Ltd.

Lynch, M. & Bogen, D. 1996. *The Spectacle of History. Speech, Text, and Memory at the Iran-contra Hearings.* Durham & London: Duke University Press.

Mabry, M. 1997. "Truth or Justice?" *Newsweek* 130 (8): 37.

Maier, Ch. S. 2000. "Doing History, Doing Justice: The Narrative of the Historian and of the Truth Commission." In *Truth versus justice: The morality of truth commissions*, R. I. Rotberg & D. Thompson (eds.), 261–278. Princeton: Princeton University Press.

Makoni, S. 2003. "From misinvention to disinvention of language: Multilingualism and the South African Constitution." In *Black Linguistics. Language, society, and politics in Africa and the Americas*, S. Makoni et al. (eds.), 132–151. London & New York: Routledge.

Maluleke, T. S. 1997. "Truth, national unity and reconciliation in South Africa. Aspects of the emerging theological agenda." *Missionalia* 25 (1): 59–86.

Mamdani, M. 1997. "Reconciliation without Justice." *Southern Review* 10 (6): 22–25.

Mamdani, M. 1998. *When does reconciliation turn into a denial of justice?* Pretoria: HSRC Publishers.

Mamdani, M. 2000. "A Diminished Truth." In *After the TRC, Reflections on truth and reconciliation in South Africa*, W. James & L. Van de Vijver (eds.), 60–63. Cape Town: David Philips Publishers.

Manda, P. 1996. "Apartheid as a crime against humanity, is the Truth and Reconciliation Commission an answer?" *Annual Conference of the African Society of International and Comparative Law* 8: 201–209.

Marlin-Curiel, S. 1999. "Truth and Consequences: Art in Response to the Truth and Reconciliation Commission." *The TRC: Commissioning the Past Conference*, Johannesburg: University of the Witwatersrand, 11–14 June 1999.

Marx, L. 1998. "Slouching towards Bethlehem: Ubu and the Truth Commission." *African Studies* 57 (2): 209–220.

Matshoba, M. 2002. "Nothing But the Truth: The Ordeal of Duma Khumalo." In *Commissioning the Past: Understanding South Africa's Truth and Reconciliation Commission*, D. Posel & G. Simpson (eds.), 131–146. Johannesburg: Witwatersrand University Press.

Mattes R. & Thiel, H. 1998. "Consolidation and Public Opinion in South Africa." *Journal of Democracy* January 1998: 95–109.

Mbembe, A. 2002. "The Power of the Archive and its Limits." In *Refiguring the Archive*, C. Hamilton et al. (eds.), 19–26. Cape Town: David Philip Publishers.

McCandless, E. 1997. "Bridging Justice and Reconciliation in the New South Africa." *Cantilevers* Volume 3: 19–22.

McClure, E. 2000. "Oral and written Assyrian-English codeswitching." In *Trends in Linguistics. Codeswitching Worldwide II*, R. Jacobson (ed.), 157–192. Berlin: Mouton de Gruyter.

McClure, E. & McClure, M. 1988. "Macro- and micro-sociolinguistic dimensions of codeswitching in Vingard (Romania)." In *Codeswitching. Anthropological and Sociolinguistic Perspectives*, M. Heller (ed.), 25–52. Berlin: Mouton de Gruyter.

McCormick, K. 2003. "Negotiating the public/private interface: Analysis of testimonies given at the first public hearing on human rights violations. Non-verbal expression of 'experiential truth': An analysis of gesture, gaze and marked intonation." *Conference "Troubled histories and identities in dicourse – the case of the South African TRC".* Antwerp, 26–27 November 2003.

McGreal, C. 1999. "The hate that won't go away." *Guardian Unlimited* Monday July 26th 1999.

McGreal, C. 2000. "Apartheid victims reject handouts. Apartheid victims push for adequate reparations after being offered a pittance." *Daily Mail & Guardian* January 3rd 2000.

McGregor, L. 2001. "Individual Accountability in South Africa: Cultural Optimum or Political facade?" *American Journal of International Law* 95 (1): 32–45.

Mda, Z. 2002. "South African theatre in an era of reconciliation." In *The Performance Arts in Africa. A reader,* F. Harding (ed.), 279–289. London: Routledge.

Meiring, P. 1999. *Chronicle of the Truth Commission.* Vanderbijlpark: Carpe Diem Books.

Meredith, M. 1999. *Coming to Terms, South Africa's Search for Truth.* New York: Public Affairs.

Merwe van der, H. 1999. "The Truth and Reconciliation Commission and Community Reconciliation: An Analysis of Competing Strategies and Conceptualisations." *Dissertation submitted in partial fulfilment of the requirements of the degree of Ph.D. at the George Mason University.*

Merwe van der, H. 2002. "National Narrative versus Local Truths: The Truth and Reconciliation Commission's Engagement with Duduza." In *Commissioning the Past: Understanding South Africa's Truth and Reconciliation Commission,* D. Posel & G. Simpson (eds.), 204–219. Johannesburg: Witwatersrand University Press.

Merwe van der, H. & Kgalema, L. 1998. "The Truth and Reconciliation Commission: A Foundation for Community Reconciliation?" *Reconciliation International* June 1998.

Mesthrie, U. S. 1999. "Land Restitution in Cape Town: Public Displays and Private Meanings." *Kronos, Journal of Cape History* 1998–1999 (25): 239–258.

Meyer, M. 2001. "Between theory, method, and politics: positioning of the approaches to CDA." In *Methods of Critical Discourse Analysis,* R. Wodak & M. Meyer (eds.), 14–31. London: SAGE Publications Ltd.

Miller, A. 1995. "A time to remember." *Odyssee* 19 (4).

Miller, A. 2001. "Truth and reconciliation: 'Many layers, many seasons.'" *M/C: A Journal of Media and Culture* 4th January 2001.

Minnaar, A. 1995. "Will the truth out? The delaying of the truth commission." *Political Update* Third Quarter 1995: 56–66.

Minow, M. 1998. *Between Vengeance and Forgiveness. Facing History after Genocide and mass Violence.* Boston: Beacon Press.

Minow, M. 2000. "The Hope for Healing: What Can Truth Commissions Do?" In *Truth versus justice: The morality of truth commissions,* R. I. Rotberg & D. Thompson (eds.), 235–260. Princeton: Princeton University Press.

MixedFolks.com. 1996. http://www.mixedfolks.com/africa.htm.

Mofokeng, T. & Hamber, B. 2000. "Recontextualising Reconciliation and Reparations in South Africa." In *From Rhetoric to Responsibility. Making Reparations to the Survivors of Past Political Violence in South Africa,* B. Hamber & T. Mofokeng (eds.), Chapter 1. Johannesburg: Centre for the Study of Violence and Reconciliation.

Mokoena, S. 1997. "Radio & reconciliation." In *Rhodes Journalism Review, Online Edition 14,* A. Garman & G. Berger (eds.). School of Journalism and Media Studies, Rhodes University, South Africa.

Moon, C. 1999. "True Fictions: Truth, Reconciliation, and the Narrativisation of Identity." *ECPR Conference.* Mannheim, March 1999.

Mooney K., Nieftagodien, N. & Ulrich, N. 1999. "Conference Report, The TRC: Commissioning the past (June 1999)." *African Studies* 58 (2): 209–218.

Moosa, E. 2000. "Truth and reconciliation as performance: Spectres of Eucharistic redemption." In *Looking Back, Reaching Forward, Reflections on the Truth and Reconciliation Commission of South Africa,* Ch. Villa-Vicencio & W. Verwoerd (eds.), 113–122. Cape Town: University of Cape Town Press.

Morson, G. S. 1986a. "Who Speaks for Bakhtin?" In *Bakhtin. Essays and Dialogues on His Work,* G. S. Morson (ed.), 1–20. Chicago: The University of Chicago Press.

Morson, G. S. 1986b. "Dialogue, Monologue, and the Social: A Reply to Ken Hirschkop." In *Bakhtin. Essays and Dialogues on His Work,* G. S. Morson (ed.), 81–88. Chicago: The University of Chicago Press.

Motala, Z. 1995. "The Promotion of National Unity and Reconciliation Act, the constitution and international law." *International Law Journal of Southern Africa* 28: 338–362.

Mpe, P. 1998. "Orality and literacy in an electronic era." *South African Archives Journal* 40: 80–88.

Mphahlele, L. 2003. "The Case for a General Amnesty." In *The Provocations of Amnesty: Memory, Justice and Impunity,* Ch. Villa-Vicencio & E. Doxtader (eds.), 9–12. Claremont: David Philip Publishers.

Muller, A. 1997. "Facing Our Shadow Side. Afrikaners must own their complicity." *Track Two:* 6 (3&4).

Mumby, D. K. 1993. "Introduction: Narrative and Social Control." In *Narrative and Social Control: Critical Perspectives,* D. K. Mumby (ed.), 1–14. Newbury Park: SAGE Publications, Inc.

Mxolisi, M. 2000. "Reconciliation: A call to action." In *Looking Back, Reaching Forward, Reflections on the Truth and Reconciliation Commission of South Africa,* Ch. Villa-Vicencio & W. Verwoerd (eds.), 210–218. Cape Town: University of Cape Town Press.

Myers-Scotton, C. 1993. *Social Motivations for Codeswitching. Evidence from Africa.* Oxford: Clarendon Press.

National Archives and Records Service Website. 2001. http://www.national.archives.gov.za/.

Nattrass, N. 1999. "The Truth and Reconciliation Commission on business and apartheid: a critical evaluation." *African Affairs* 98: 373–391.

Nattrass, N. 2000. "Inequality, unemployment and wage-setting institutions in South Africa." *Journal for studies in Economics and Econometrics* 24 (3): 129–142.

Ndebele, N. 1999. "South Africa: Quandaries of compromise." *UNESCO Courier,* December 1999: 22–25.

Ndungane, N. 2000. "An opportunity for peace." In *Looking Back, Reaching Forward, Reflections on the Truth and Reconciliation Commission of South Africa,* Ch. Villa-Vicencio & W. Verwoerd (eds.), 258–264. Cape Town: University of Cape Town Press.

Newham, G. 1995. "Investigation Units: The Teeth of the Truth and Reconciliation Commission." *Paper Online:* http://www.csvr.org.za/papers/papnwhm2.htm.

Newsom, D. 1997. "A crucial few weeks for South Africa's truth seekers." *Christian Science Monitor* 89 (181): 19–20.

Nolutshungu, S. C. 1993. "Reflections on national unity in South Africa: A comparative approach." *Third World Quarterly* 13 (4): 607–624.

North, J. 1998. "The "Ideal" of Forgiveness: A Philosopher's Exploration." In *Exploring Forgiveness,* R. D. Enright & J. North (eds.), 15–34. Madison: The University of Wisconsin Press.

Norval, A. J. 1996a. *Deconstructing Apartheid Discourse.* London: Verso.

Norval, A. J. 1996b. "Thinking Identities: Against a Theory of Ethnicity." In *The Politics of Difference. Ethnic premises in a world of power,* E. N. Wilmsen & P. McAllister (eds.), 59–70. Chicago: The University of Chicago Press.

Norval, A. J. 1999. "Truth and reconciliation: The birth of the present and the reworking of history." *Journal of Southern African Studies* 25 (3): 499–528.

Norval, A. J. 2001. "Reconstructing National identity and Renegotiating Memory: The Work of the TRC." In *States of Imagination: Ethnographic Explorations of the Postcolonial State,* Th. B. Hansen & F. Stepputat (eds.), 182–202. Durham & London: Duke University Press.

Ntsebeza, D. B. 2000a. "A Lot More to Live For." In *After the TRC, Reflections on truth and reconciliation in South Africa*, W. James & L. Van de Vijver (eds.), 103–108. Cape Town: David Philips Publishers.

Ntsebeza, D. B. 2000b. "The Uses of Truth Commissions: Lessons for the World." In *Truth versus justice: The morality of truth commissions*, R. I. Rotberg & D. Thompson (eds.), 158–169. Princeton: Princeton University Press.

Ntsebeza, D. B. 2001. "Truth, Justice and Reconciliation – The Legacy of the South African Truth and Reconciliation Commission." *African Legal Aid Quarterly* July–September 2001: 23–24.

Nyatsumba, K. 2000. "Neither Dull nor Tiresome." In *After the TRC, Reflections on truth and reconciliation in South Africa*, W. James & L. Van de Vijver (eds.), 90–94. Cape Town: David Philips Publishers.

O'Barr, W. M. & Conley, J. M. 1996. "Ideological Dissonance in the American Legal." In *Disorderly Discourse. Narrative, Conflict, and Inequality*, Ch. L. Briggs (ed.), 114–134. New York: Oxford University Press.

Ochs, E. 1997. "Narrative." In *Discourse as Structure and Process*, T. A. Van Dijk (ed.), 185–207. London: SAGE Publications Ltd.

Ochs, E. & Capps, L. 2001. *Living Narrative. Creating Lives in Everyday Storytelling*. Cambridge: Harvard University Press.

Odendaal, A. 1997. "For All Its Flaws. The TRC as a Peacebuilding Tool." *Track Two* 6 (3&4).

Official TRC Website. 2003. http://www.doj.gov.za/trc/trc_frameset.htm.

Official Website of the Department of Foreign Affairs, Republic of South Africa. 2005. http://www.dfa.gov.za/docs/speeches/mbeki.htm.

Orr, W. 2000a. *From Biko to Basson*. Saxonwold: Contra Press.

Orr, W. 2000b. "Reparation delayed is healing retarded." In *Looking Back, Reaching Forward, Reflections on the Truth and Reconciliation Commission of South Africa*, Ch. Villa-Vicencio & W. Verwoerd (eds.), 239–249. Cape Town: University of Cape Town Press.

Oxford Advanced Learner's Dictionary. 1992. *Dictionary of Current English*. Oxford: Oxford University Press.

Parlevliet, M. 1998a. "Considering Truth. Dealing with a Legacy of Gross Human Rights Violations." *Netherlands Quarterly of Human Rights* 16 (2): 141–174.

Parlevliet, M. 1998b. "Between Facilitator and Advocate: The South African Truth and Reconciliation Commission." *National Institute for Dispute Resolution Forum* 36: 6–15.

Patel, R. 2003. "Narratives of Trauma and Resilience." In *Telling Wounds. Narrative, Trauma & Memory. Working through the SA armed conflicts of the 20th century. Proceedings of the conference*, C. van der Merwe & R. Wolfswinkel (eds.), 289–294. Stellenbosch: Van Schaik Content Solutions.

Pauw, J. 1998. "Inside the Mind of Torture, The Story of Apartheid's Electrician." *Covert Action Quarterly* 63: 18–25.

Payne, L. A. 1999. "Confessions of Torturers. Reflections from Argentina." *The TRC: Commissioning the Past Conference* University of the Witwatersrand, 11–14 June 1999.

Pêcheux, M. 1982. *Language, Semantics and Ideology. Stating the Obvious*. London: The MacMillan Press Ltd.

Pentzold, C. & Seidenglanz, S. 2006. "First Steps Towards a Conceptual Framework for the Analysis of Wiki Discourses." *Paper Online*: www.wikisym.org/ws2006/proceedings/p59.pdf.

Pérouse de Montclos, M.-A. 1997. 'Les nouveau enjeux de l'immigration en Afrique du Sud.' *Afrique Contemporaine* 4ᵉ trimestre: 223–232.

Peterson, B. 2002. "The Archives and the Political Imaginary." In *Refiguring the Archive*, C. Hamilton et al. (eds.), 29–37. Cape Town: David Philip Publishers.

Phakathi, T. S. & Van der Merwe, H. 2003. "The Impact of the TRC's Amnesty Process on Survivors of Human Rights Violations." *Unpublished Paper*. Johannesburg: CSVR.

Phaswana, N. 2003. "Contradiction or affirmation? The South African language policy and the South African national government." In *Black Linguistics. Language, society, and politics in Africa and the Americas*, S. Makoni et al. (eds.), 117–131. London & New York: Routledge.

Philips, N. & Hardy, C. 2002. *Discourse Analysis. Investigating Processes of Social Construction*. Thousand Oaks: Sage Publications.

Philips, S. U. 1998. "Language Ideologies in Institutions of Power: A Commentary." In *Language Ideologies. Practice and Theory*, B. B. Schieffelin, K. A. Woolard & P. V. Kroskrity (eds.), 211–228. New York: Oxford University Press.

Philips, S. U. 2000. "Constructing a Tongan Nation-State through Language Ideology in the Courtroom." In *Regimes of Language. Ideologies, Polities, and Identities*, P. V. Kroskrity (ed.), 229–258. Santa Fe: School of American Research Press.

Picker, R. 2003. "Victim's Perspectives about the Hearings." *Paper Online:* http://www.csvr.org.za/papcrs/pappick.htm.

Pienaar, A. 1995. "The Truth and Reconciliation Commission in South Africa, 'Settling Accounts' or 'Burning the Hatchet'?" *Annual Conference of the African Society of International and Comparative Law* Volume 7: 453–467.

Pigou, P. 2003. "Degrees of Truth: Amnesty and Limitations of the Truth Recovery Project." In *The Provocations of Amnesty: Memory, Justice and Impunity*, Ch. Villa-Vicencio & E. Doxtader (eds.), 217–236. Claremont: David Philip Publishers.

Pityana, B. N. 2000. "South Africa's inquiry into racism in the media: The role of national institutions in the promotion and protection of human rights." *African Affairs* 99: 525–532.

Plessis du, Th. & Wiegand, C. 1997. "Report on interpreting at the hearings of the Truth and Reconciliation Commission: April 1996 to February 1997." *Acta Varia. Onderweg na vertaal- en tolkopleiding in Suid-Afrika* 3: 10–29.

Plessis du, T. 1998. "Newspaper management keeps quiet about its role in Apartheid: In the Afrikaans press, some reporters decide to testify." *Nieman Reports* 52 (4): 55–58.

Pons, S. 2000. *Apartheid, l'aveu et le Pardon*. Saint-Amand-Montrond: Bayard Editions.

Posel, D. 2002. "The TRC Report: What Kind of History? What Kind of Truth?" In *Commissioning the Past: Understanding South Africa's Truth and Reconciliation Commission*, D. Posel & G. Simpson (eds.), 147–172. Johannesburg: Witwatersrand University Press.

Posel, D. & Simpson, G. 2002. "The Power of Truth: South Africa's Truth and Reconciliation Commission in Context." In *Commissioning the Past: Understanding South Africa's Truth and Reconciliation Commission*, D. Posel & G. Simpson (eds.), 1–16. Johannesburg: Witwatersrand University Press.

Powell, I. 2000. "Where have all the apartheid bastards gone?" *Daily Mail & Guardian* June 21st 2000.

Praeg, L. 2000. *African Philosophy and the Quest for Autonomy. A philosophical investigation*. Amsterdam: Rodopi.

Preez du, M. 1998. "When Cowboys Cry." In *Rhodes Journalism Review, Online Edition 14*, A. Garman & G. Berger (eds.). School of Journalism and Media Studies, Rhodes University, South Africa.

Preez du, M. 1999. "The price of truth." *UNESCO Courier* December 1999: 24–26.

Pretoria News Online Edition. 2004. http://www.pretorianews.co.za/index.php?fSectionId=670&fArticleId=2257751.

Price, R. M. 1994. "South Africa: The Political Economy of Growth and Democracy." In *South Africa. The Political Economy of Transformation*, S. J. Stedman (ed.), 181–198. Boulder & London: Lynne Rienner Publishers.

Promotion of Access to Information Act Online. 2000. http://www.acts.co.za/prom_of_access_to_info/index.htm.

Quinn, J. R. 2001. "Dealing with a Legacy of Mass Atrocity: Truth Commissions in Uganda and Chile." *Netherlands Quarterly of Human Rights* 19 (4): 383–402.

Qwelane, J. 1997. "South Africa, a rainbow nation: Fiction or reality?" In *Echoes of Violence. Niza Cahier no 1, April 1997*, De Balie & the Netherlands Institute for Southern Africa (eds.), 13–20. Amsterdam: NiZa.

Rakate, P. T. K. 1998. "Truth Commissions and International Criminal Tribunals As Mechanisms for Conflict Resolution in Transitional Societies with Specific Reference to South Africa and the Former Yugoslavia." *Lesotho Law Journal* 11 (1): 177–198.

Rakate, P. T. K. 1999. *Domestic truth commissions and international criminal tribunals as mechanisms for conflict resolution in transitional societies, with specific reference to South Africa and the former Yugoslavia*. Thesis submitted in fulfilment of the Degree of Masters of Laws, University of Stellenbosch.

Ransome, P. 1992. *Antonio Gramsci. A New Introduction*. New York: Harvester Wheatsheaf.

Rassool, C. 2000. "The Rise of Heritage and the Reconstitution of History in South Africa." *Kronos: Journal for Cape History* 26: 1–21.

Renan, E. 1990. "What is a nation?" In *Nation and Narration*, Homi K. Bhabha (ed.), 8–22. London: Routledge.

Rey de la, C. 1997. "On political activism and discourse analysis in South Africa." In *Culture, Power & Difference, Discourse Analysis in South Africa*, A. Levett, A. Kottlet, E. Burman & I. Parker (eds.), 189–197. Cape Town: University of Cape Town Press.

Reynolds, A. 1999. "The results." In *Election '99 South Africa. From Mandela to Mbeki*, A. Reynolds (ed.), 173–209. Claremont: David Philip Publishers Ltd.

Richards, Th. 1993. *The Imperial Archive. Knowledge and the Fantasy of Empire*. London: Verso.

Ridder de, T. 1997. "The Trauma of Testifying. Deponents' difficult healing process." *Track Two* 6 (3&4).

Rigby, A. 2001. *Justice and Reconciliation. After the Violence*. Boulder: Lynne Riener Publisher.

Robbins, D. 1991 *The Work of Pierre Bourdieu*. Milton Keynes: Open University Press.

Robins, S. 1998a. "Silence in my father's house: Memory, nationalism, and the narratives of the body." In *Negotiating the Past: The making of memory in South Africa*, S. Nuttall & C. Coetzee (eds.), 120–142. Cape Town: Oxford University Press.

Robins, S. 1998b. "The Truth Shall Make You Free? Reflections on the TRC." *Southern African Report* August 1998: 9–13.

Rogers, K. L. & Leydesdorff, S. with Dawson, G. (eds.). 1999. *Trauma and Life Stories. International Perspectives*. London: Routledge.

Rojo, L. M. & Pujol, A. G. 2002. "Michel Foucault: On 'problematization.'" In *The Handbook of Pragmatics 4*, J. Verschueren, J.-O. Ostman, J. Blommaert & C. Bulcaen (eds.). Amsterdam: John Benjamins.

Rombouts, H. 2002. "The Legal Profession and the TRC: A Study of a Tense Relationship." *Research Paper*. Johannesburg: Centre for the Study of Violence and Reconciliation, February 2002.

Roodt, D. 2000. *Om die waarheidskommissie te vergeet*. Dainfern: Praag.

Rose, S. 1999. "Naming and claiming: the integration of traumatic experience and the reconstruction of self in survivors' stories of sexual abuse." In *Trauma and Life Stories. International Perspectives*, K. L. Rogers & S. Leydesdorff with G. Dawson (eds.), 160–179. London: Routledge.

Roseberry, W. 1996. "Hegemony, Power, and Languages of Contention." In *The Politics of Difference. Ethnic premises in a world of power*, E. N. Wilmsen & P. McAllister (eds.), 71–84. Chicago: The University of Chicago Press.

Ross, F. C. 1996. "Existing in Secret Places: Women's Testimony in the First Five Weeks of Public Hearings of the Truth and Reconciliation Commission." *Unpublished Paper*.

Ross, F. C. 1997. "Blood Feuds and Childbirth. The TRC as Ritual." *Track Two* 6 (3&4).

Ross, F. C. 1999. "Speech and Silence: Women's Testimony in the First Five Weeks of the Public Hearings of the South African Truth and Reconciliation Commission." In *Remaking a World. Violence, Social Suffering and Recovery*, V. Das, A. Kleinman, M. Lock, M. Ramphele & P. Reynolds (eds.), 250–280. Berkeley: University of California Press.

Ross, F. C. 2003a. *Bearing Witness: Women and the Truth and Reconciliation Commission in South Africa*. London: Pluto Press.

Ross, F. C. 2003b. "On having voice and being heard: Some aftereffects of testifying before the South African Truth and Reconciliation Commission." *Annual Conference of the Canadian Association of African Studies*. Halifax, Canada, 1–4 June 2003.

Ross, F. C. 2003c. "The Construction of Voice and Identity in the South African Truth and Reconciliation Commission." In *Political Transition: Politics and Cultures*, P. Gready (ed.), 165–180. London, Sterling, Virginia: Pluto Press.

Ross, M. H. 2002. "The Political Psychology of Competing Narratives: September 11 and Beyond." *Paper Online*: http://www.ssrc.org/sept11/essays/ross.htm.

Rotberg, R. I. 2000. "Truth Commissions and the Provision of Truth, Justice, and Reconciliation." In *Truth versus justice: The morality of truth commissions*, R. I. Rotberg & D. Thompson (eds.), 3–21. Princeton: Princeton University Press.

Rotberg, R. I. 2002. *Ending autocracy, enabling democracy. The tribulations of Southern Africa, 1960–2000*. Cambridge, Massachusetts: World Peace Foundation.

Sachs, A. 2000. "His name was Henry." In *After the TRC, Reflections on truth and reconciliation in South Africa*, W. James & L. Van de Vijver (eds.), 95–102. Cape Town: David Philips Publishers.

Sampson, A. 1997. "Looking back at the press." In *Rhodes Journalism Review, Online Edition 14*, A. Garman & G. Berger (eds.). School of Journalism and Media Studies, Rhodes University, South Africa.

Sanford, V. 2003. "'What is Written in Our Hearts': Memory, Justice and the Healing of Fragmented Communities." In *Political Transition: Politics and Cultures*, P. Gready (ed.), 70–89. London, Sterling, Virginia: Pluto Press.

Sarbin, Th. R. 2001. "Embodiment and the Narrative Structure of Emotional Life." *Narrative Inquiry* 11 (1): 217–225.

Satyo, S. 1999. "Eleven Official Languages: One Plus One Equals Two." In *Knowledge in Black and White*, Kwesi Kwaa Prah (ed.), 149–158. Cape Town: Centre for Advanced Studies of African Society.

Schieffelin, B. B. & Doucet, R. C. 1998. "The 'Real' Haitian Creole: Ideology, Metalinguistics, and Orthographic Choice." In *Language Ideologies. Practice and Theory*, B. B. Schieffelin, K. A. Woolard & P. V. Kroskrity (eds.), 285–316. New York: Oxford University Press.

Schiffrin, D. 1987. *Discourse markers. Studies in Interactional Sociolinguistics 5*. Cambridge: Cambridge University Press.

Schiffrin, D. 1996. "Narrative as self-portrait: Sociolinguistic constructions of identity." *Language and Society* 25: 167–203.

Schillinger, K. 1998. "Forging a new South Africa with contrition, mercy." *Christian Science Monitor* 90 (153): 6–10.

Schimmel, S. 2002. *Wounds not Healed by Time. The Power of Repentance and Forgiveness*. Oxford: Oxford University Press.

Scholes, R. 1980. "Language, Narrative and Anti–Narrative." In *On Narrative*, W. J. T. Mitchell (ed.), 200–208. Chicago: University of Chicago Press.

Scott, C. J. 1990. *Domination and the Arts of Resistance*. New Haven: Yale University Press.

Seremane, W.-O. 1998. "Where lies my brother?" *Siyaya* 3: 46–47.

Shea, D. 2000. *The South African Truth Commission: The Politics of Reconciliation*. Washington DC: United States Institute of Peace Press.

Shriver Jr., D. W. 1998. "Is There Forgiveness in Politics? Germany, Vietnam, and America." In *Exploring Forgiveness*, R. D. Enright & J. North (eds.), 131–149. Madison: The University of Wisconsin Press.

Silverstein, M. 1998. "The Uses and Utility of Ideology: A Commentary." In *Language Ideologies. Practice and Theory*, B.B. Schieffelin, K. A. Woolard & P. V. Kroskrity (eds.), 123–148. New York: Oxford University Press.

Silverstein, M. & Urban, G. 1996. "The Natural History of Discourse." In *The Natural Histories of Discourse*, M. Silverstein & G. Urban (eds.), 1–20. Chicago: University of Chicago Press.

Simpson, G. 1993. "Explaining Endemic Violence in South Africa." Published under the title 'Gewalt in Südafrica', *Weltfriedensdienst Quesrbrief* 3.

Simpson, G. 1997a. "Reconstruction and Reconciliation: Emerging from transition." *Development in Practice* 7 (4): 475–478.

Simpson, G. 1997b. "A 'culture of impunity'. Successive amnesties may send out wrong signals: Encouraging rather than alarming criminals." *The Star* 24th January 1997.

Simpson, G. 1998. "A Brief Evaluation of South Africa's Truth and Reconciliation Commission: Some lessons for societies in transition." *Paper Online:* http://www.csvr.org.za/papers/paptrce2.htm.

Simpson, G. 2004. "'A snake gives birth to a snake': Politics and Crime in the Transition to Democracy in South Africa." In *Justice Gained? Crime and Crime Control in South Africa's Transition*, B. Dixon & E. van der Spuy (eds.), 1–28. Cape Town/Cullompton, Devon: UCT Press/Willan Publishing.

Slembrouck, S. 2001. "Explanation, Interpretation and Critique in the Analysis of Discourse." In *Critique of Anthropology* 21(1), J. Gledhill & S. Nugent (eds.), 33–58. London: SAGE Publications.

Slovo, G. 2001. *Red Dust*. Kettering: Virago.

Slye, R. C. 2000a. "Amnesty, Truth and Reconciliation: Reflections on the South African Amnesty Process." In *Truth versus justice: The morality of truth commissions*, R. I. Rotberg & D. Thompson (eds.), 170–188. Princeton: Princeton University Press.

Slye, R. C. 2000b. "Justice and amnesty." In *Looking Back, Reaching Forward, Reflections on the Truth and Reconciliation Commission of South Africa*, Ch. Villa-Vicencio & W. Verwoerd (eds.), 174–183. Cape Town: University of Cape Town Press.

Sooka, Y. 2000. "The Unfinished Business of the TRC." In *From Rhetoric to Responsibility. Making Reparations to the Survivors of Past Political Violence in South Africa*, B. Hamber & T. Mofokeng (eds.), Chapter 4. Johannesburg: Centre for the Study of Violence and Reconciliation.

Sooka, Y. 2003. "Apartheid's Victims in the Midst of Amnesty's Promise." In *The Provocations of Amnesty: Memory, Justice and Impunity*, Ch. Villa-Vicencio & E. Doxtader (eds.), 309–314. Claremont: David Philip Publishers.

South African Government Information Online. 2004. http://www.info.gov.za/speeches/.

South African Government Information Online. 2005. http://www.info.gov.za/yearbook/2004/landpeople.htm.

South Africa Government Online. 2005. http://www.gov.za/.

South African History Archive Website. 1999. http://www.wits.ac.za/saha/history.htm.

South Africa's Human Spirit Website. 2000. http://www.sabctruth.co.za/.

South African Language Policy Online. 2004. http://www.polity.org.za/pdf/languagepolicy.pdf.

Soyinka, W. 1999. *The Burden of Memory: The Muse of Forgiveness*. New York City: Oxford University Press.

Sparks, A. 1995. *Tomorrow is Another Country. The Inside Story of South Africa's Road to Change*. Chicago: the University of Chicago Press.

Sparks, A. 2003. *Beyond the Miracle. Inside the New South Africa*. Johannesburg & Cape Town: Jonathan Ball Publishers.

Spears, I. S. 2002. "Evolutions in African Conflict. Power and Strategy in Africa's Civil Wars, 1985–1995." *Canadian Association for African Studies Conference: The Global and the Local*. 29/5–1/6/2002. Toronto, Ontario: University of Toronto.

Spence, D. P. 1982. *Narrative Truth and Historical Truth. Meaning and Interpretation in Psychoanalysis*. New York: W. W. Norton & Company.

Spitulnik, D. 1998. "Mediating Unity and Diversity: The Production of Language Ideologies in Zambian Broadcasting." In *Language Ideologies. Practice and Theory*, B. B. Schieffelin, K. A. Woolard & P. V. Kroskrity (eds.), 163–188. New York: Oxford University Press.

Stacey, S. 1999. "A 'New South Africa': The South African Truth and Reconciliation Commission's vexed nation-building project." *The TRC: Commissioning the Past Conference*. The University of the Witwatersrand, Johannesburg, June 11–14, 1999.

Stanley, E. 2001. "Identities, Truth and Reconciliation in South Africa: Some International Concerns." In *Globalisation, National Identities. Crisis or Opportunity*, P. Kennedy & C. J. Danks (eds.), 175–189. Houndmills: Palgrave.

Statman, J. 2000. "Performing the truth: The social-psychological context of TRC narratives." *South African Journal of Psychology* 30 (1): 23–45.

Stauffer, C. & Hamber, B. 1995. "Putting a Face on the Past: Survivor-Offender Mediation and the Truth and Reconciliation Commission." *Paper Online:* http://www.csvr.org.za/papers/papcsbh.htm.

Steward, S. 1986. "Shouts on the Street: Bakhtin's Anti-Linguistics." In *Bakhtin. Essays and Dialogues on His Work,* G. S. Morson (ed.), 41–58. Chicago: The University of Chicago Press.

Stibbe, A. & Ross, A. 1997. "The Truth Commission: At the Crossroads of Discourse." *Sajals* 5 (1): 14–28.

Stoppard, A. 2003. "South Africa: Compensating apartheid victims." *Inter Press Service (IPS),* 16 April 2003.

Streek, B. 1999. "Truth commission pays out a pittance." *Daily Mail & Guardian,* December 14th 1999.

Taylor, J. 1997. "Truth or Reconciliation?" In *Rhodes Journalism Review, Online Edition 14,* A. Garman & G. Berger (eds.). School of Journalism and Media Studies, Rhodes University, South Africa.

Taylor, J. 1998. *UBU and the Truth Commission.* Cape Town: University of Cape Town Press.

Taylor, J. 2002. "Yours sincerely: A history and theory of affect and the performance of feeling." *Practices of the Self and Experiences of Worldliness Conference,* Wits Institute for Social and Economic Research, Johannesburg, 7–8 August 2002.

Teitel, R. 2002. "Transitional Justice as Liberal Narrative." In *Experiments with Truth. Documenta 11_Platform2,* O. Enwezor et al. (eds.), 241–257. Ostfildern-Ruit: Hatje Cantz Publishers.

Terreblanche, S. 2000. "Dealing with systematic economic injustice." In *Looking Back, Reaching Forward, Reflections on the Truth and Reconciliation Commission of South Africa,* Ch. Villa-Vicencio & W. Verwoerd (eds.), 265–276. Cape Town: University of Cape Town Press.

Thamm, M. 2003. "Demonen Uitdrijven". *De Standaard,* 14 maart 2003.

Theissen, G. 1998. *Amnesty for Apartheid Crimes? The South African Truth and Reconciliation Commission and International Law.* Thesis presented in fulfilment of the requirements for the degree of Magister Legum in the Faculty of Law, University of the Western Cape.

Theissen, G. & Hamber, B. 1998. "A State of Denial: White South Africans' Attitudes to the Truth and Reconciliation Commission." *Indicator South Africa* 15 (1): 8–12.

Therborn, G. 1980. *The Ideology of Power and the Power of Ideology.* London: Verso.

The Truth in Translation Project website. 2007. http://www.truthintranslation.org/.

Thloloe, J. 1998. "Showing faces, hearing voices, tugging at emotions: Televising the Truth and Reconciliation Commission." *Nieman Reports* 52 (4): 53–56.

Thompson, J. B. 1984. *Studies in the Theory of Ideology.* Cambridge: Polity Press.

Thompson, J. B. 1994. "Ideology and Modern Culture." In *The Polity Reader in Social Theory:* 133–141. Cambridge: Polity Press.

Thornborrow, J. 1999a. "Language and the media." In *Language, Society and Power. An introduction,* L. Thomas & S. Wareing (eds.), 49–64. London: Routledge.

Thornborrow, J. 1999b. "Language and identity." In *Language, Society and Power. An introduction,* L. Thomas & S. Wareing (eds.), 135–150. London: Routledge.

Tobias, S. 1999. "History, Memory and the Ethics of Writing: Antjie Krog's 'Country of My Skull'." *The TRC: Commissioning the Past Conference,* Johannesburg: University of the Witwatersrand, 11–14 June 1999.

Toit du, A. 2002. "Transitional Justice and the Problems of Accountability and Responsibility in the New Politics of Memory and History in South Africa." *Research Workshop 'History, Truth and Reconciliation: Memory Matters in Africa'.* Basel, October 2002.

Toit du, F. 2003. *Learning to live together. Practices of social reconciliation.* Cape Town: Institute of Justice and Reconciliation.

Toit du, F. 2006. "The road ahead: Beyond the TRC". In *Truth & Reconciliation in South Africa: 10 years on*, Ch. Villa-Vicencio & F. du Toit (eds.), 199–204. Claremont: David Philip.

Toolan, M. J. 1988. *Narrative. A Critical Linguistic Introduction.* London: Routledge.

Torfing, J. 1999. *New Theories of Discourse. Laclau, Mouffe and Zizek.* Oxford: Blackwell Publishers ltd.

TRC Act Online. 1995. http://www.doj.gov.za/trc/trc_frameset.htm.

TRC: Commissioning the Past Website. 2000. http://www.trcresearch.org.za/network.

TRC Research Website. 2007. http://cas1.elis.rug.ac.be/avrug/trc.htm.

Truth and Reconciliation Commission of South Africa Report. 1998. *Volumes 1–5.* Cape Town: Juta & Co Ltd.

Truth and Reconciliation Commission of South Africa Report. 2002. *Volume 7.* Cape Town: Juta & Co Ltd.

Truth and Reconciliation Commission of South Africa Report. 2003. *Volume 6.* Cape Town: Juta & Co Ltd.

Truth Talk. Truth, the road to reconciliation. 1996, 1997, 1998. *The official newsletter of the Truth and Reconciliation Commission.* Cape Town: The Truth and Reconciliation Commission.

Tutu, D. 1998. "Between a nightmare and a dream." *Christianity Today* 42 (2): 25–28.

Tutu, D. 1999a. "No Future without Forgiveness." *New Perspectives Quarterly* 16 (5): 29–31.

Tutu, D. 1999b. *No Future without Forgiveness: A personal overview of South Africa's truth and reconciliation commission.* London: Rider Books.

United States Institute of Peace Website. 2005. http://www.usip.org/library/truth.html.

University of Georgia Libraries Research Guide. 2003. http://www.libs.uga.edu/researchcentral/choosing/what/primary.html.

Vandergucht, L. 2003. *De Notie Brotherhood binnen Umkhonto we Sizwe.* Master thesis. Department of African Languages and Cultures, Ghent University.

VanZanten-Gallagher, S. 1998. "Cry with a Beloved Country." *Christianity Today* 42 (2): 23–24.

VanZanten-Gallagher, S. 2002. *Truth and Reconciliation. The Confessional Mode in South African Literature.* Portsmouth: Heinemann.

Van Zyl Slabbert, F. 2000. "Truth without Reconciliation, Reconciliation without Truth." In *After the TRC, Reflections on truth and reconciliation in South Africa,* W. James & L. Van de Vijver (eds.), 64–73. Cape Town: David Philips Publishers.

Van Zyl Slabbert, F. 2003. "Truth Without Reconciliation, Reconciliation Without Truth." In *The Provocations of Amnesty: Memory, Justice and Impunity,* Ch. Villa-Vicencio & E. Doxtader (eds.), 315–326. Claremont: David Philip Publishers.

Verdoolaege, A. 2002. "The Human Rights Violations Hearings of the South African TRC: A bridge between individual narratives of suffering and a contextualizing master-story of reconciliation." *Paper Online:* http://cas1.elis.rug.ac.be/avrug/trc/02_08.htm.

Verdoolaege, A. 2004. "The South African Truth and Reconciliation Commission and the Belgian Lumumba Commission, a comparison." *Africa Today* 50 (3): 75–92.

Verdoolaege, A. 2005. "Media Representations of the South African Truth and Reconciliation Commission and their commitment to reconciliation". *The Journal of African Cultural Studies* 17 (2): 181–199.

Verdoolaege, A. 2006. "The debate on truth and reconciliation: A survey of literature on the South African Truth and Reconciliation Commission." *The Journal of Language and Politics* 5 (1): 15–35.

Verdoolaege, A. 2006. "Managing reconciliation at the human rights violations hearings of the South African Truth and Reconciliation Commission." *Journal of Human Rights* 5 (1): 61–80.

Verschueren, J. 1998. *Understanding Pragmatics.* London: Edward Arnold.

Verschueren, J. 2001. "Predicaments of Criticism." In *Critique of Anthropology* 21 (1), J. Gledhill & S. Nugent (eds.), 59–82. London: SAGE Publications.

Verwoerd, W. 1996. "Continuing Discussion: Reflections from within the Truth and Reconciliation Commission." *Current Writing* 8 (2): 66–85.

Verwoerd, W. 2000. "Towards the recognition of our past injustices." In *Looking Back, Reaching Forward, Reflections on the Truth and Reconciliation Commission of South Africa*, Ch. Villa-Vicencio & W. Verwoerd (eds.), 155–165. Cape Town: University of Cape Town Press.

Verwoerd, W. & Mabizela, M. 2000. *Truths Drawn in Jest. Commentary on the Truth and Reconciliation Commission through Cartoons.* Cape Town: David Philip Publishers.

Villa-Vicencio, Ch. 1996. "On Taking Responsibility." In *To Remember and to Heal. Theological and Psychological Reflections on Truth and Reconciliation*, R. H. Botman & R. Petersen (eds.), 145–166. Cape Town: Human & Rousseau.

Villa-Vicencio, Ch. 2000a. "On the Limitations of Academic History." In *After the TRC, Reflections on truth and reconciliation in South Africa*, W. James & L. Van de Vijver (eds.), 14–32. Cape Town: David Philips Publishers.

Villa-Vicencio, Ch. 2000b. "Restorative justice: Dealing with the past differently." In *Looking Back, Reaching Forward, Reflections on the Truth and Reconciliation Commission of South Africa*, Ch. Villa-Vicencio & W. Verwoerd (eds.), 68–76. Cape Town: University of Cape Town Press.

Villa-Vicencio, Ch. 2000c. "Getting on with life: A move towards reconciliation." In *Looking Back, Reaching Forward, Reflections on the Truth and Reconciliation Commission of South Africa*, Ch. Villa-Vicencio & W. Verwoerd (eds.), 199–209. Cape Town: University of Cape Town Press.

Villa-Vicencio, Ch. 2000d. "Reconciliation: A Concept that Lures and Infuriates." *New South African Outlook* Winter 2000, 2 (3): 1–2.

Villa-Vicencio, Ch. 2002. "Reconciliation as Metaphor." *Paper Online:* http://www. justicereparatrice.org/articlesdb/articles/3328.

Villa-Vicencio, Ch. 2003a. "Debating the Questions of Amnesty: A Symposium Convened in Cape Town, 4 October 2001. Introductory Remarks." In *The Provocations of Amnesty: Memory, Justice and Impunity*, Ch. Villa-Vicencio & E. Doxtader (eds.), 1–4. Claremont: David Philip Publishers.

Villa-Vicencio, Ch. 2003b. "Restorative Justice: Ambiguities and Limitations of a Theory." In *The Provocations of Amnesty: Memory, Justice and Impunity*, Ch. Villa-Vicencio & E. Doxtader (eds.), 30–50. Claremont: David Philip Publishers.

Villa-Vicencio, Ch. & Ngesi, S. 2003. "South Africa: Beyond the "Miracle"." In *Through Fire with Water. The roots of division and the potential for reconciliation in Africa*, E. Doxtader & Ch. Villa-Vicencio (eds.), 267–304. Claremont: David Philip Publishers.

Villa-Vicencio, Ch. & Verwoerd, W. 2000. "Constructing a Report: Writing Up the 'Truth'." In *Truth versus justice: The morality of truth commissions*, R. I. Rotberg & D. Thompson (eds.), 279–294. Princeton: Princeton University Press.

Waldmeir, P. 1997. *Anatomy of a Miracle: The end of apartheid and the birth of the new South Africa.* London: Penguin.

Walt Van der, B. J. & Van der Walt, T. 1996. *Die Waarheids- en Versoeningskommissie*. Potchefst-roomse Universiteit vir Christelike Hoër Onderwys: Instituut vir Reformatoriese Studie.

Wareing, S. 1999. "What is language and what does it do?" In *Language, Society and Power. An introduction*, L. Thomas & S. Wareing (eds.), 1–16. London: Routledge.

Webb, V. 2002. *Language in South Africa. The role of language in national transformation, recon-struction and development*. Amsterdam: John Benjamins Publishing Company.

Werle, G. 1996. "Without Truth, No Reconciliation. The South African *Rechtsstaat* and the Apartheid Past." *Verfassung und Recht in Ubersee. Law and Politics in Africa, Asia and Latin America* 29 (1): 58–72.

West, G. 1997. "Don't Stand on My Story: The Truth and Reconciliation Commission, Intellec-tuals, Genre and Identity." *Journal of Theology for Southern Africa* 97: 3–12.

Wetherell, M. & Potter, J. 1992. *Mapping the Language of Racism Discourse and the Legitimation of Exploitation*. New York: Harvester Wheatsheaf.

White, H. 1980. "The Value of Narrativity in the Representation of Reality." In *On Narrative*, W. J. T. Mitchell (ed.), 1–24. Chicago: University of Chicago Press.

White, M. & Epston, D. 1990. *Narrative Means to Therapeutic Ends*. New York: W. W. Norton & Company.

Williams, C. 1998. "The TRC: A project of Public Education." *The TRC: Commissioning the Past Conference*. The University of the Witwatersrand, Johannesburg, 11–14 June 1999.

Williams, D. E. 1999. "Liberating the Past from the Future, Liberating the Future from the Past. Race and Reconciliation in the US and the New South Africa." *The TRC: Commission-ing the Past Conference*. The University of the Witwatersrand, Johannesburg, 11–14 June 1999.

Williams, J. J. 2000. "Truth and reconciliation – Beyond the TRC process and findings." *Ecquid Novi* 21 (2): 207–219.

Williams, J. J. 2001. "Human Rights and Citizenship in Post-apartheid South Africa." *Critical Arts: A Journal of south-north culture and media studies* 15 (1&2): 24–46.

Wilson, F. 2000. "Addressing Poverty and Inequality." In *After the TRC, Reflections on truth and reconciliation in South Africa*, W. James & L. Van de Vijver (eds.), 183–197. Cape Town: David Philips Publishers.

Wilson, R. A. 1995. "Manufacturing Legitimacy. The Truth and Reconciliation Commission and the Rule of Law." *Indicator South Africa* 13 (1): 41–46.

Wilson, R. A. 1996. "The Sizwe Will Not Go Away. The Truth and Reconciliation Commission, Human Rights and Nation-Building in South Africa." *African Studies* 55 (2): 1–18.

Wilson, R. A. 2000. "Reconciliation and Revenge in Post-Apartheid South Africa. Rethinking Legal Pluralism and Human Rights." *Current Anthropology* 41 (1): 75–98.

Wilson, R. A. 2001a. *The politics of Truth and Reconciliation in South Africa. Legitimising the Post-Apartheid State*. Cambridge: Cambridge University Press.

Wilson, R. A. 2001b. "Justice and Legitimacy in the South African Transition." In *The Politics of Memory. Transitional Justice in Democratizing Societies*, A. Barahona de Brito, C. Gonza-lez-Enriquez & P. Aguilar (eds.), 190–217. Oxford: Oxford University Press.

Winslow, T. 1997. "Reconciliation: TShe road to healing? Collective good, individual harm?" *Track Two* 6 (3&4): 24–42.

Wodak, R. 1985. "The Interaction between Judge and Defendant." In *Handbook of Discourse Analysis, Volume 4: Discourse Analysis in Society*, T. A. Van Dijk (ed.), 181–192. London: Academic Press.

Wodak, R. 1989. "Introduction." In *Languages, Power and Ideology. Studies in Political Discourse,* R. Wodak (ed.), xiii–xx. Amsterdam: John Benjamins Publishing Company.

Wodak, R. 1995. "Critical linguistics and critical discourse analysis." In *Handbook of Pragmatics: Manual,* J. Verschueren et al. (eds.), 204–210. Amsterdam: John Benjamins.

Wodak, R. 2001. "What CDA is about – a summary of its history, important concepts and its developments." In *Methods of Critical Discourse Analysis,* R. Wodak & M. Meyer (eds.), 1–13. London: SAGE Publications Ltd.

Wodak, R. 2001. "The discourse-historical approach." In *Methods of Critical Discourse Analysis,* R. Wodak & M. Meyer (eds.), 63–94. London: SAGE Publications Ltd.

Wodak, R. 2006. "Review focus: Boundaries in discourse analysis." *Language in Society* 35 (4): 595–611.

World List Afrikaans-Dutch Online. 2002. http://roepstem2.tripod.com/snaaks.html.

Wordic.com. 2005. http://www.wordiq.com/definition/Afrikaans_language.

Yandell, K. E. 1998. "The Metaphysics and Morality of Forgiveness." In *Exploring Forgiveness*, R. D. Enright & J. North (eds.), 35–46. Madison: The University of Wisconsin Press.

Zehr, H. 1997. "Restorative Justice. When justice and healing go together." *Track Two* 6 (3&4): 20.

Zelizer, B. 1993. "American Journalists and the Death of Lee Harvey Oswald: Narratives of Self-Legitimation." In *Narrative and Social Control: Critical Perspectives,* D. K. Mumby (ed.), 189–206. Newbury Park: SAGE Publications, Inc.

Zyl van, J. 1997. "Human Rights and Wrongs." In *Rhodes Journalism Review, Online Edition 14*, A. Garman & G. Berger (eds.). School of Journalism and Media Studies, Rhodes University, South Africa.

Zyl van, P. 1995. "Hiding behind the truth." *Mail & Guardian,* January 27th to February 2nd, 1995.

Zyl van, P. 1999. "Dilemmas of transitional justice: The case of South Africa's Truth and Reconciliation Commission." *Journal of International Affairs* 52 (2): 648–664.

# Index

In the series *Discourse Approaches to Politics, Society and Culture* the following titles have been published thus far or are scheduled for publication: